CREATED BY **JOSS WHEDON**

GREG **PAK**   DAN **McDAID**   LALIT KUMAR **SHARMA**
DANIEL **BAYLISS**   MARCELO **COSTA**

BLUE SUN RISING PART ONE

Published by

Designer
Marie Krupina with **Scott Newman**

Assistant Editor
Gavin Gronenthal

Executive Editor
Jeanine Schaefer

Special Thanks to **Sierra Hahn**, **Becca J. Sadowsky**,
and **Nicole Spiegel** & **Carol Roeder**.

FIREFLY: BLUE SUN RISING Volume One, March 2021.
Published by BOOM! Studios, a division of Boom Entertainment,
Inc. © 2021 20th Television. Originally published in single magazine
form as FIREFLY: BLUE SUN RISING No. 0, FIREFLY No.
21-22. © 2020 20th Television. BOOM! Studios™ and the
BOOM! Studios logo are trademarks of Boom Entertainment,
Inc., registered in various countries and categories. All characters,
events, and institutions depicted herein are fictional. Any similarity
between any of the names, characters, persons, events, and/or
institutions in this publication to actual names, characters, and
persons, whether living or dead, events, and/or institutions is
unintended and purely coincidental. BOOM! Studios does not
read or accept unsolicited submissions of ideas, stories, or artwork.

BOOM! Studios, 5670 Wilshire Boulevard, Suite 400, Los
Angeles, CA 90036-5679. Printed in China. First Printing.

ISBN: 978-1-68415-659-7, eISBN: 978-1-64668-144-0

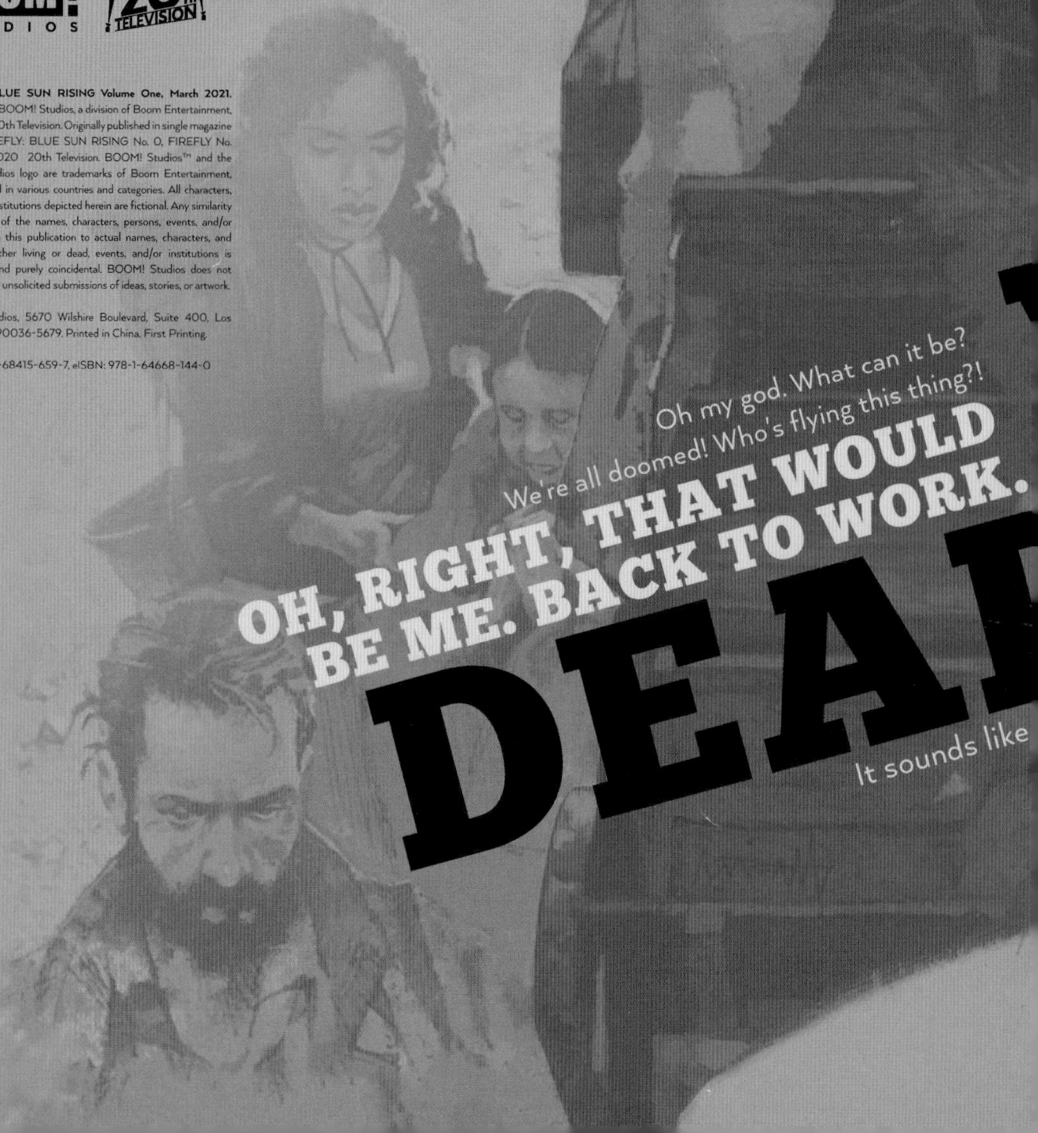

Oh my god. What can it be?

We're all doomed! Who's flying this thing?!

OH, RIGHT, THAT WOULD
BE ME. BACK TO WORK.

DEAD

It sounds like

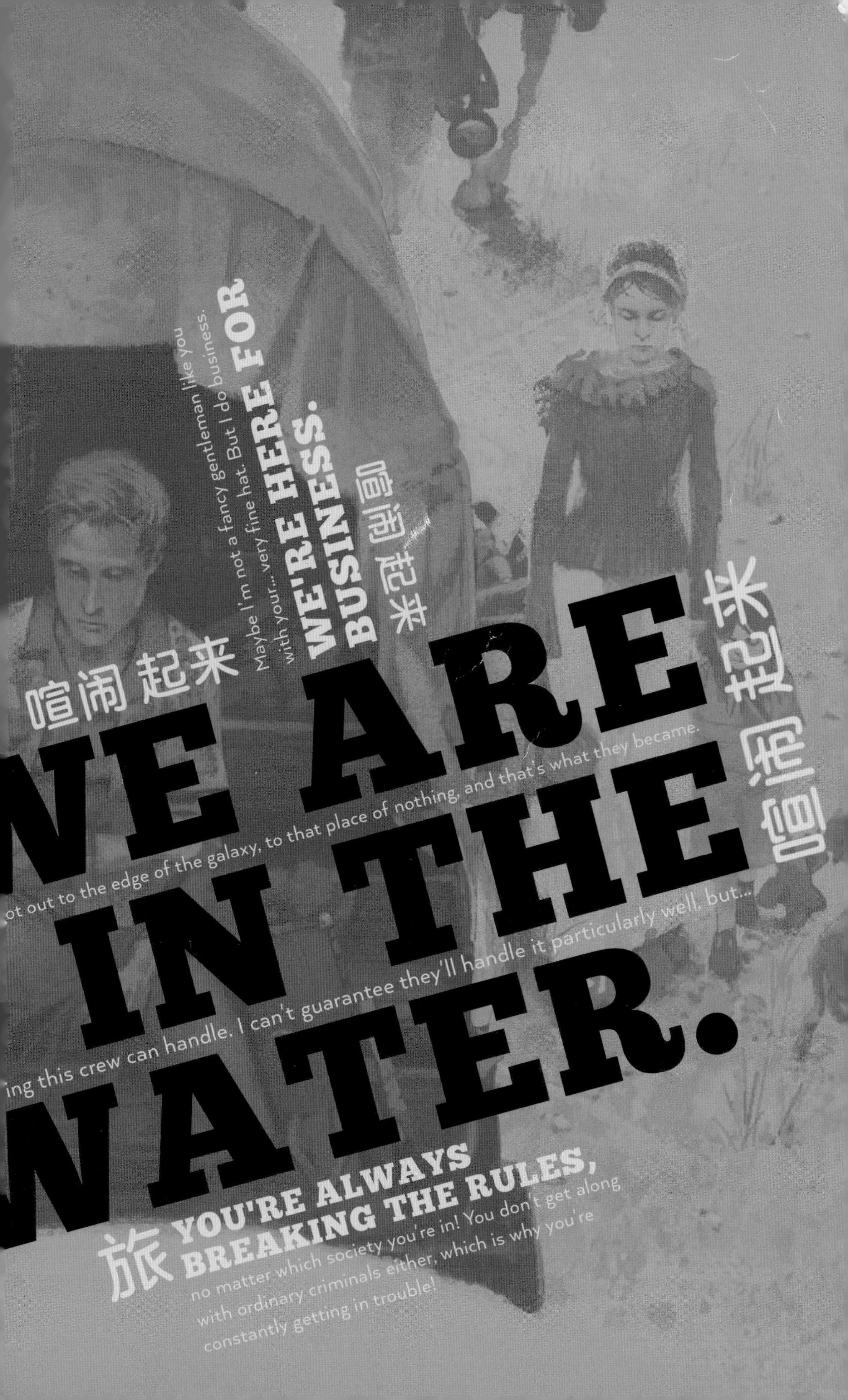

Maybe I'm not a fancy gentleman like you
with your... very fine hat. But I do business.
WE'RE HERE FOR
BUSINESS.
喧闹起来
喧闹起来
喧闹起来
E ARE
IN THE
ATER.
ot out to the edge of the galaxy, to that place of nothing, and that's what they became.
ing this crew can handle. I can't guarantee they'll handle it particularly well, but...
旅
YOU'RE ALWAYS
BREAKING THE RULES,
no matter which society you're in! You don't get along
with ordinary criminals either, which is why you're
constantly getting in trouble!

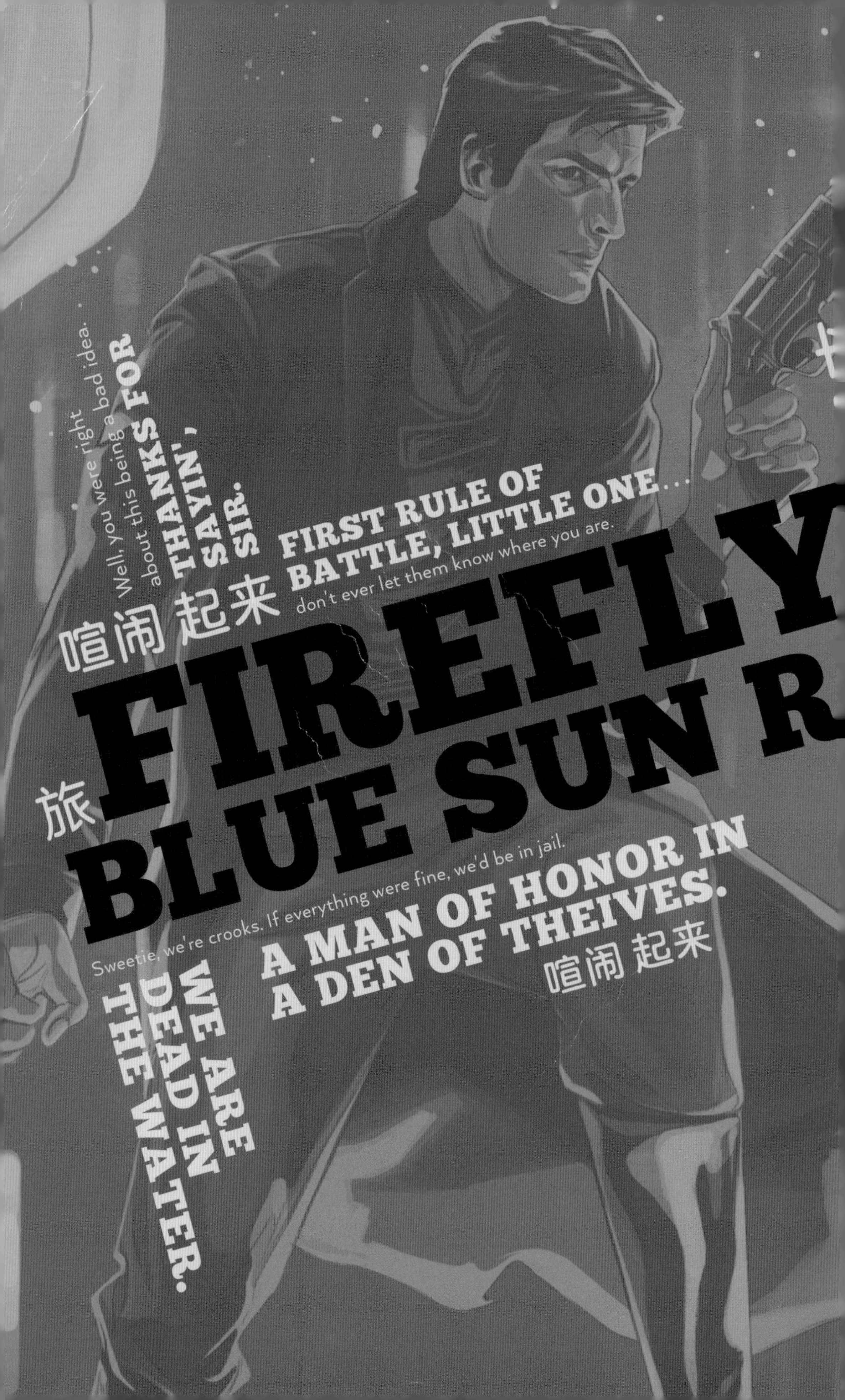
Well, you were right about this being a bad idea.
THANKS FOR SAYIN', SIR.
FIRST RULE OF BATTLE, LITTLE ONE...
don't ever let them know where you are.
喧闹起来
旅
FIREFLY
BLUE SUN R
Sweetie, we're crooks. If everything were fine, we'd be in jail.
A MAN OF HONOR IN A DEN OF THEIVES.
喧闹起来
WE ARE DEAD IN THE WATER.

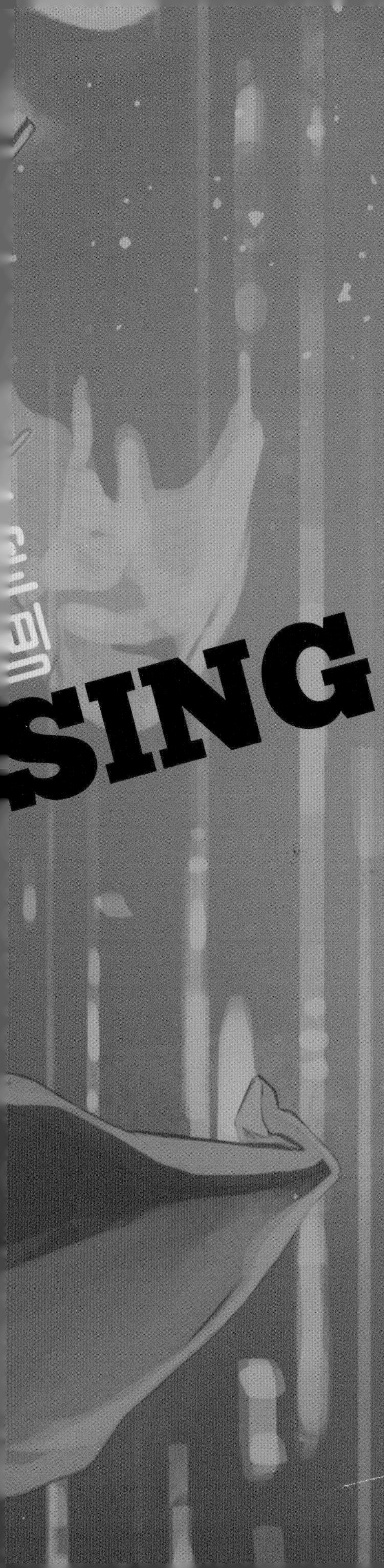
SING

Created by
Joss Whedon

Blue Sun Rising Part One

Written by
Greg Pak

Illustrated by
Dan McDaid
Lalit Kumar Sharma
Daniel Bayliss

Colored by
Marcelo Costa

Lettered by
Jim Campbell

Cover by
Nimit Malavia

BLUE SUN RISING

CHAPTER ONE 喧闹起来

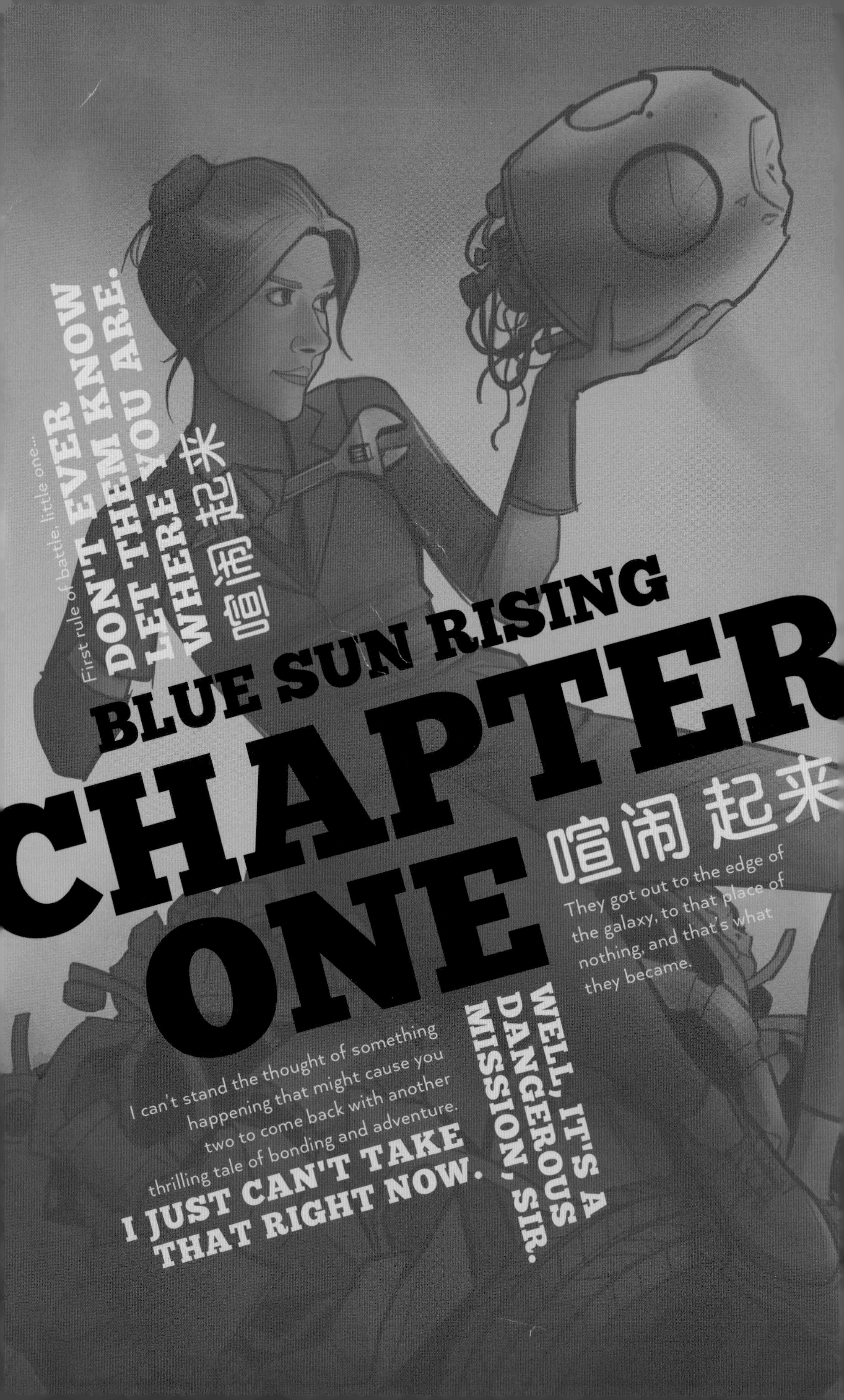
First rule of battle, little one...
DON'T EVER LET THEM KNOW WHERE YOU ARE.
喧闹起来
They got out to the edge of the galaxy, to that place of nothing, and that's what they became.
I can't stand the thought of something happening that might cause you two to come back with another thrilling tale of bonding and adventure.
I JUST CAN'T TAKE THAT RIGHT NOW.
WELL, IT'S A DANGEROUS MISSION, SIR.

Chapter One
The 'Verse in Flux

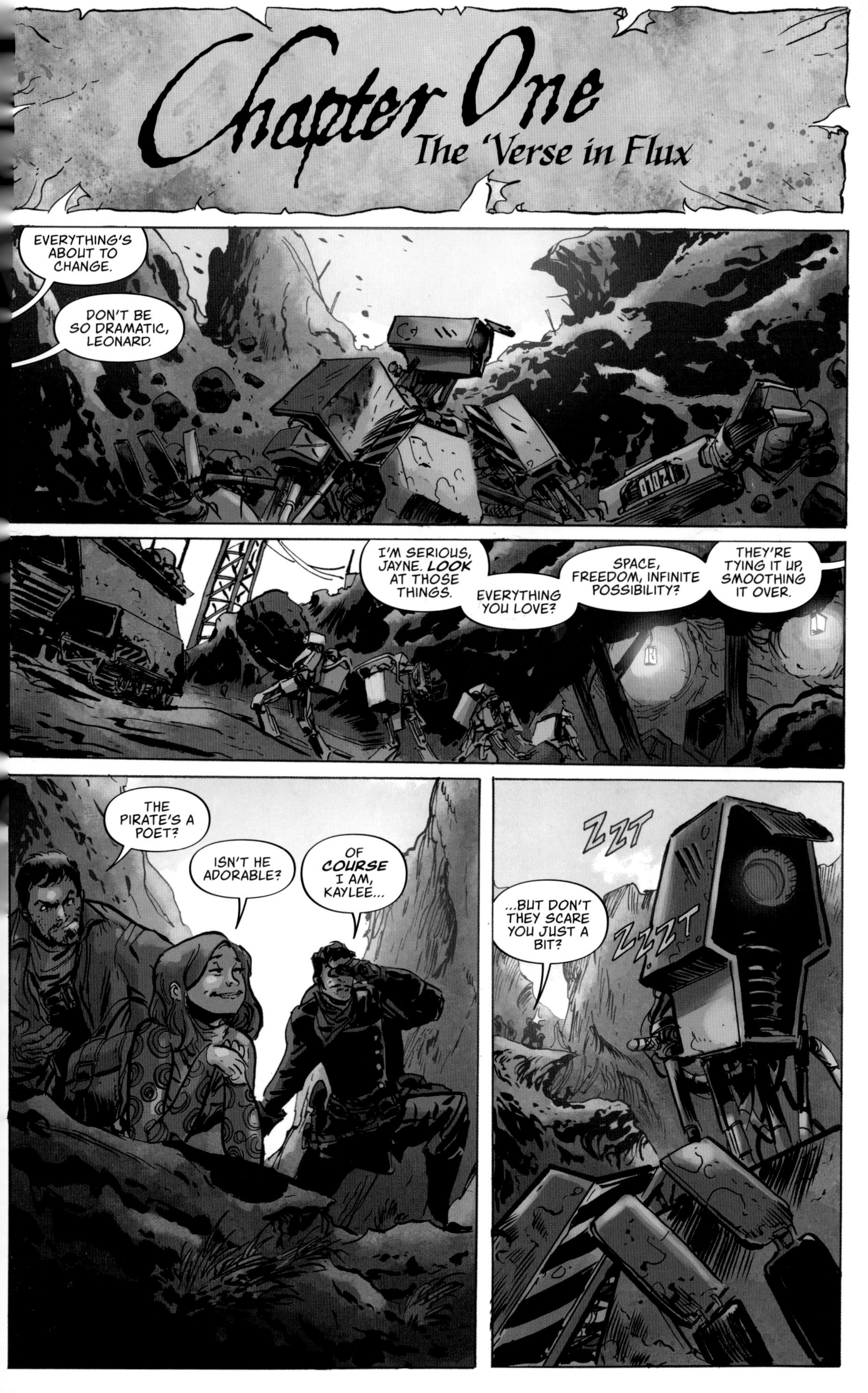
EVERYTHING'S ABOUT TO CHANGE.
DON'T BE SO DRAMATIC, LEONARD.
I'M SERIOUS, JAYNE. LOOK AT THOSE THINGS.
EVERYTHING YOU LOVE?
SPACE, FREEDOM, INFINITE POSSIBILITY?
THEY'RE TYING IT UP, SMOOTHING IT OVER.
THE PIRATE'S A POET?
ISN'T HE ADORABLE?
OF COURSE I AM, KAYLEE...
ZZT
...BUT DON'T THEY SCARE YOU JUST A BIT?
ZZZT
01021

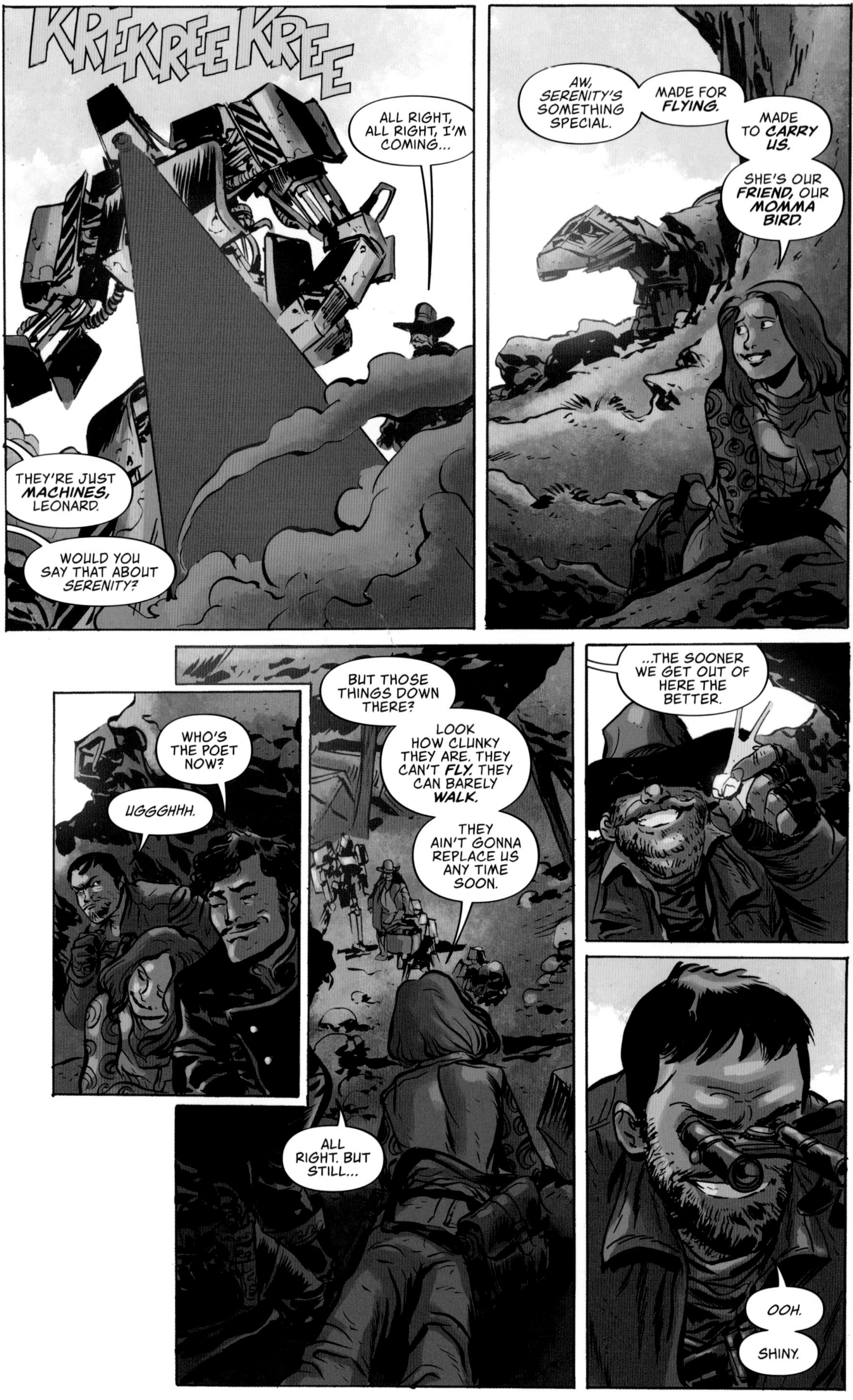
KREE KREE KREE
ALL RIGHT, ALL RIGHT, I'M COMING...
THEY'RE JUST MACHINES, LEONARD.
WOULD YOU SAY THAT ABOUT SERENITY?
AW, SERENITY'S SOMETHING SPECIAL.
MADE FOR FLYING.
MADE TO CARRY US.
SHE'S OUR FRIEND, OUR MOMMA BIRD.
WHO'S THE POET NOW?
UGGGHHH.
BUT THOSE THINGS DOWN THERE?
LOOK HOW CLUNKY THEY ARE. THEY CAN'T FLY. THEY CAN BARELY WALK.
THEY AIN'T GONNA REPLACE US ANY TIME SOON.
ALL RIGHT. BUT STILL...
...THE SOONER WE GET OUT OF HERE THE BETTER.
OOH.
SHINY.

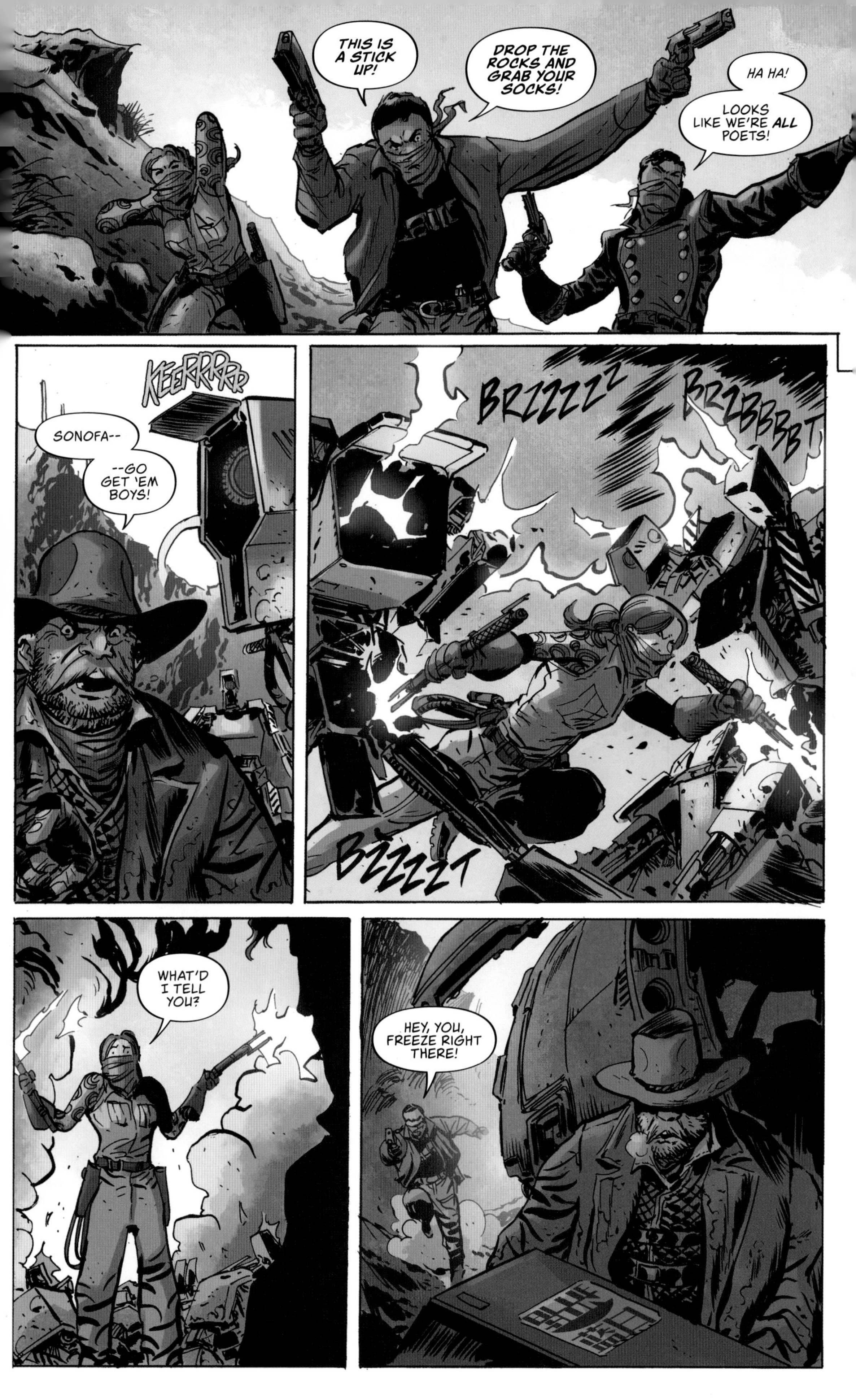
THIS IS A STICK UP!
DROP THE ROCKS AND GRAB YOUR SOCKS!
HA HA!
LOOKS LIKE WE'RE ALL POETS!
KEERRRRR
SONOFA--
--GO GET 'EM BOYS!
BRZZZZZ
BRZZBBBBT
BZZZZZT
WHAT'D I TELL YOU?
HEY, YOU, FREEZE RIGHT THERE!

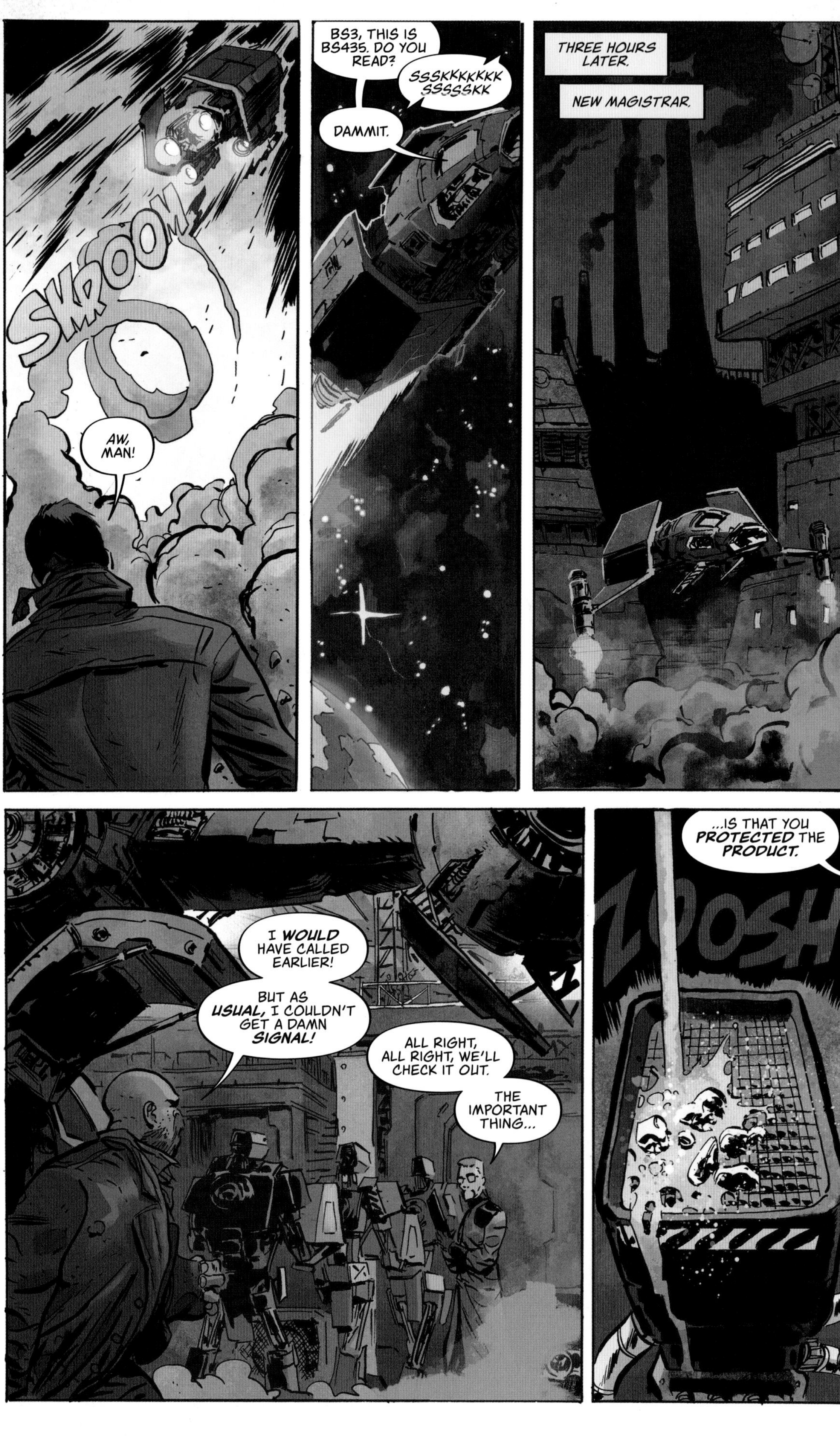
SKROOM
AW, MAN!
BS3, THIS IS BS435. DO YOU READ?
SSSKKKKKKK SSSSSKK
DAMMIT.
THREE HOURS LATER.
NEW MAGISTRAR.
I WOULD HAVE CALLED EARLIER!
BUT AS USUAL, I COULDN'T GET A DAMN SIGNAL!
ALL RIGHT, ALL RIGHT, WE'LL CHECK IT OUT.
THE IMPORTANT THING...
...IS THAT YOU PROTECTED THE PRODUCT.
ZOOSH

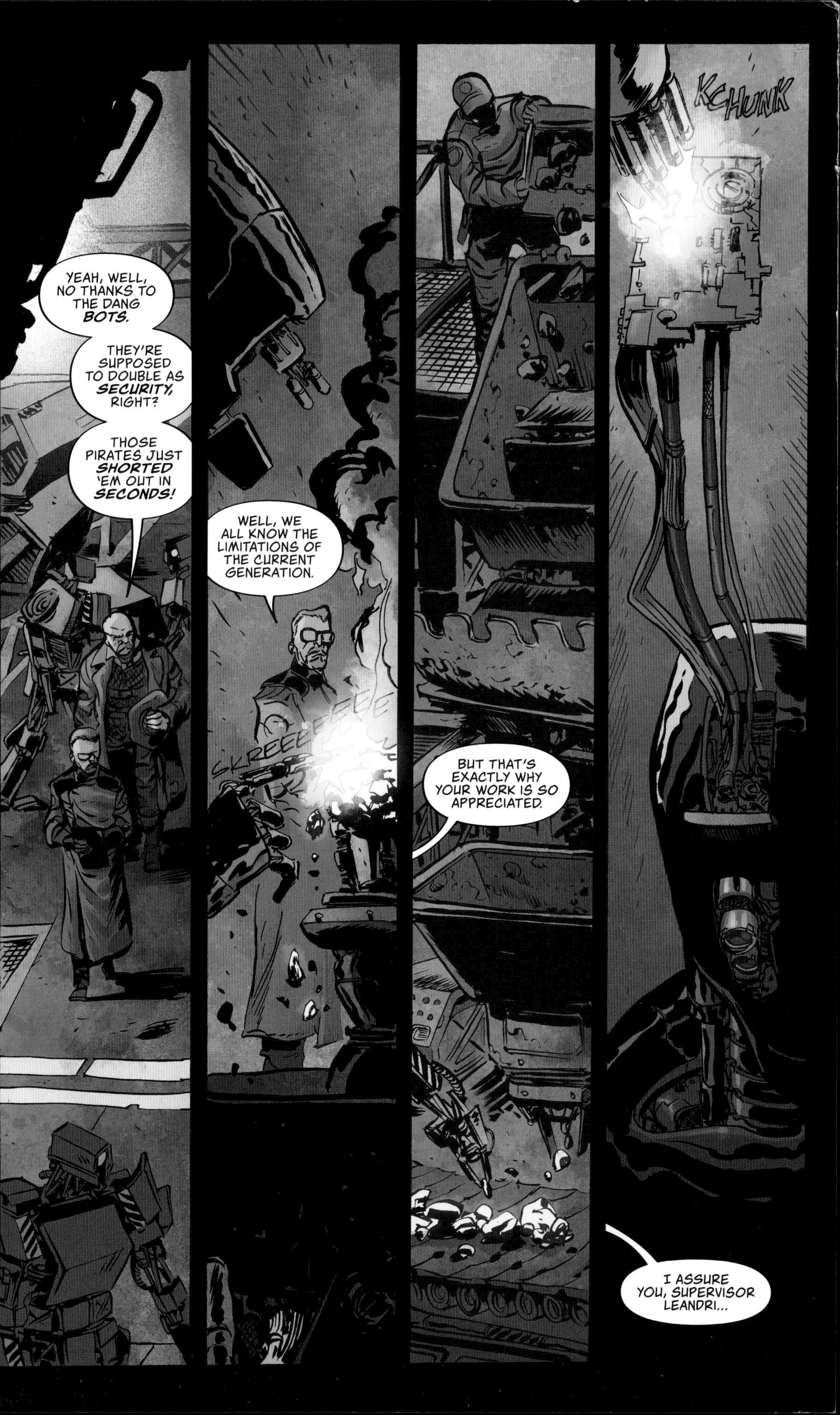
YEAH, WELL, NO THANKS TO THE DANG BOTS.
THEY'RE SUPPOSED TO DOUBLE AS SECURITY, RIGHT?
THOSE PIRATES JUST SHORTED 'EM OUT IN SECONDS!
WELL, WE ALL KNOW THE LIMITATIONS OF THE CURRENT GENERATION.
BUT THAT'S EXACTLY WHY YOUR WORK IS SO APPRECIATED.
KCHUNK
I ASSURE YOU, SUPERVISOR LEANDRI...

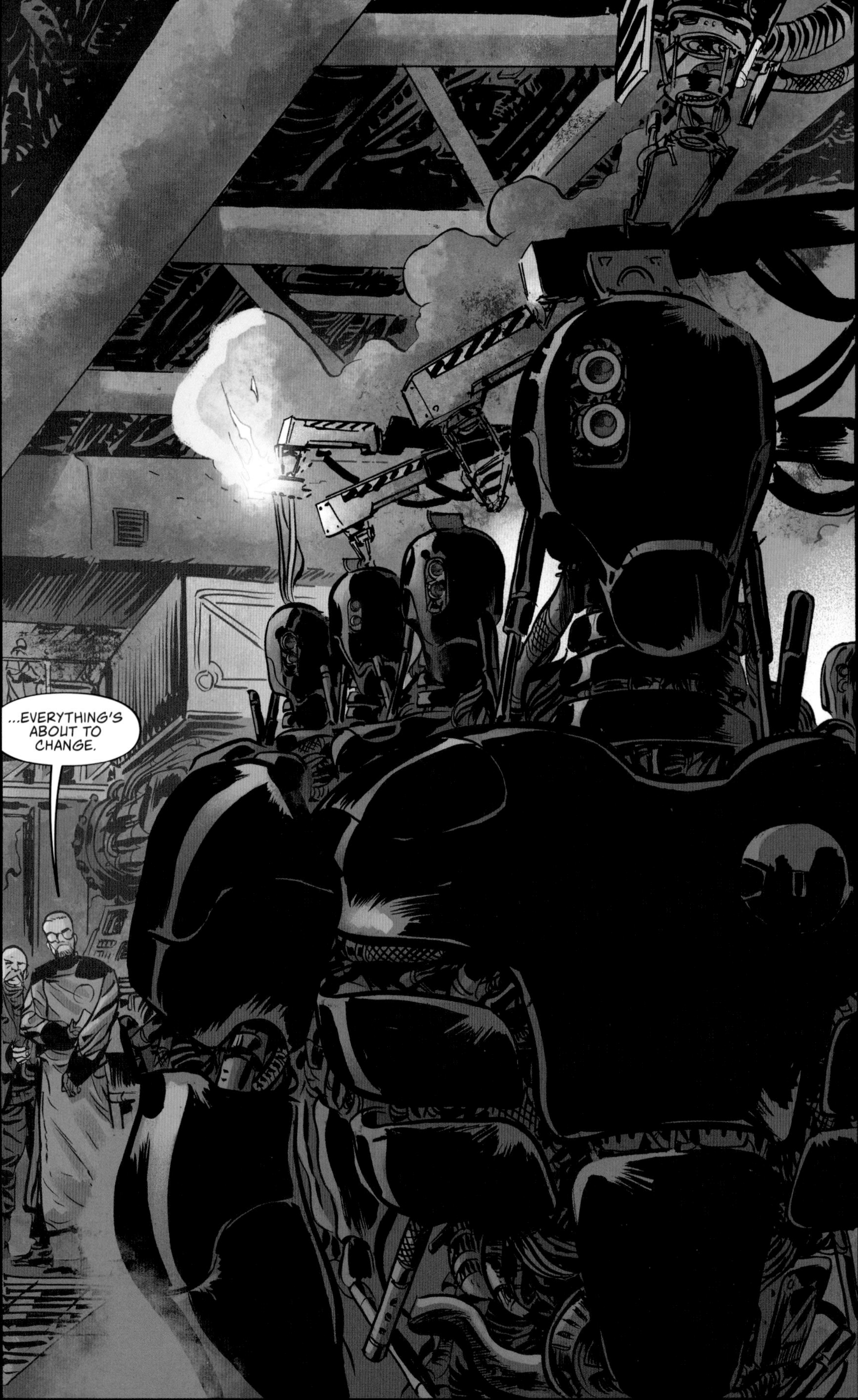
...EVERYTHING'S ABOUT TO CHANGE.

Chapter Two
In the Cool of the Sun

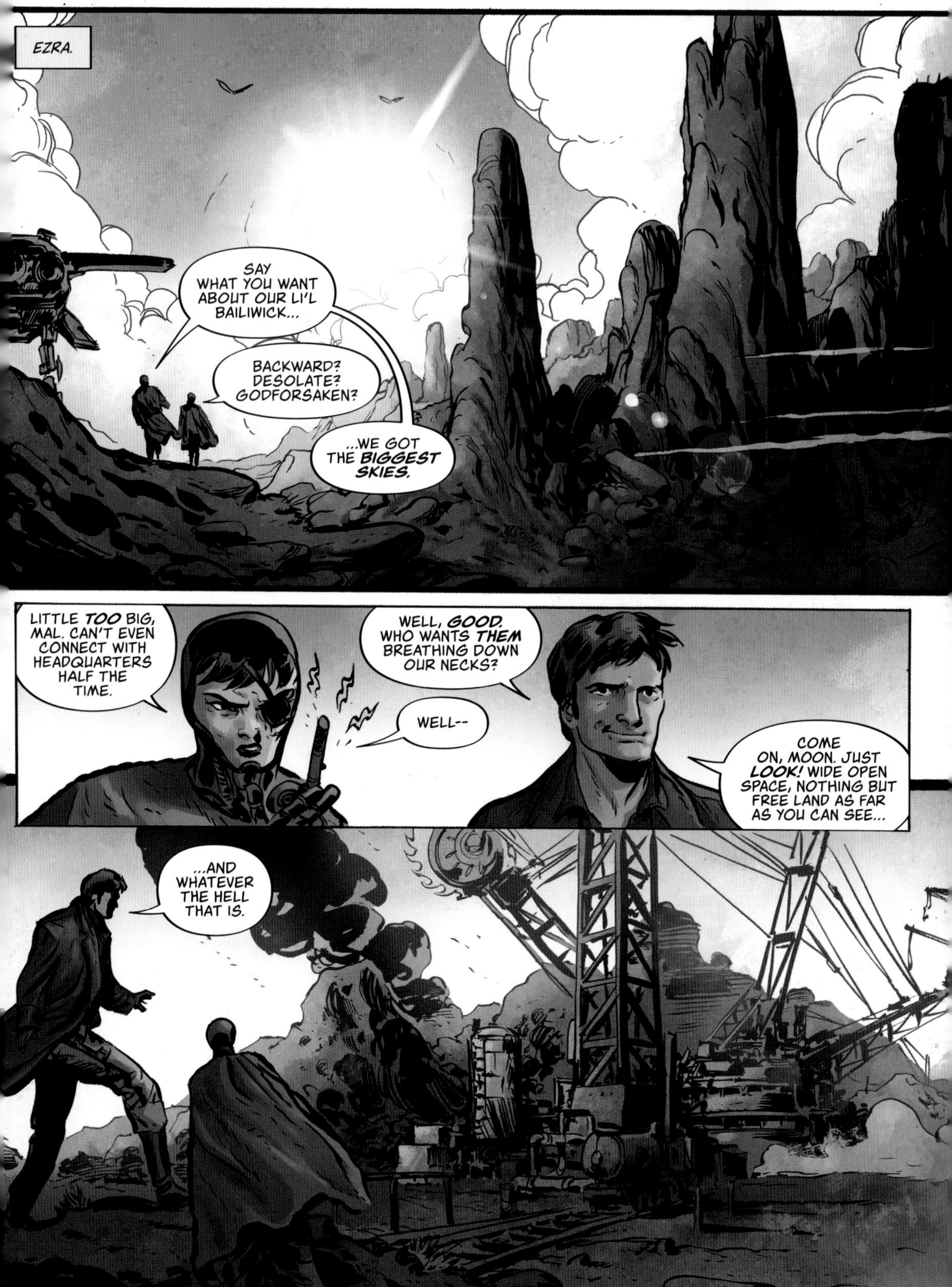
EZRA.
SAY WHAT YOU WANT ABOUT OUR LI'L BAILIWICK...
BACKWARD? DESOLATE? GODFORSAKEN?
...WE GOT THE BIGGEST SKIES.
LITTLE TOO BIG, MAL. CAN'T EVEN CONNECT WITH HEADQUARTERS HALF THE TIME.
WELL, GOOD. WHO WANTS THEM BREATHING DOWN OUR NECKS?
WELL--
COME ON, MOON. JUST LOOK! WIDE OPEN SPACE, NOTHING BUT FREE LAND AS FAR AS YOU CAN SEE...
...AND WHATEVER THE HELL THAT IS.

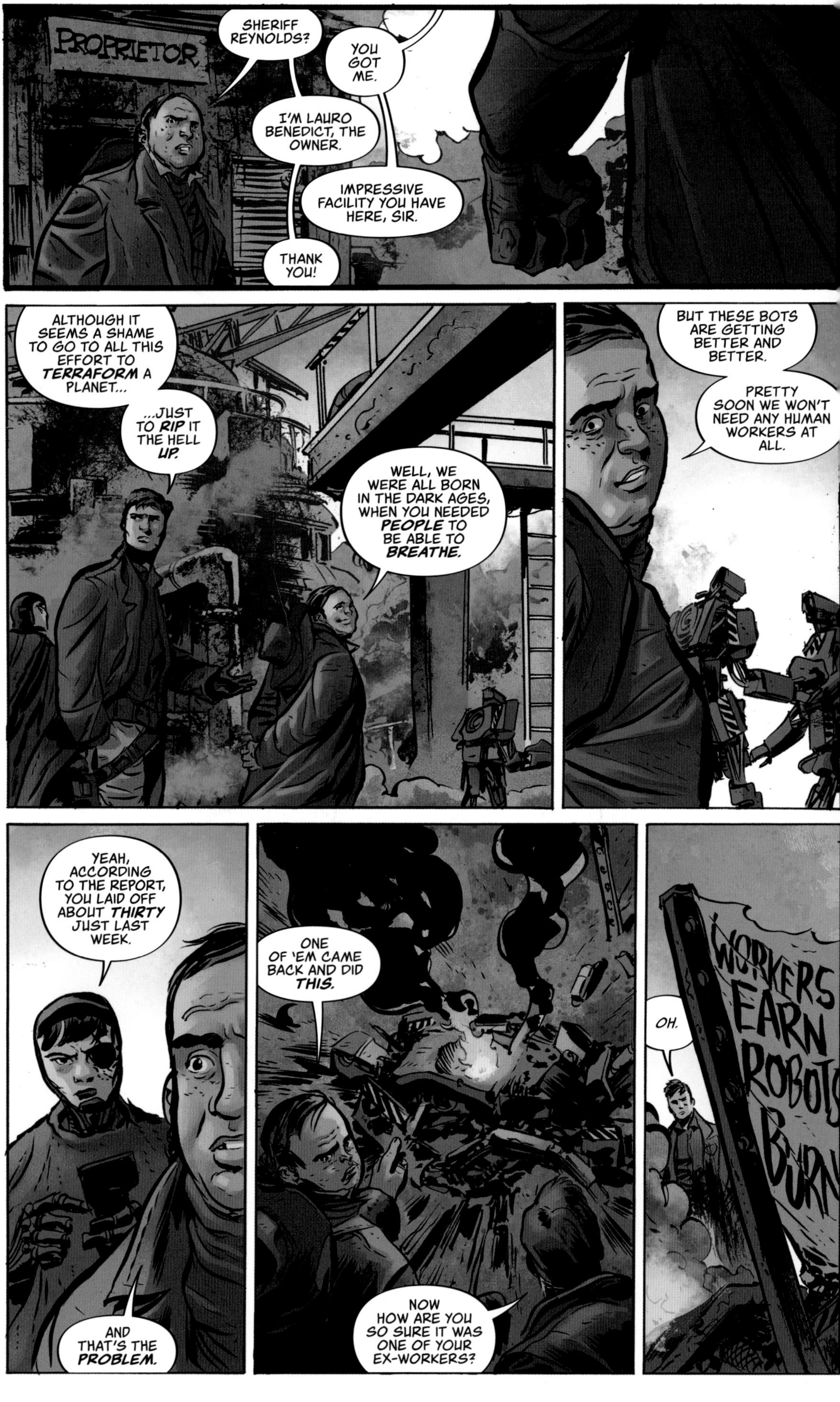
PROPRIETOR
SHERIFF REYNOLDS?
YOU GOT ME.
I'M LAURO BENEDICT, THE OWNER.
IMPRESSIVE FACILITY YOU HAVE HERE, SIR.
THANK YOU!
ALTHOUGH IT SEEMS A SHAME TO GO TO ALL THIS EFFORT TO TERRAFORM A PLANET...
...JUST TO RIP IT THE HELL UP.
WELL, WE WERE ALL BORN IN THE DARK AGES, WHEN YOU NEEDED PEOPLE TO BE ABLE TO BREATHE.
BUT THESE BOTS ARE GETTING BETTER AND BETTER.
PRETTY SOON WE WON'T NEED ANY HUMAN WORKERS AT ALL.
YEAH, ACCORDING TO THE REPORT, YOU LAID OFF ABOUT THIRTY JUST LAST WEEK.
AND THAT'S THE PROBLEM.
ONE OF 'EM CAME BACK AND DID THIS.
NOW HOW ARE YOU SO SURE IT WAS ONE OF YOUR EX-WORKERS?
OH.
WORKERS EARN ROBOTS BURN

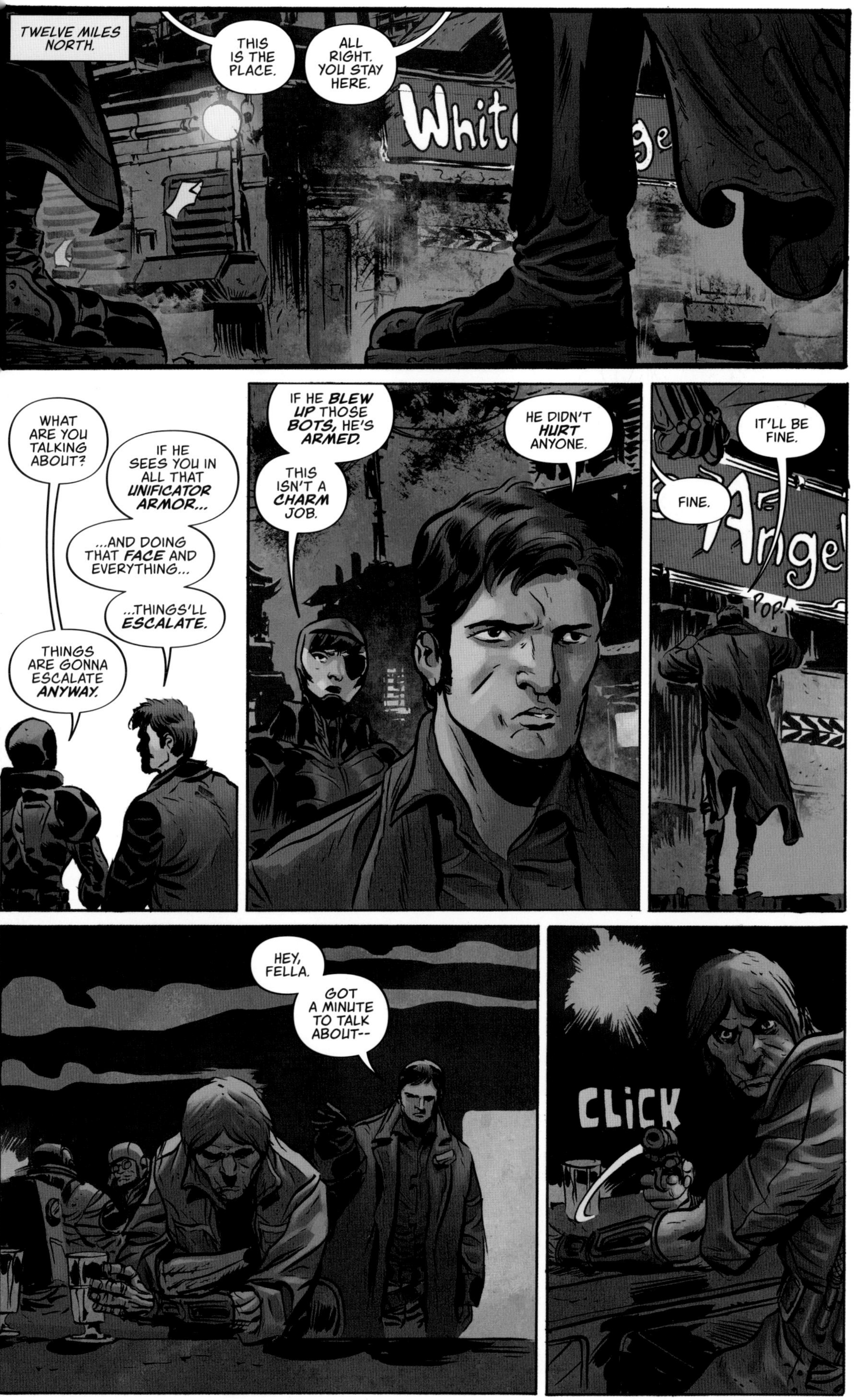
TWELVE MILES NORTH.
THIS IS THE PLACE.
ALL RIGHT. YOU STAY HERE.
WHAT ARE YOU TALKING ABOUT?
IF HE SEES YOU IN ALL THAT UNIFICATOR ARMOR...
...AND DOING THAT FACE AND EVERYTHING...
...THINGS'LL ESCALATE.
THINGS ARE GONNA ESCALATE ANYWAY.
IF HE BLEW UP THOSE BOTS, HE'S ARMED.
THIS ISN'T A CHARM JOB.
HE DIDN'T HURT ANYONE.
IT'LL BE FINE.
FINE.
POP!
HEY, FELLA.
GOT A MINUTE TO TALK ABOUT--
CLICK

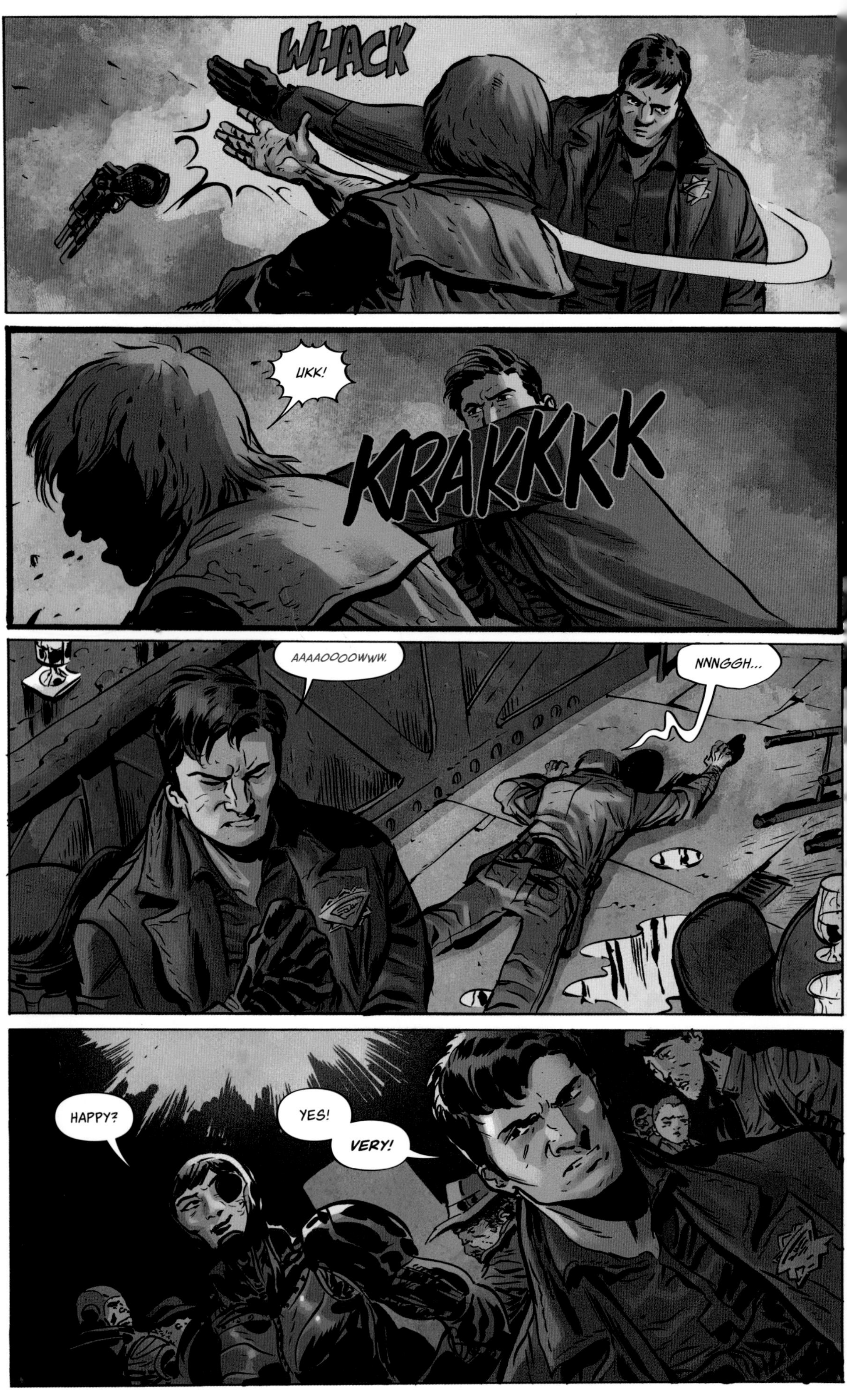
WHACK
UKK!
KRAKKKK
AAAAOOOOWWW.
NNNGGH...
HAPPY?
YES!
VERY!

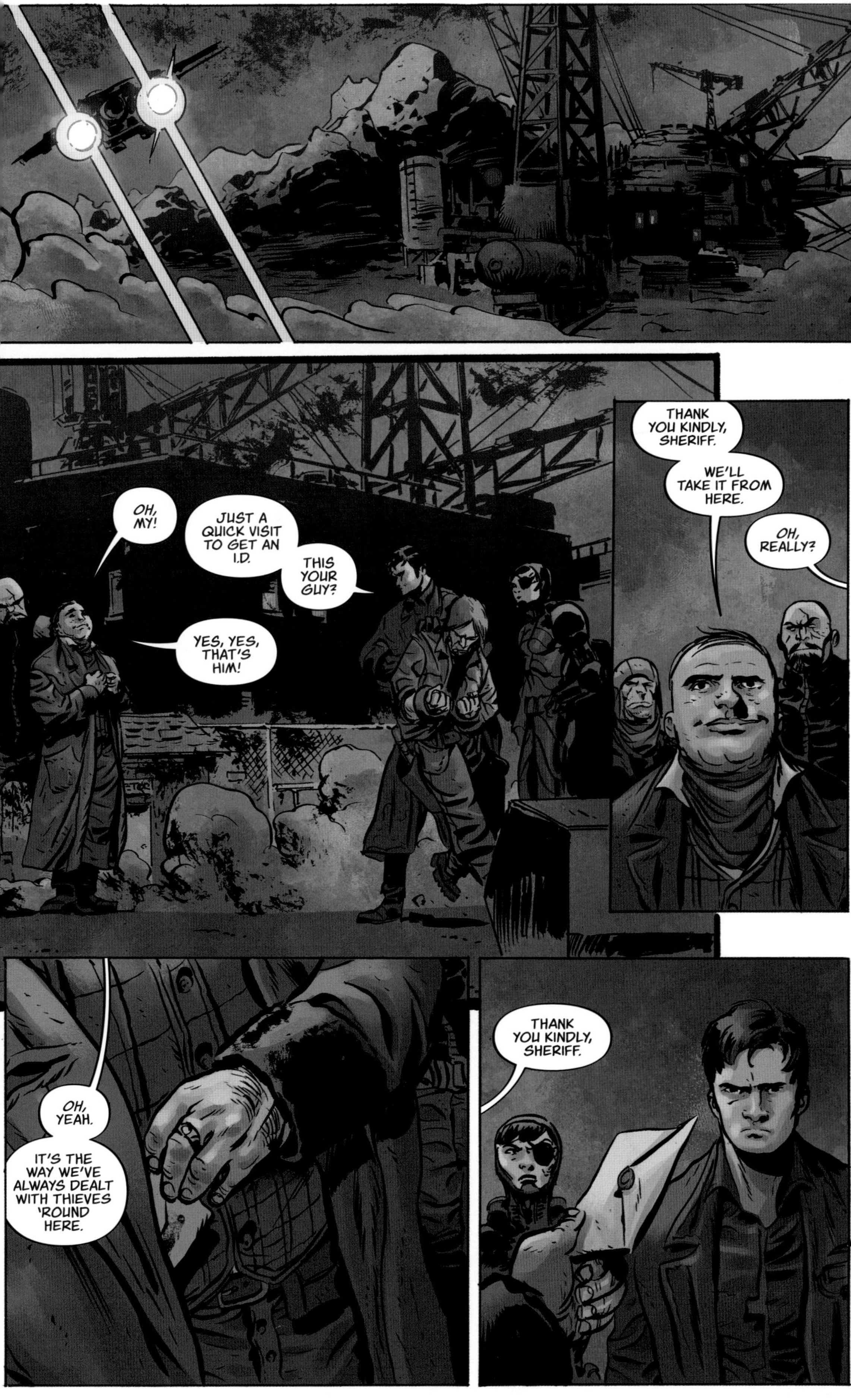
OH, MY!
JUST A QUICK VISIT TO GET AN I.D.
THIS YOUR GUY?
YES, YES, THAT'S HIM!
THANK YOU KINDLY, SHERIFF.
WE'LL TAKE IT FROM HERE.
OH, REALLY?
OH, YEAH.
IT'S THE WAY WE'VE ALWAYS DEALT WITH THIEVES 'ROUND HERE.
THANK YOU KINDLY, SHERIFF.

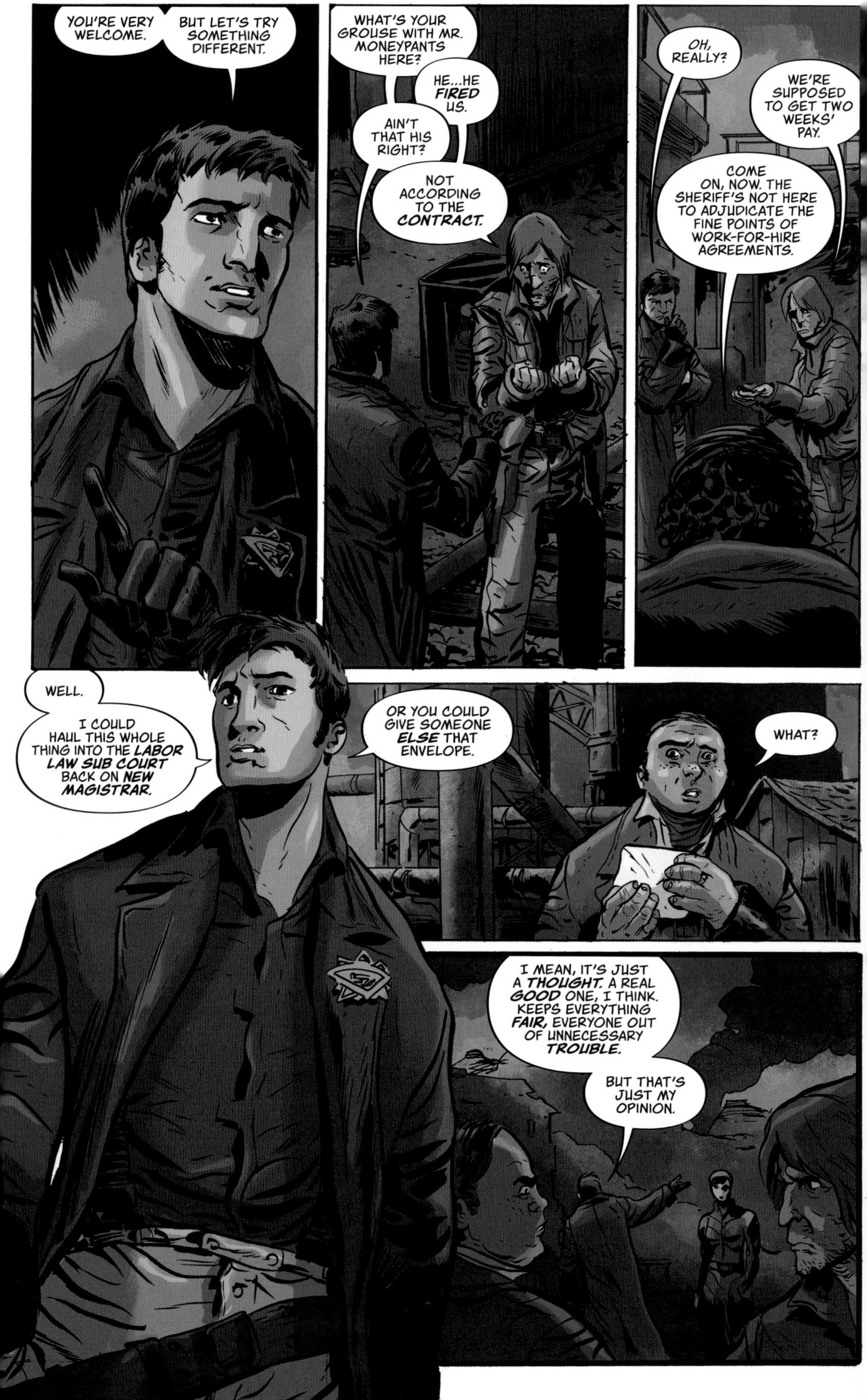
YOU'RE VERY WELCOME.
BUT LET'S TRY SOMETHING DIFFERENT.
WHAT'S YOUR GROUSE WITH MR. MONEYPANTS HERE?
HE...HE FIRED US.
AIN'T THAT HIS RIGHT?
NOT ACCORDING TO THE CONTRACT.
OH, REALLY?
WE'RE SUPPOSED TO GET TWO WEEKS' PAY.
COME ON, NOW. THE SHERIFF'S NOT HERE TO ADJUDICATE THE FINE POINTS OF WORK-FOR-HIRE AGREEMENTS.
WELL.
I COULD HAUL THIS WHOLE THING INTO THE LABOR LAW SUB COURT BACK ON NEW MAGISTRAR.
OR YOU COULD GIVE SOMEONE ELSE THAT ENVELOPE.
WHAT?
I MEAN, IT'S JUST A THOUGHT. A REAL GOOD ONE, I THINK. KEEPS EVERYTHING FAIR, EVERYONE OUT OF UNNECESSARY TROUBLE.
BUT THAT'S JUST MY OPINION.

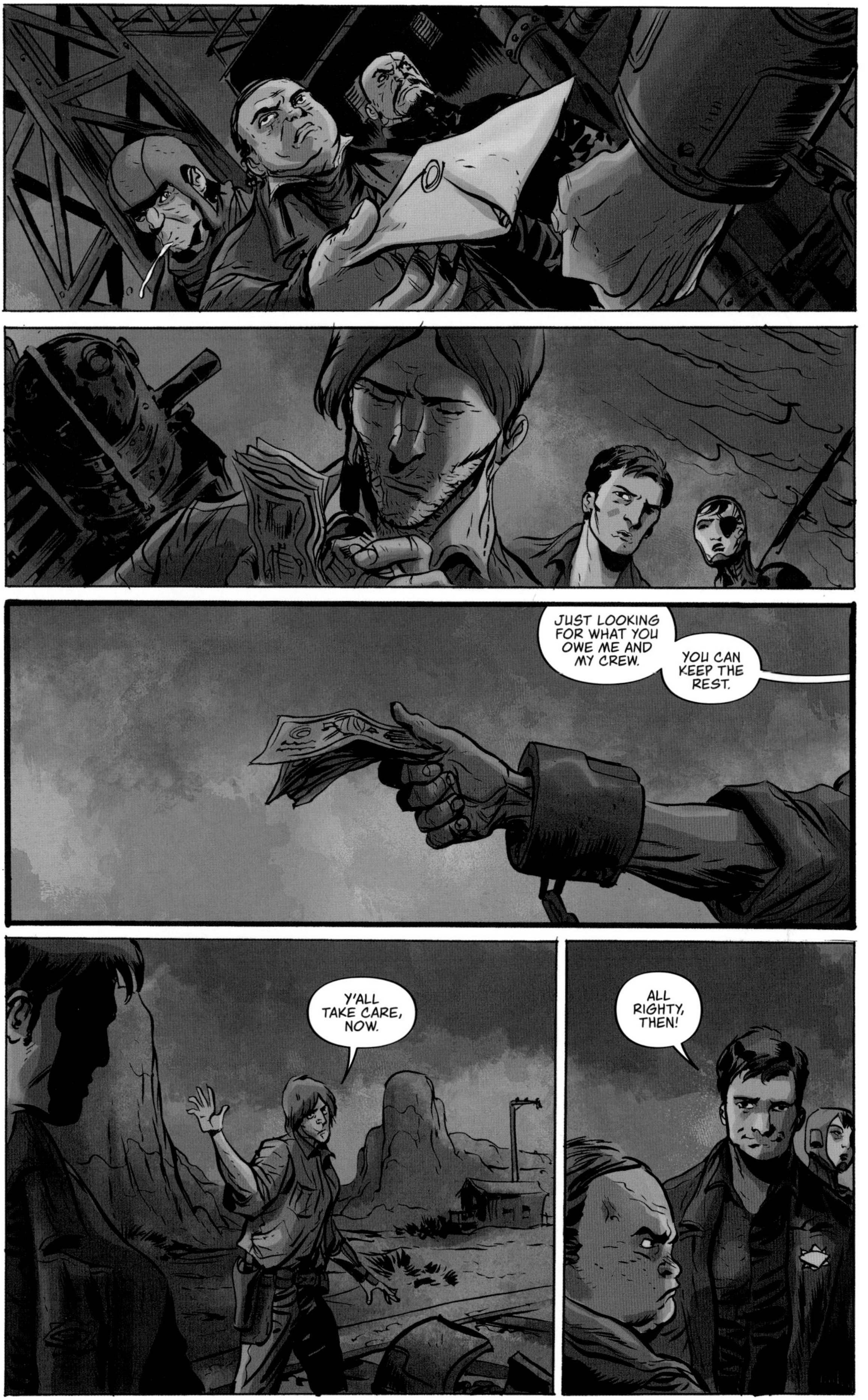
JUST LOOKING FOR WHAT YOU OWE ME AND MY CREW.
YOU CAN KEEP THE REST.
Y'ALL TAKE CARE, NOW.
ALL RIGHTY, THEN!

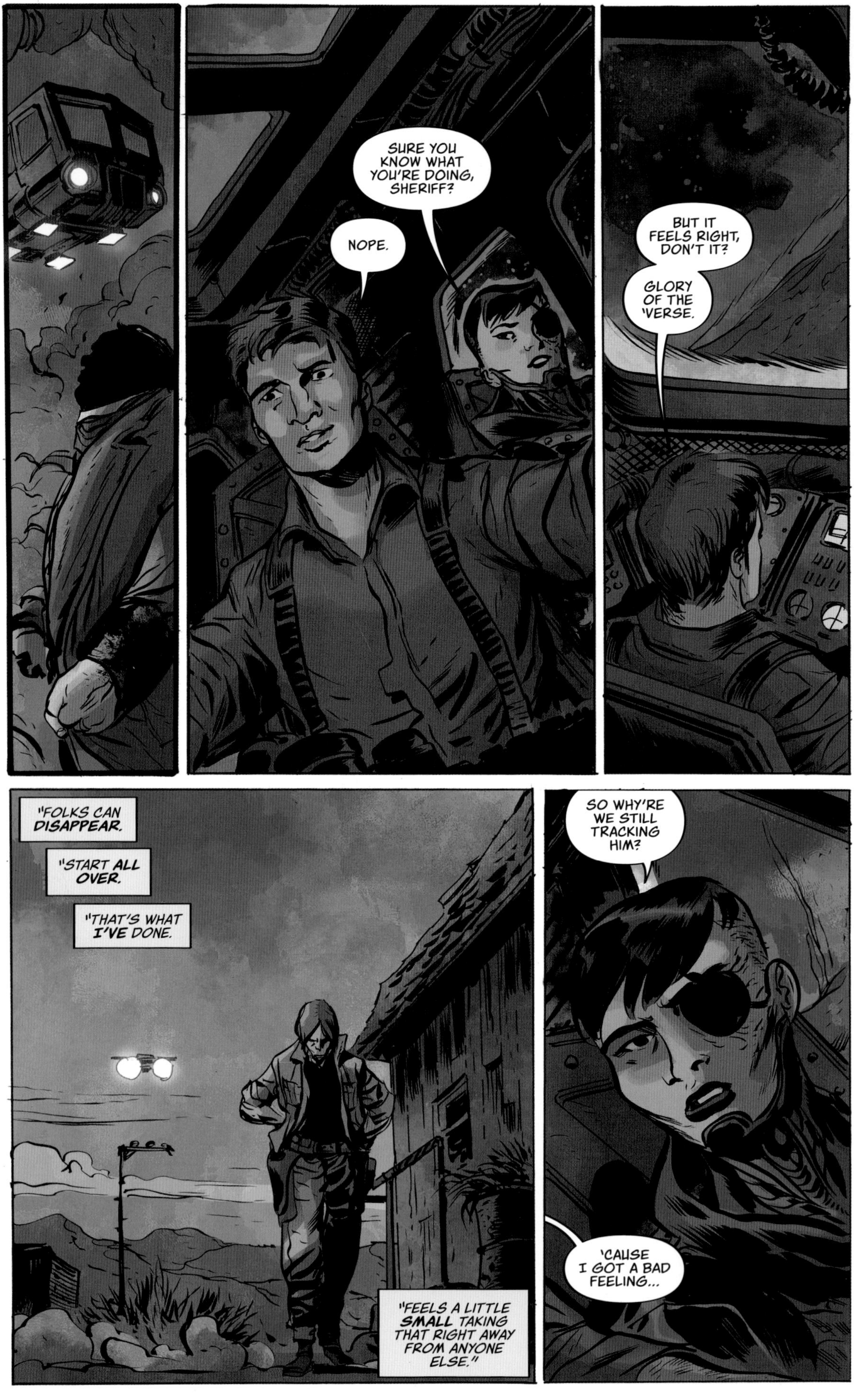
SURE YOU KNOW WHAT YOU'RE DOING, SHERIFF?
NOPE.
BUT IT FEELS RIGHT, DON'T IT?
GLORY OF THE 'VERSE.
"FOLKS CAN DISAPPEAR.
"START ALL OVER.
"THAT'S WHAT I'VE DONE.
"FEELS A LITTLE SMALL TAKING THAT RIGHT AWAY FROM ANYONE ELSE."
SO WHY'RE WE STILL TRACKING HIM?
'CAUSE I GOT A BAD FEELING...

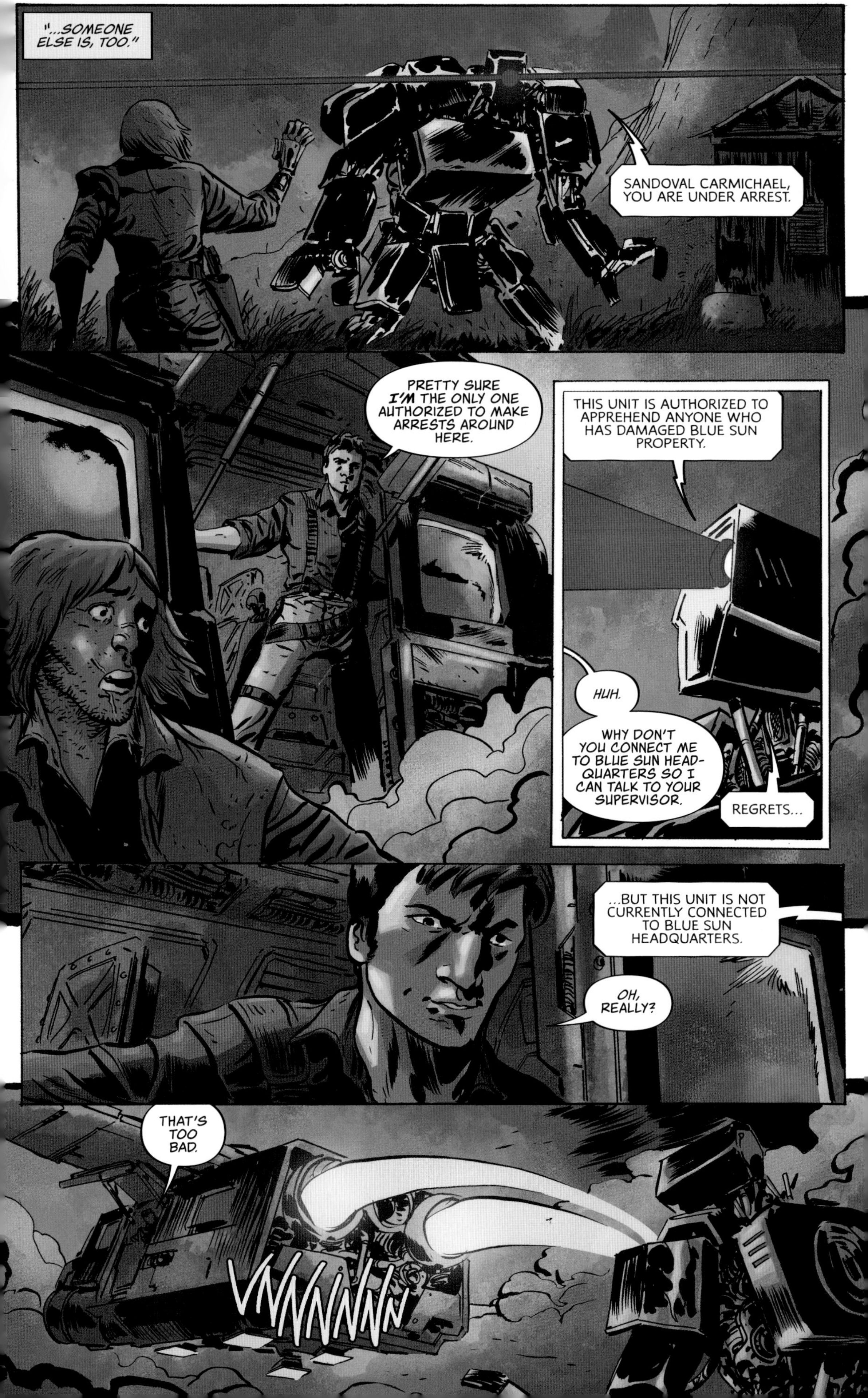
"...SOMEONE ELSE IS, TOO."
SANDOVAL CARMICHAEL, YOU ARE UNDER ARREST.
PRETTY SURE I'M THE ONLY ONE AUTHORIZED TO MAKE ARRESTS AROUND HERE.
THIS UNIT IS AUTHORIZED TO APPREHEND ANYONE WHO HAS DAMAGED BLUE SUN PROPERTY.
HUH.
WHY DON'T YOU CONNECT ME TO BLUE SUN HEAD-QUARTERS SO I CAN TALK TO YOUR SUPERVISOR.
REGRETS...
...BUT THIS UNIT IS NOT CURRENTLY CONNECTED TO BLUE SUN HEADQUARTERS.
OH, REALLY?
THAT'S TOO BAD.
VNNNNNNN

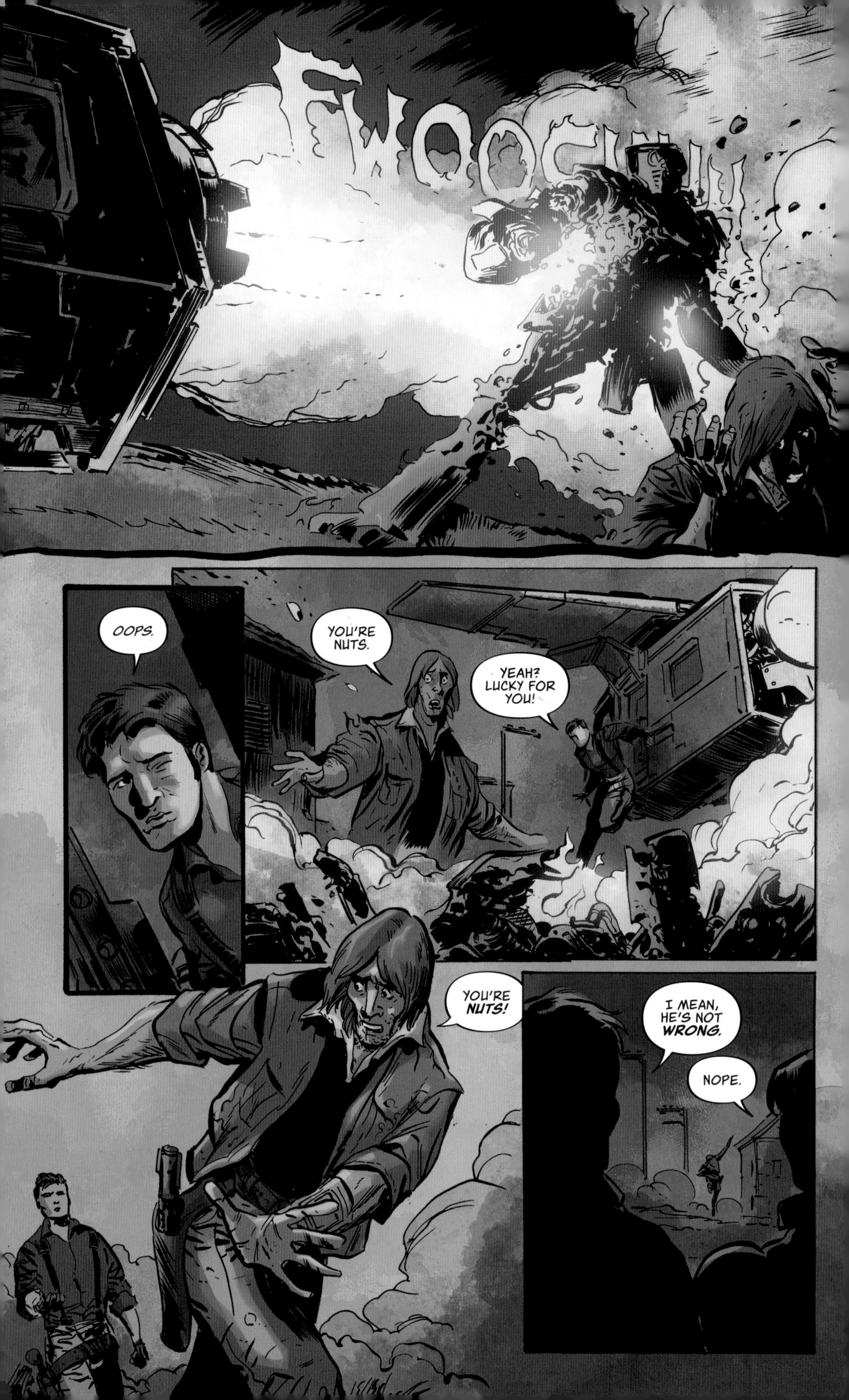
FWOOCHHH
OOPS.
YOU'RE NUTS.
YEAH? LUCKY FOR YOU!
YOU'RE NUTS!
I MEAN, HE'S NOT WRONG.
NOPE.

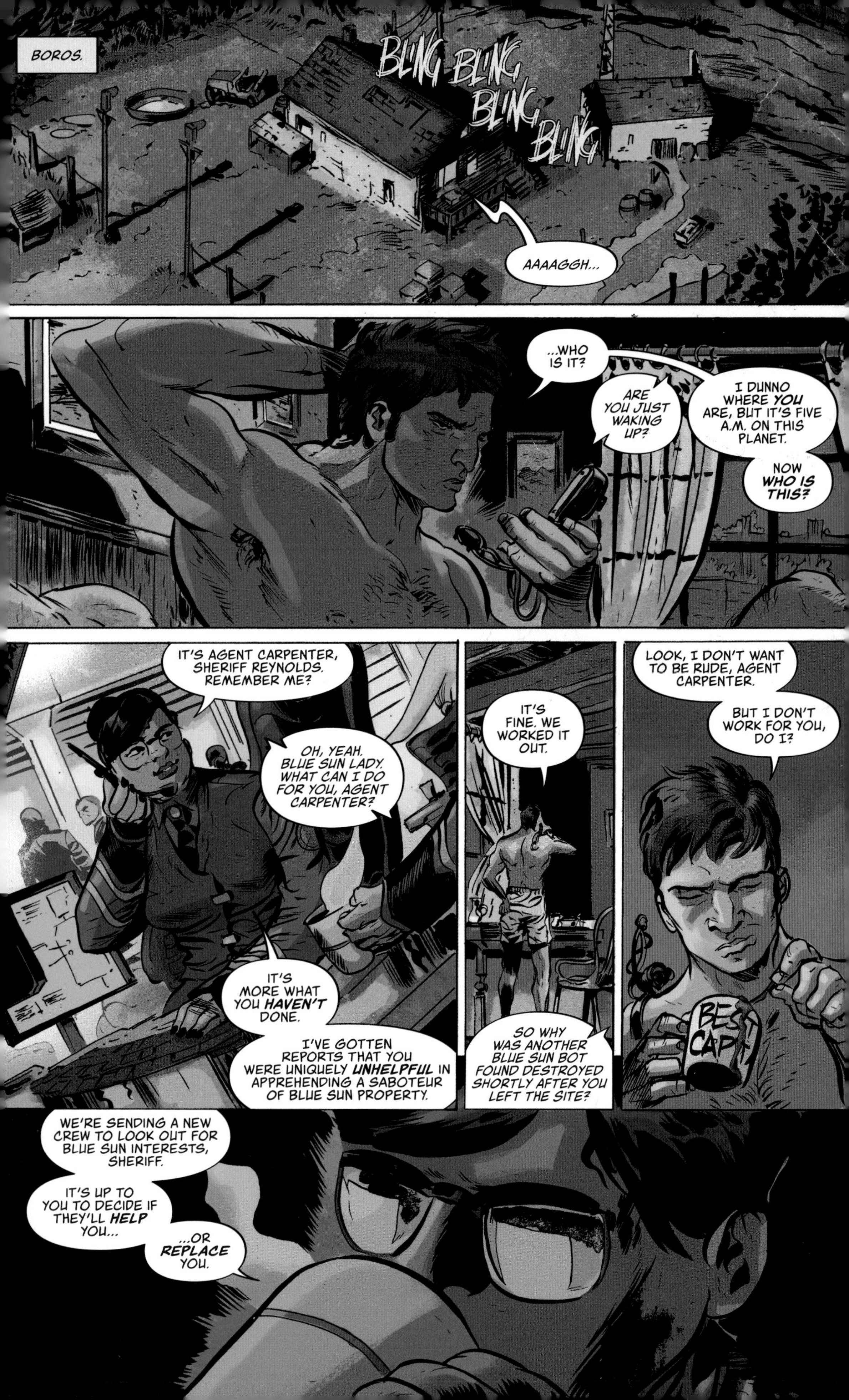
BOROS.
BLING BLING BLING BLING
AAAAGGH...
...WHO IS IT?
ARE YOU JUST WAKING UP?
I DUNNO WHERE YOU ARE, BUT IT'S FIVE A.M. ON THIS PLANET.
NOW WHO IS THIS?
IT'S AGENT CARPENTER, SHERIFF REYNOLDS. REMEMBER ME?
OH, YEAH. BLUE SUN LADY. WHAT CAN I DO FOR YOU, AGENT CARPENTER?
IT'S MORE WHAT YOU HAVEN'T DONE.
I'VE GOTTEN REPORTS THAT YOU WERE UNIQUELY UNHELPFUL IN APPREHENDING A SABOTEUR OF BLUE SUN PROPERTY.
IT'S FINE. WE WORKED IT OUT.
SO WHY WAS ANOTHER BLUE SUN BOT FOUND DESTROYED SHORTLY AFTER YOU LEFT THE SITE?
LOOK, I DON'T WANT TO BE RUDE, AGENT CARPENTER.
BUT I DON'T WORK FOR YOU, DO I?
WE'RE SENDING A NEW CREW TO LOOK OUT FOR BLUE SUN INTERESTS, SHERIFF.
IT'S UP TO YOU TO DECIDE IF THEY'LL HELP YOU...
...OR REPLACE YOU.

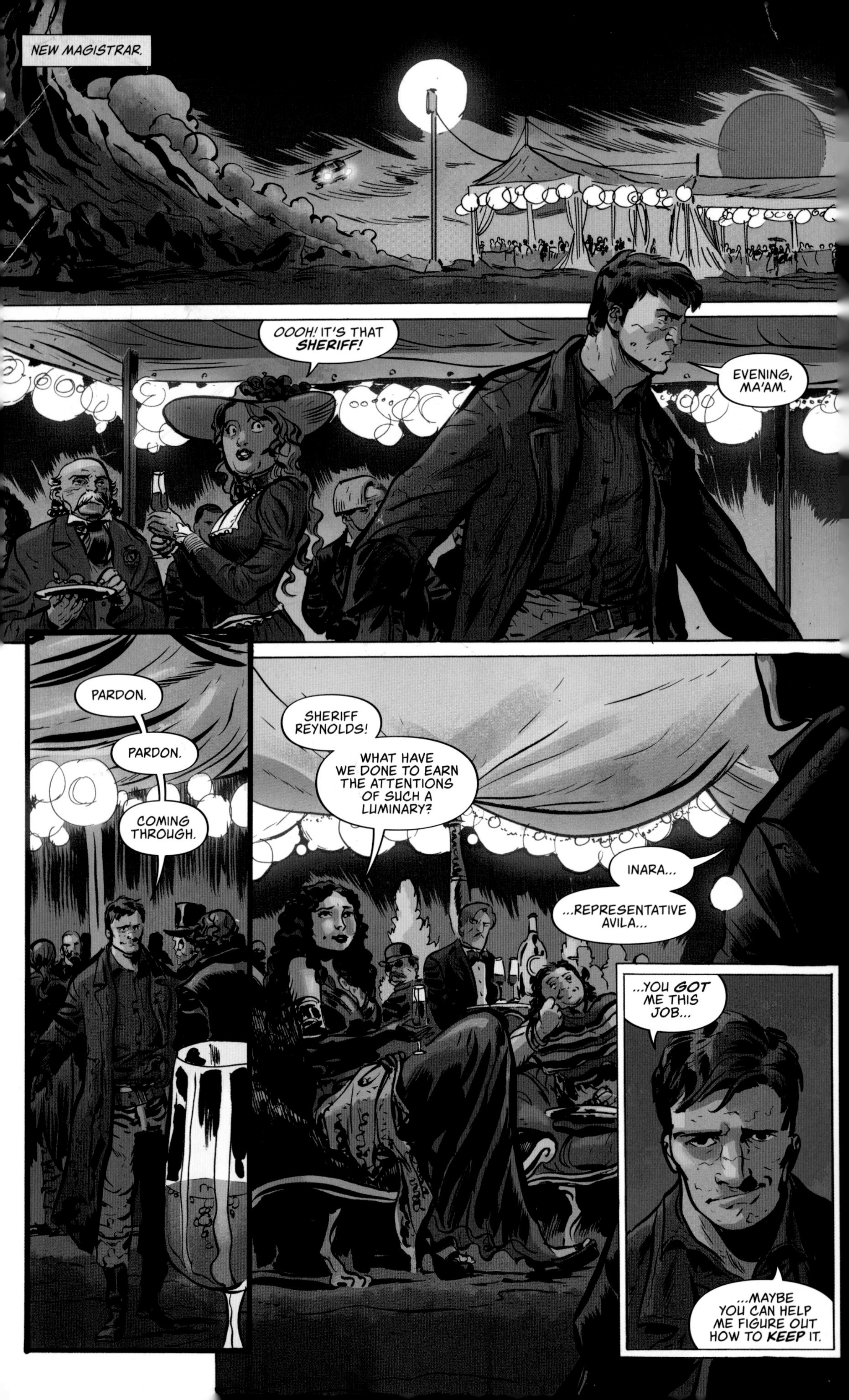
NEW MAGISTRAR.
OOOH! IT'S THAT SHERIFF!
EVENING, MA'AM.
PARDON.
PARDON.
COMING THROUGH.
SHERIFF REYNOLDS!
WHAT HAVE WE DONE TO EARN THE ATTENTIONS OF SUCH A LUMINARY?
INARA...
...REPRESENTATIVE AVILA...
...YOU GOT ME THIS JOB...
...MAYBE YOU CAN HELP ME FIGURE OUT HOW TO KEEP IT.

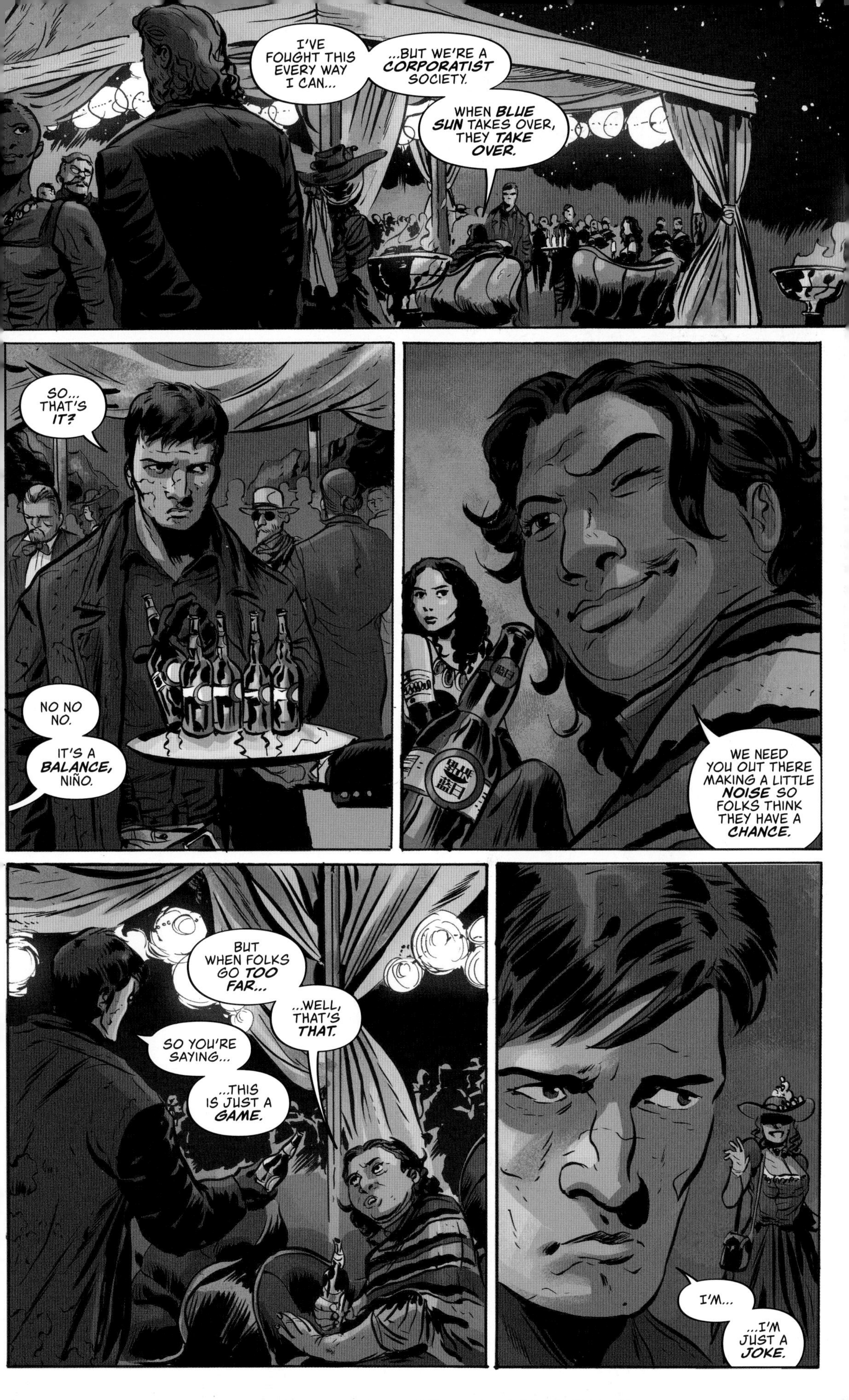

I'VE FOUGHT THIS EVERY WAY I CAN...
...BUT WE'RE A CORPORATIST SOCIETY.
WHEN BLUE SUN TAKES OVER, THEY TAKE OVER.
SO... THAT'S IT?
NO NO NO.
IT'S A BALANCE, NIÑO.
WE NEED YOU OUT THERE MAKING A LITTLE NOISE SO FOLKS THINK THEY HAVE A CHANCE.
BUT WHEN FOLKS GO TOO FAR...
...WELL, THAT'S THAT.
SO YOU'RE SAYING...
...THIS IS JUST A GAME.
I'M...
...I'M JUST A JOKE.

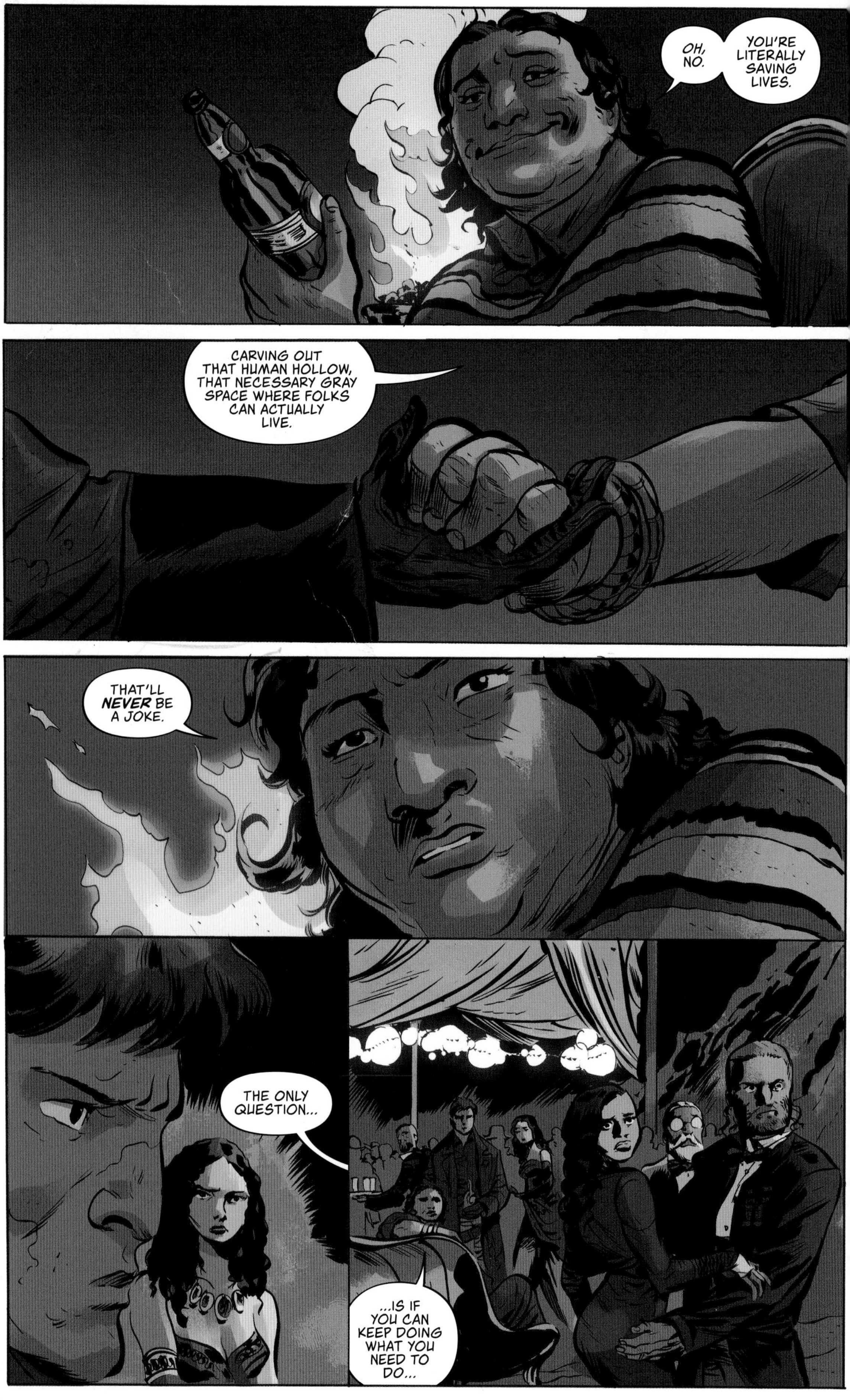
OH, NO.
YOU'RE LITERALLY SAVING LIVES.
CARVING OUT THAT HUMAN HOLLOW, THAT NECESSARY GRAY SPACE WHERE FOLKS CAN ACTUALLY LIVE.
THAT'LL NEVER BE A JOKE.
THE ONLY QUESTION...
...IS IF YOU CAN KEEP DOING WHAT YOU NEED TO DO...

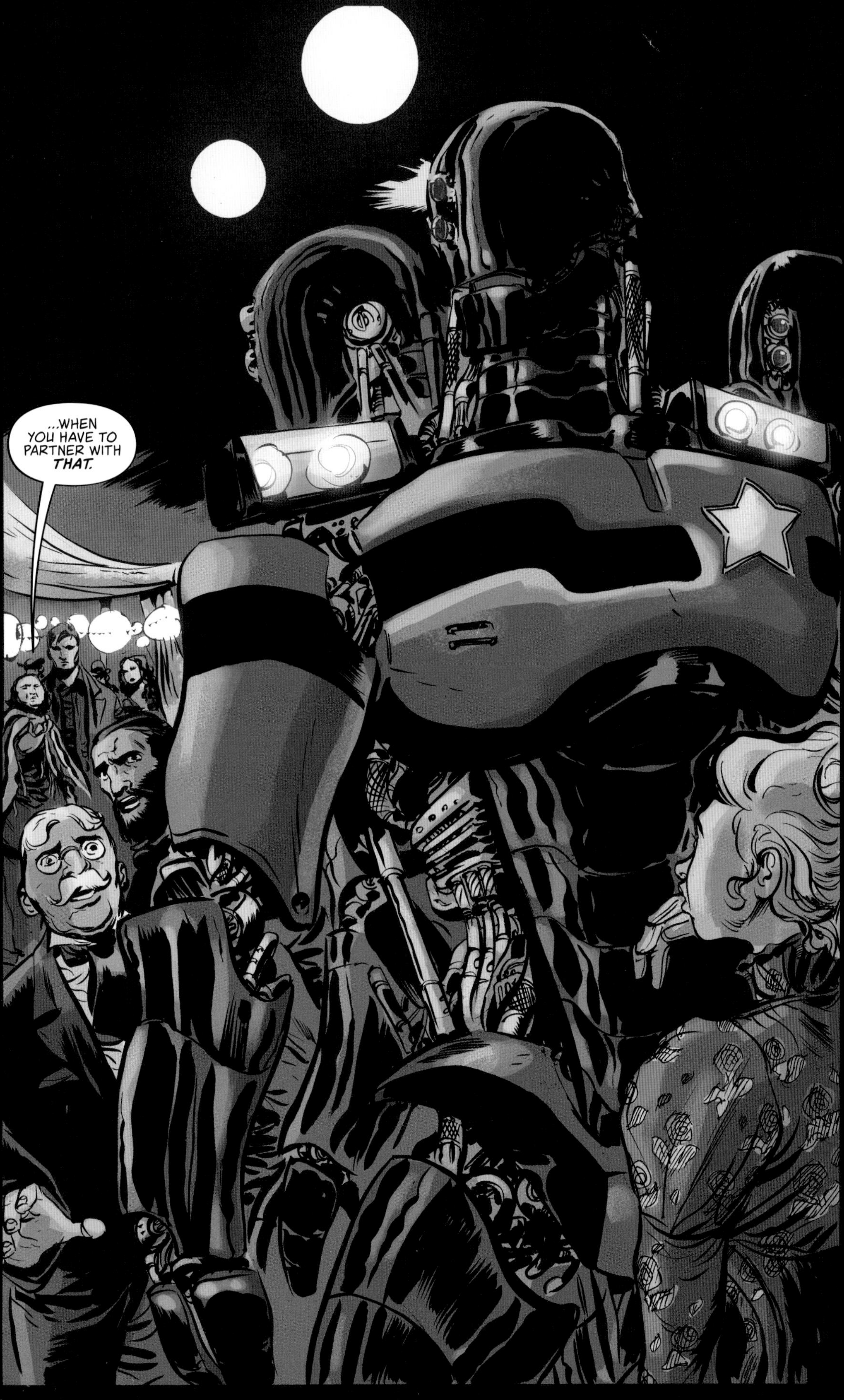
...WHEN YOU HAVE TO PARTNER WITH THAT.

Chapter Three
The Human Touch

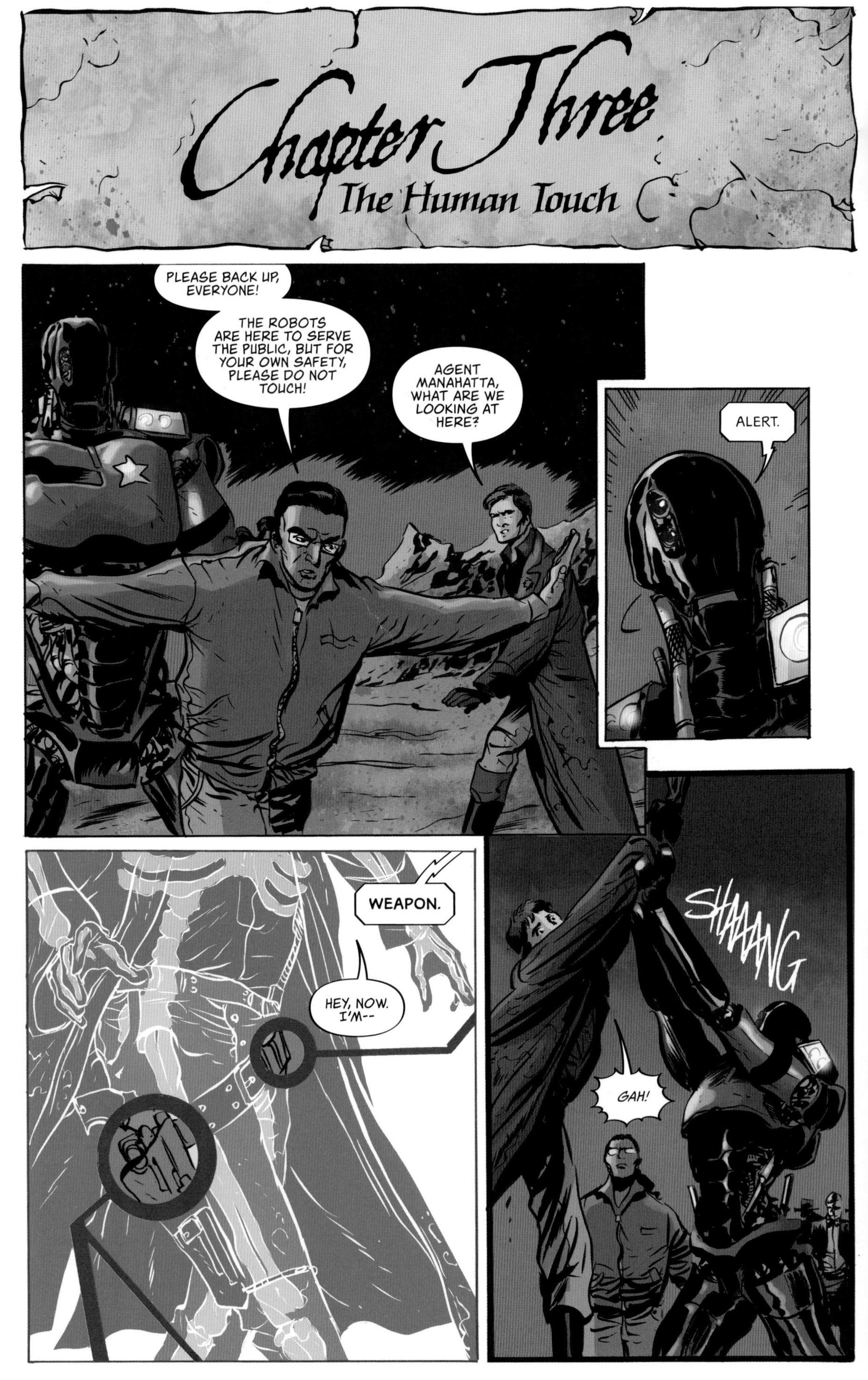

PLEASE BACK UP, EVERYONE!
THE ROBOTS ARE HERE TO SERVE THE PUBLIC, BUT FOR YOUR OWN SAFETY, PLEASE DO NOT TOUCH!
AGENT MANAHATTA, WHAT ARE WE LOOKING AT HERE?
ALERT.
WEAPON.
HEY, NOW. I'M--
SHAAAANG
GAH!

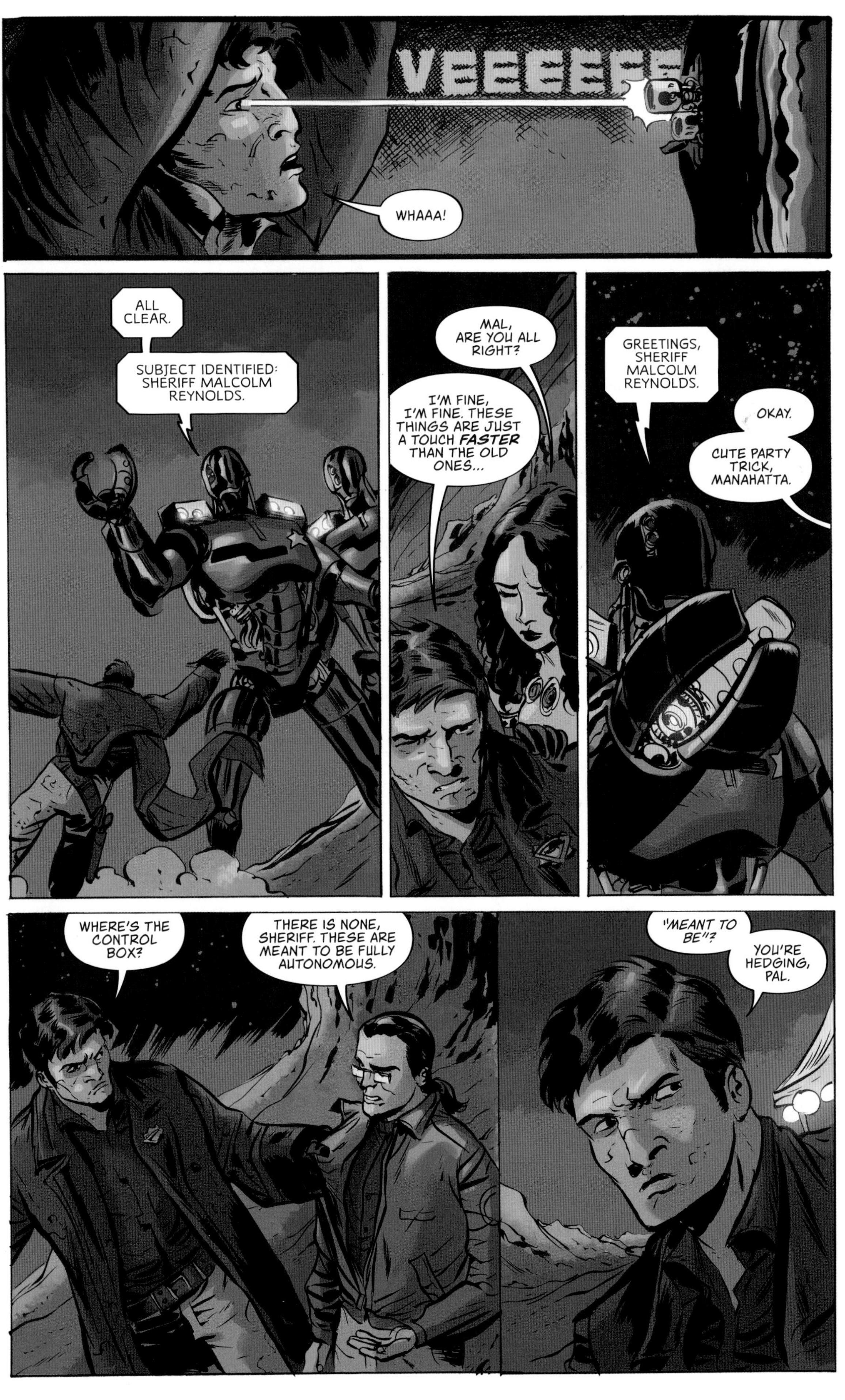
VEEEEEE
WHAAA!
ALL CLEAR.
SUBJECT IDENTIFIED: SHERIFF MALCOLM REYNOLDS.
MAL, ARE YOU ALL RIGHT?
I'M FINE, I'M FINE. THESE THINGS ARE JUST A TOUCH FASTER THAN THE OLD ONES...
GREETINGS, SHERIFF MALCOLM REYNOLDS.
OKAY.
CUTE PARTY TRICK, MANAHATTA.
WHERE'S THE CONTROL BOX?
THERE IS NONE, SHERIFF. THESE ARE MEANT TO BE FULLY AUTONOMOUS.
"MEANT TO BE"?
YOU'RE HEDGING, PAL.

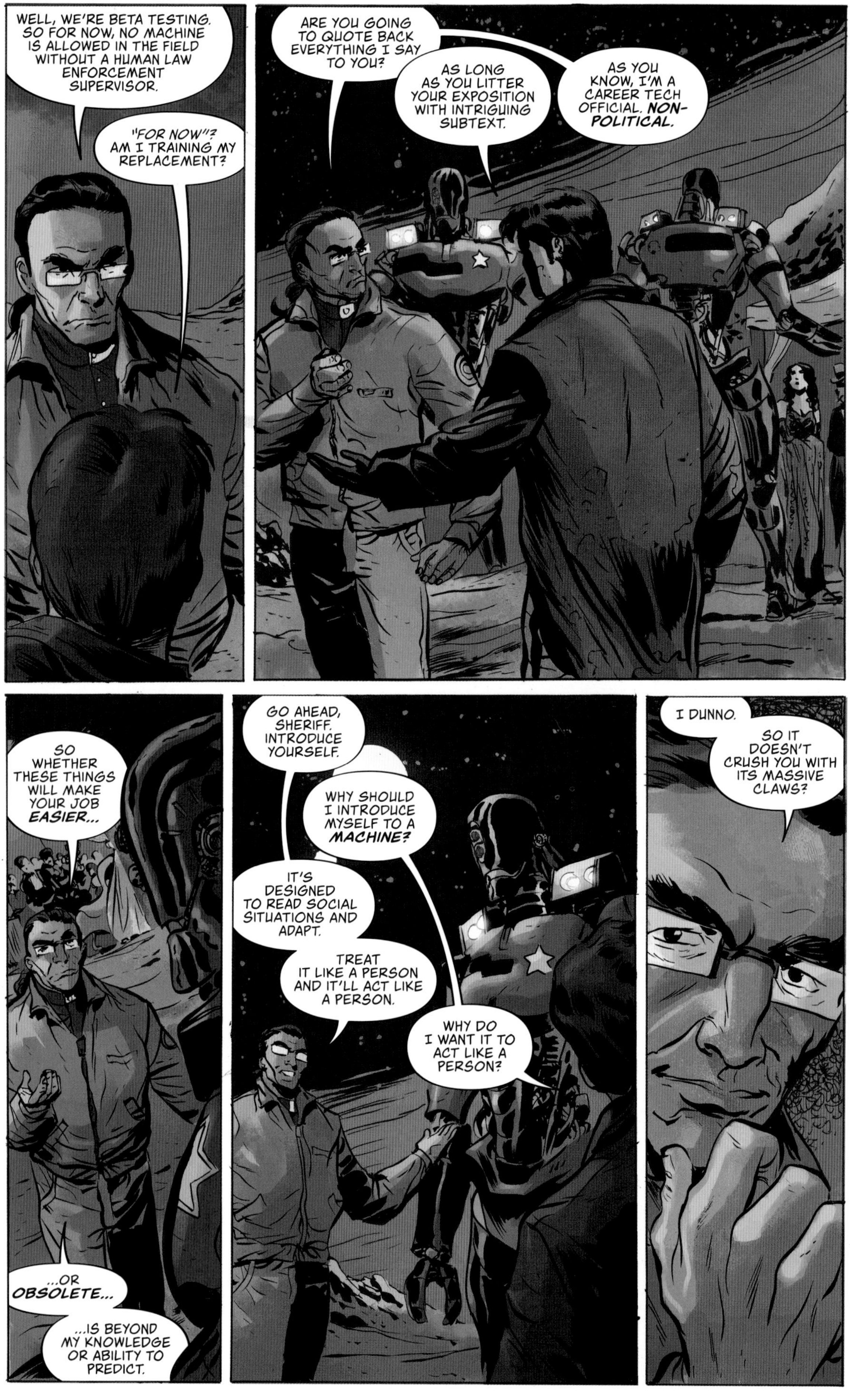
WELL, WE'RE BETA TESTING. SO FOR NOW, NO MACHINE IS ALLOWED IN THE FIELD WITHOUT A HUMAN LAW ENFORCEMENT SUPERVISOR.
"FOR NOW"? AM I TRAINING MY REPLACEMENT?
ARE YOU GOING TO QUOTE BACK EVERYTHING I SAY TO YOU?
AS LONG AS YOU LITTER YOUR EXPOSITION WITH INTRIGUING SUBTEXT.
AS YOU KNOW, I'M A CAREER TECH OFFICIAL. NON-POLITICAL.
SO WHETHER THESE THINGS WILL MAKE YOUR JOB EASIER...
...OR OBSOLETE...
...IS BEYOND MY KNOWLEDGE OR ABILITY TO PREDICT.
GO AHEAD, SHERIFF. INTRODUCE YOURSELF.
WHY SHOULD I INTRODUCE MYSELF TO A MACHINE?
IT'S DESIGNED TO READ SOCIAL SITUATIONS AND ADAPT.
TREAT IT LIKE A PERSON AND IT'LL ACT LIKE A PERSON.
WHY DO I WANT IT TO ACT LIKE A PERSON?
I DUNNO.
SO IT DOESN'T CRUSH YOU WITH ITS MASSIVE CLAWS?

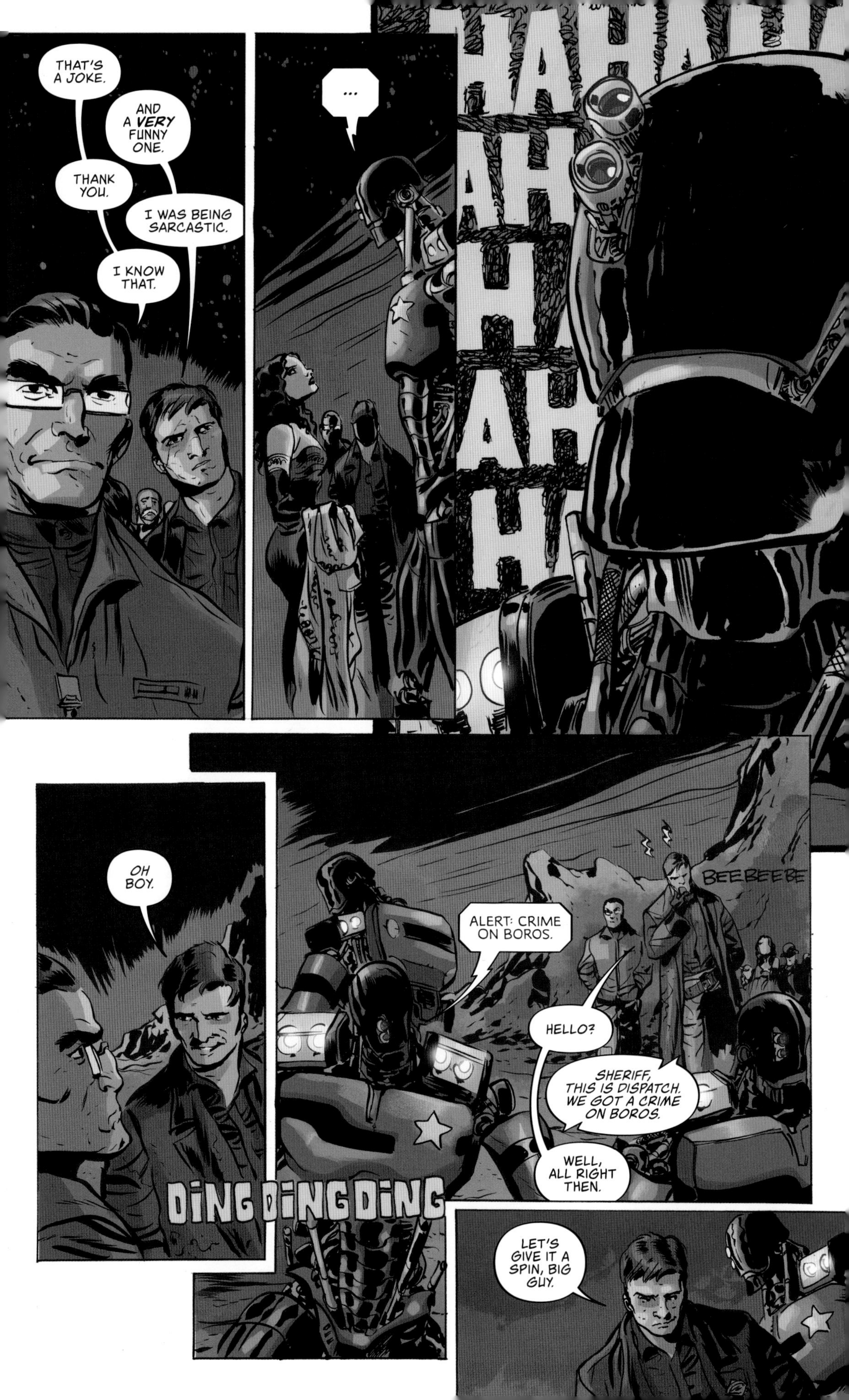
THAT'S A JOKE.
AND A VERY FUNNY ONE.
THANK YOU.
I WAS BEING SARCASTIC.
I KNOW THAT.
...
OH BOY.
DING DING DING
ALERT: CRIME ON BOROS.
BEEBEEBEE
HELLO?
SHERIFF, THIS IS DISPATCH. WE GOT A CRIME ON BOROS.
WELL, ALL RIGHT THEN.
LET'S GIVE IT A SPIN, BIG GUY.

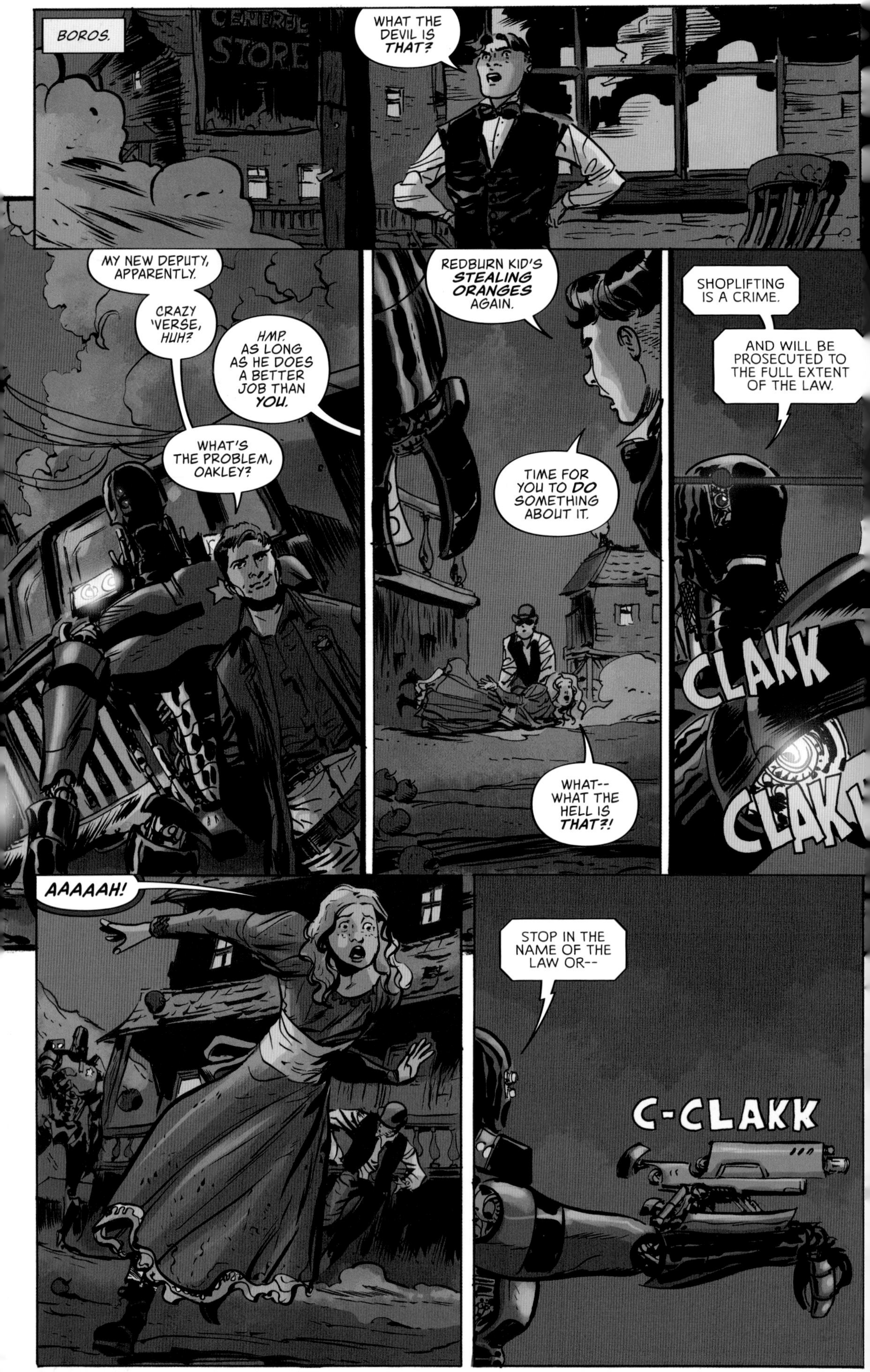
BOROS.
CENTRAL STORE
WHAT THE DEVIL IS THAT?
MY NEW DEPUTY, APPARENTLY.
CRAZY 'VERSE, HUH?
HMP. AS LONG AS HE DOES A BETTER JOB THAN YOU.
WHAT'S THE PROBLEM, OAKLEY?
REDBURN KID'S STEALING ORANGES AGAIN.
TIME FOR YOU TO DO SOMETHING ABOUT IT.
WHAT-- WHAT THE HELL IS THAT?!
SHOPLIFTING IS A CRIME.
AND WILL BE PROSECUTED TO THE FULL EXTENT OF THE LAW.
CLAKK
AAAAAH!
STOP IN THE NAME OF THE LAW OR--
C-CLAKK

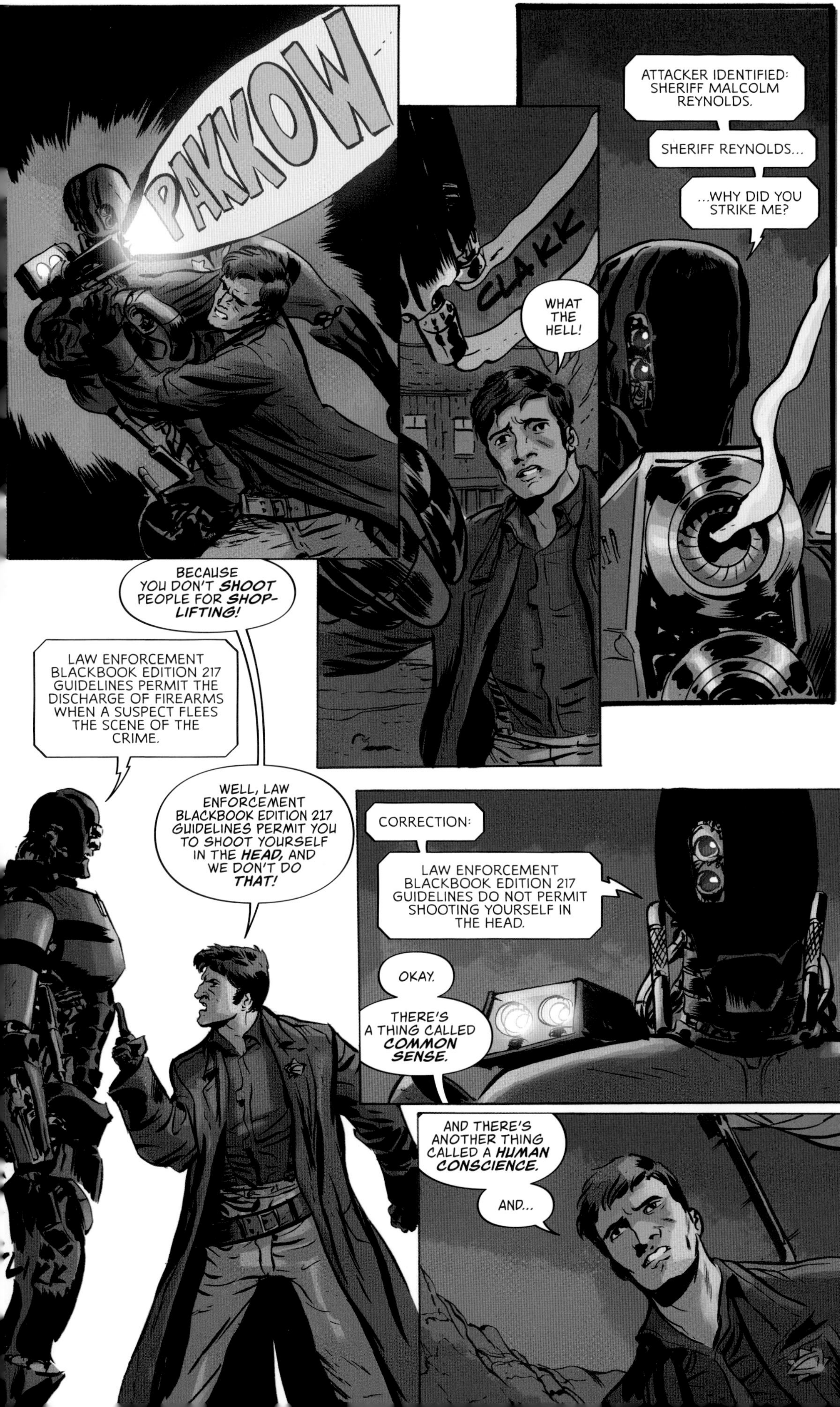
PAKKOW
CLAKK
WHAT THE HELL!
ATTACKER IDENTIFIED: SHERIFF MALCOLM REYNOLDS.
SHERIFF REYNOLDS...
...WHY DID YOU STRIKE ME?
BECAUSE YOU DON'T SHOOT PEOPLE FOR SHOP-LIFTING!
LAW ENFORCEMENT BLACKBOOK EDITION 217 GUIDELINES PERMIT THE DISCHARGE OF FIREARMS WHEN A SUSPECT FLEES THE SCENE OF THE CRIME.
WELL, LAW ENFORCEMENT BLACKBOOK EDITION 217 GUIDELINES PERMIT YOU TO SHOOT YOURSELF IN THE HEAD, AND WE DON'T DO THAT!
CORRECTION:
LAW ENFORCEMENT BLACKBOOK EDITION 217 GUIDELINES DO NOT PERMIT SHOOTING YOURSELF IN THE HEAD.
OKAY.
THERE'S A THING CALLED COMMON SENSE.
AND THERE'S ANOTHER THING CALLED A HUMAN CONSCIENCE.
AND...

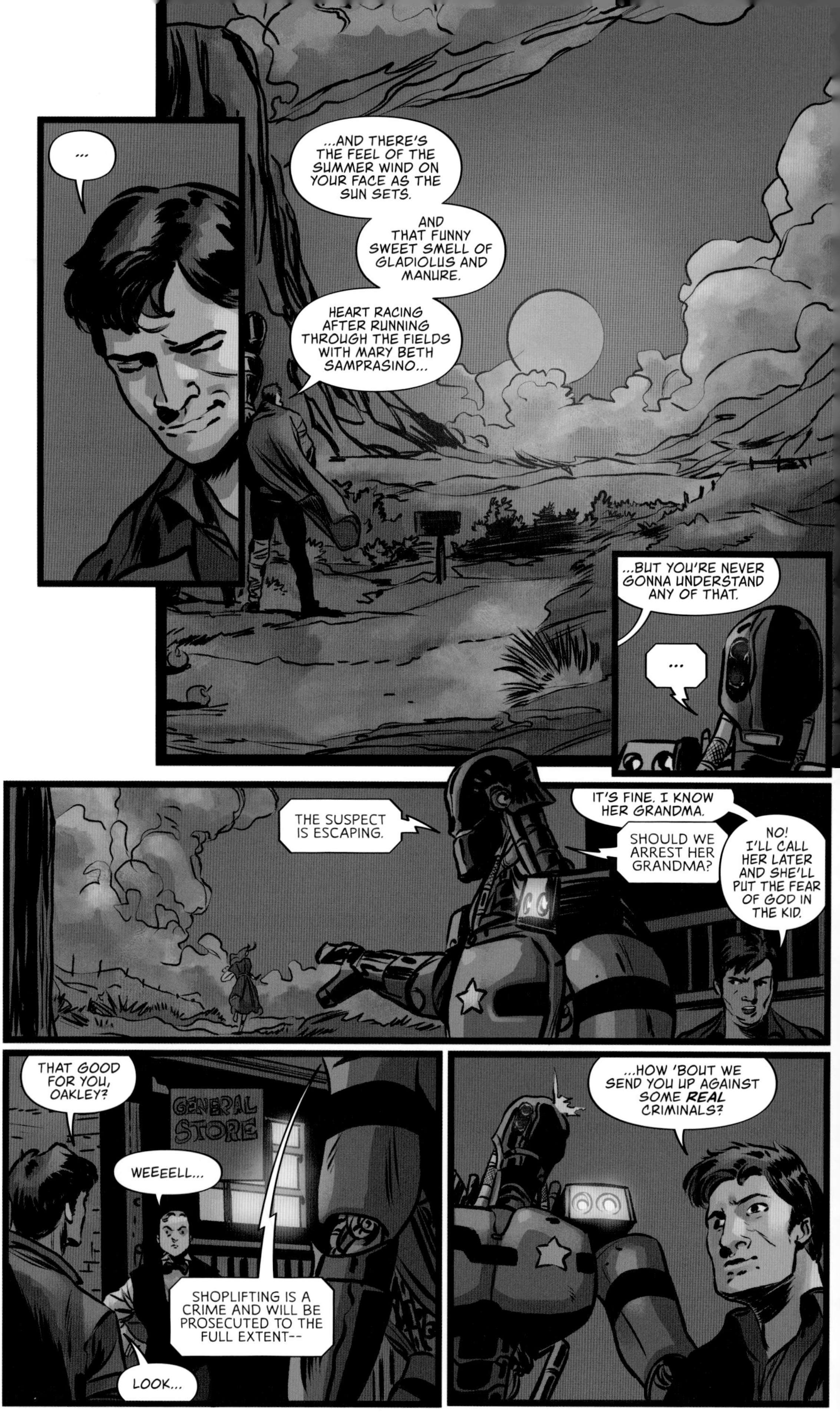
...
...AND THERE'S THE FEEL OF THE SUMMER WIND ON YOUR FACE AS THE SUN SETS.
AND THAT FUNNY SWEET SMELL OF GLADIOLUS AND MANURE.
HEART RACING AFTER RUNNING THROUGH THE FIELDS WITH MARY BETH SAMPRASINO...
...BUT YOU'RE NEVER GONNA UNDERSTAND ANY OF THAT.
...
THE SUSPECT IS ESCAPING.
IT'S FINE. I KNOW HER GRANDMA.
SHOULD WE ARREST HER GRANDMA?
NO! I'LL CALL HER LATER AND SHE'LL PUT THE FEAR OF GOD IN THE KID.
THAT GOOD FOR YOU, OAKLEY?
GENERAL STORE
WEEEELL...
SHOPLIFTING IS A CRIME AND WILL BE PROSECUTED TO THE FULL EXTENT--
LOOK...
...HOW 'BOUT WE SEND YOU UP AGAINST SOME REAL CRIMINALS?

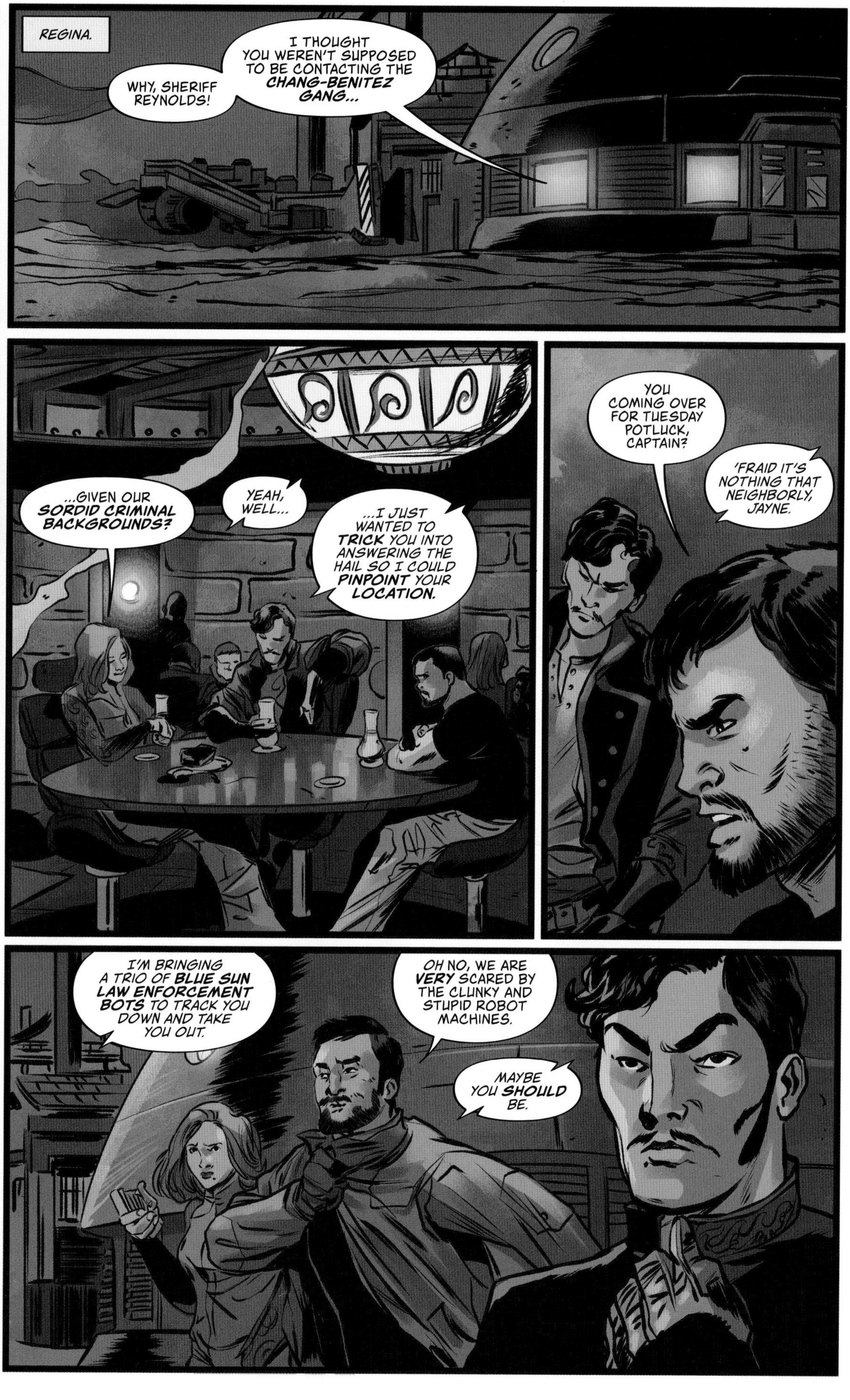
REGINA.
WHY, SHERIFF REYNOLDS!
I THOUGHT YOU WEREN'T SUPPOSED TO BE CONTACTING THE CHANG-BENITEZ GANG...
...GIVEN OUR SORDID CRIMINAL BACKGROUNDS?
YEAH, WELL...
...I JUST WANTED TO TRICK YOU INTO ANSWERING THE HAIL SO I COULD PINPOINT YOUR LOCATION.
YOU COMING OVER FOR TUESDAY POTLUCK, CAPTAIN?
'FRAID IT'S NOTHING THAT NEIGHBORLY, JAYNE.
I'M BRINGING A TRIO OF BLUE SUN LAW ENFORCEMENT BOTS TO TRACK YOU DOWN AND TAKE YOU OUT.
OH NO, WE ARE VERY SCARED BY THE CLUNKY AND STUPID ROBOT MACHINES.
MAYBE YOU SHOULD BE.

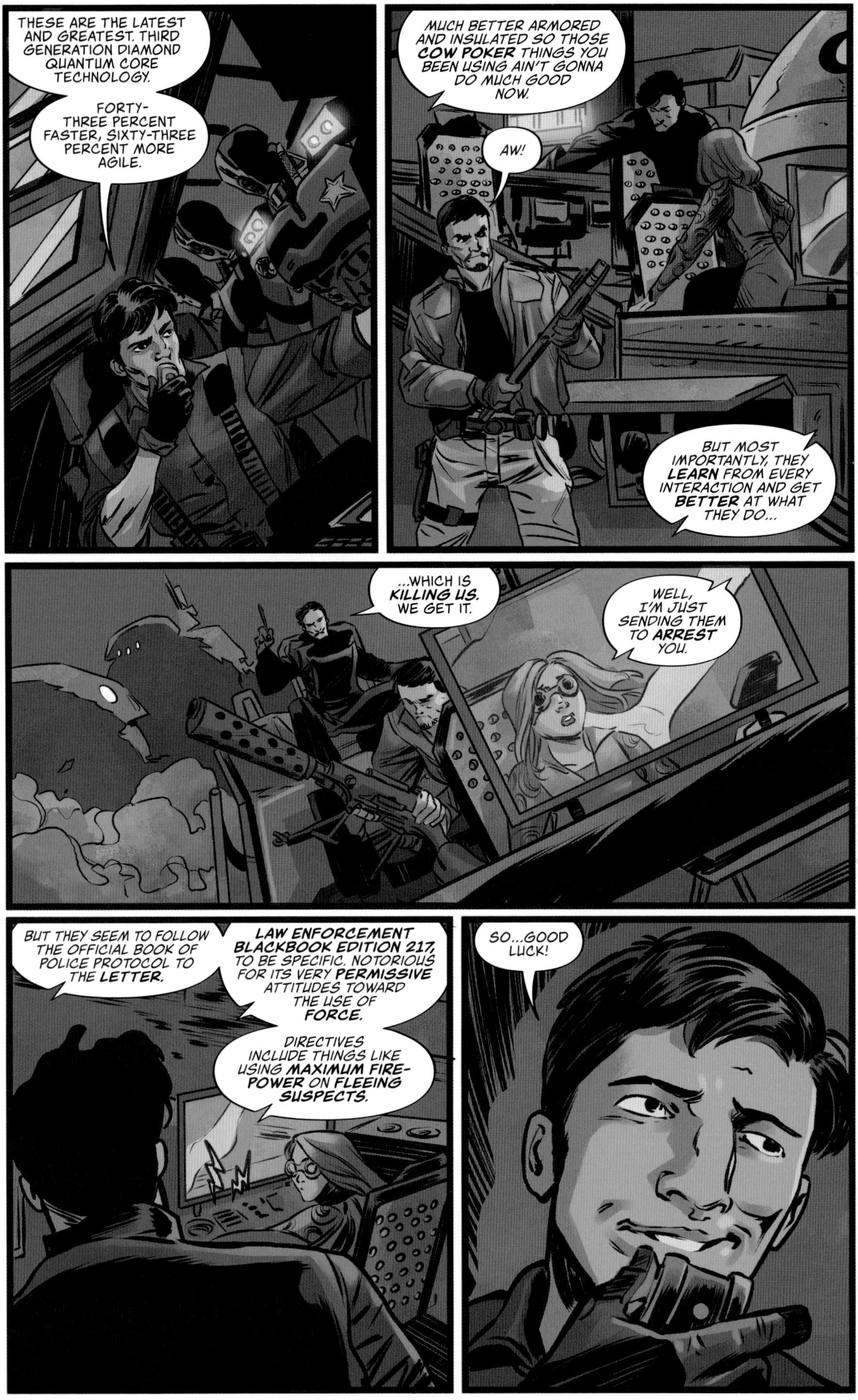
THESE ARE THE LATEST AND GREATEST. THIRD GENERATION DIAMOND QUANTUM CORE TECHNOLOGY.
FORTY-THREE PERCENT FASTER, SIXTY-THREE PERCENT MORE AGILE.
MUCH BETTER ARMORED AND INSULATED SO THOSE COW POKER THINGS YOU BEEN USING AIN'T GONNA DO MUCH GOOD NOW.
AW!
BUT MOST IMPORTANTLY, THEY LEARN FROM EVERY INTERACTION AND GET BETTER AT WHAT THEY DO...
...WHICH IS KILLING US. WE GET IT.
WELL, I'M JUST SENDING THEM TO ARREST YOU.
BUT THEY SEEM TO FOLLOW THE OFFICIAL BOOK OF POLICE PROTOCOL TO THE LETTER.
LAW ENFORCEMENT BLACKBOOK EDITION 217, TO BE SPECIFIC. NOTORIOUS FOR ITS VERY PERMISSIVE ATTITUDES TOWARD THE USE OF FORCE.
DIRECTIVES INCLUDE THINGS LIKE USING MAXIMUM FIRE-POWER ON FLEEING SUSPECTS.
SO...GOOD LUCK!

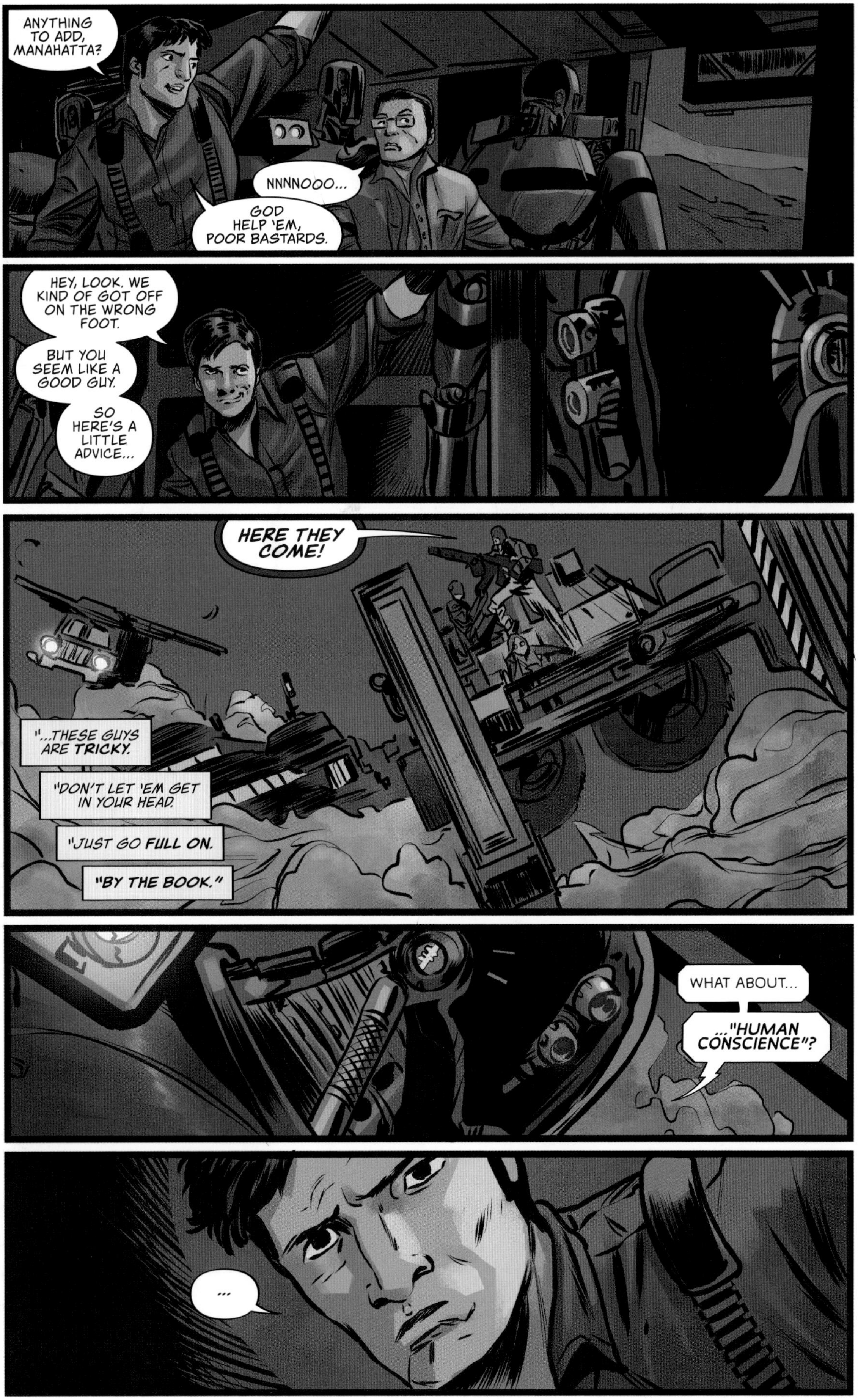
ANYTHING TO ADD, MANAHATTA?
NNNNOOO...
GOD HELP 'EM, POOR BASTARDS.
HEY, LOOK. WE KIND OF GOT OFF ON THE WRONG FOOT.
BUT YOU SEEM LIKE A GOOD GUY.
SO HERE'S A LITTLE ADVICE...
HERE THEY COME!
"...THESE GUYS ARE TRICKY.
"DON'T LET 'EM GET IN YOUR HEAD.
"JUST GO FULL ON.
"BY THE BOOK."
WHAT ABOUT...
..."HUMAN CONSCIENCE"?
...

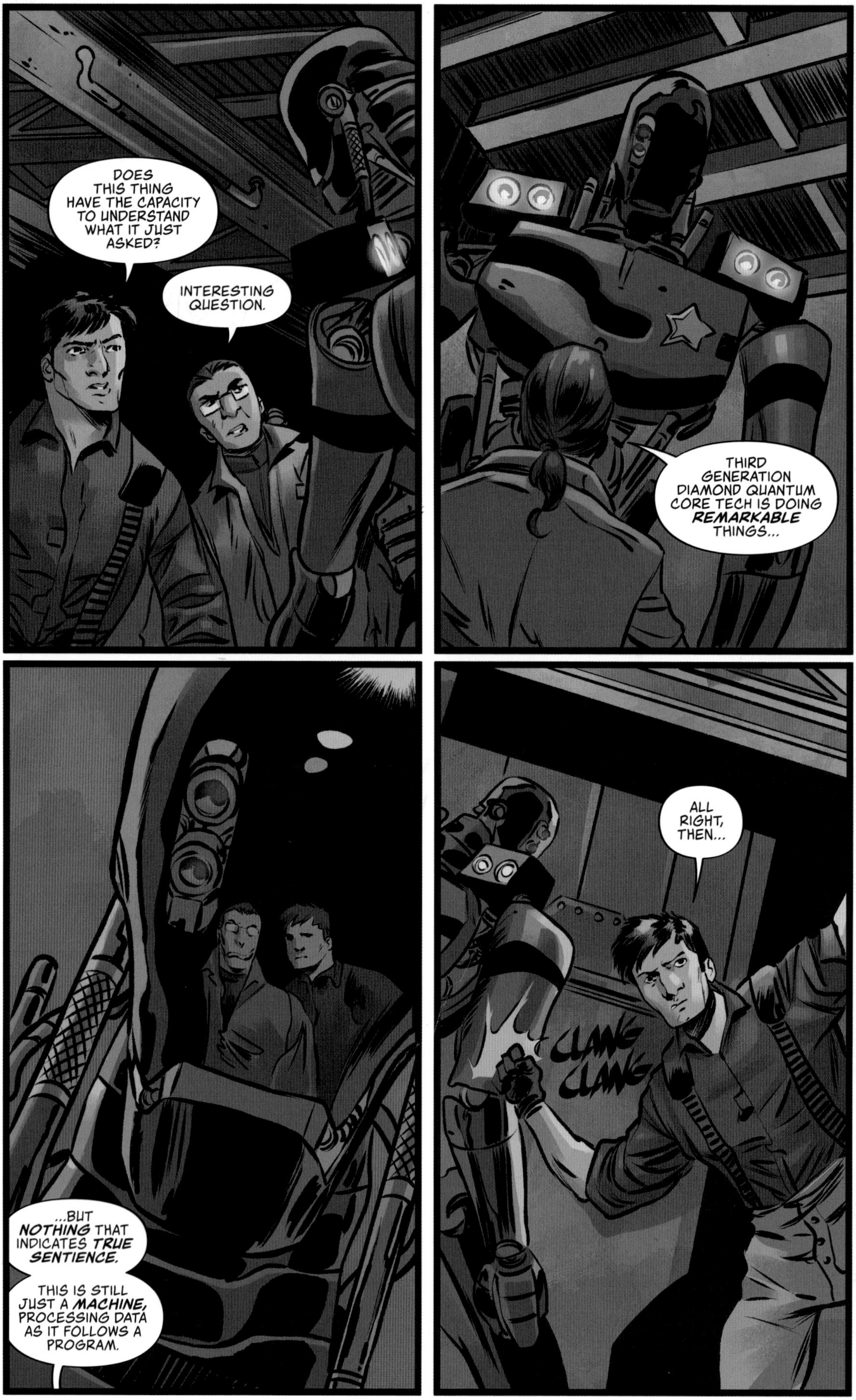
DOES THIS THING HAVE THE CAPACITY TO UNDERSTAND WHAT IT JUST ASKED?
INTERESTING QUESTION.
THIRD GENERATION DIAMOND QUANTUM CORE TECH IS DOING **REMARKABLE** THINGS...
...BUT **NOTHING** THAT INDICATES **TRUE SENTIENCE.**
THIS IS STILL JUST A **MACHINE,** PROCESSING DATA AS IT FOLLOWS A PROGRAM.
ALL RIGHT, THEN...
CLANG CLANG

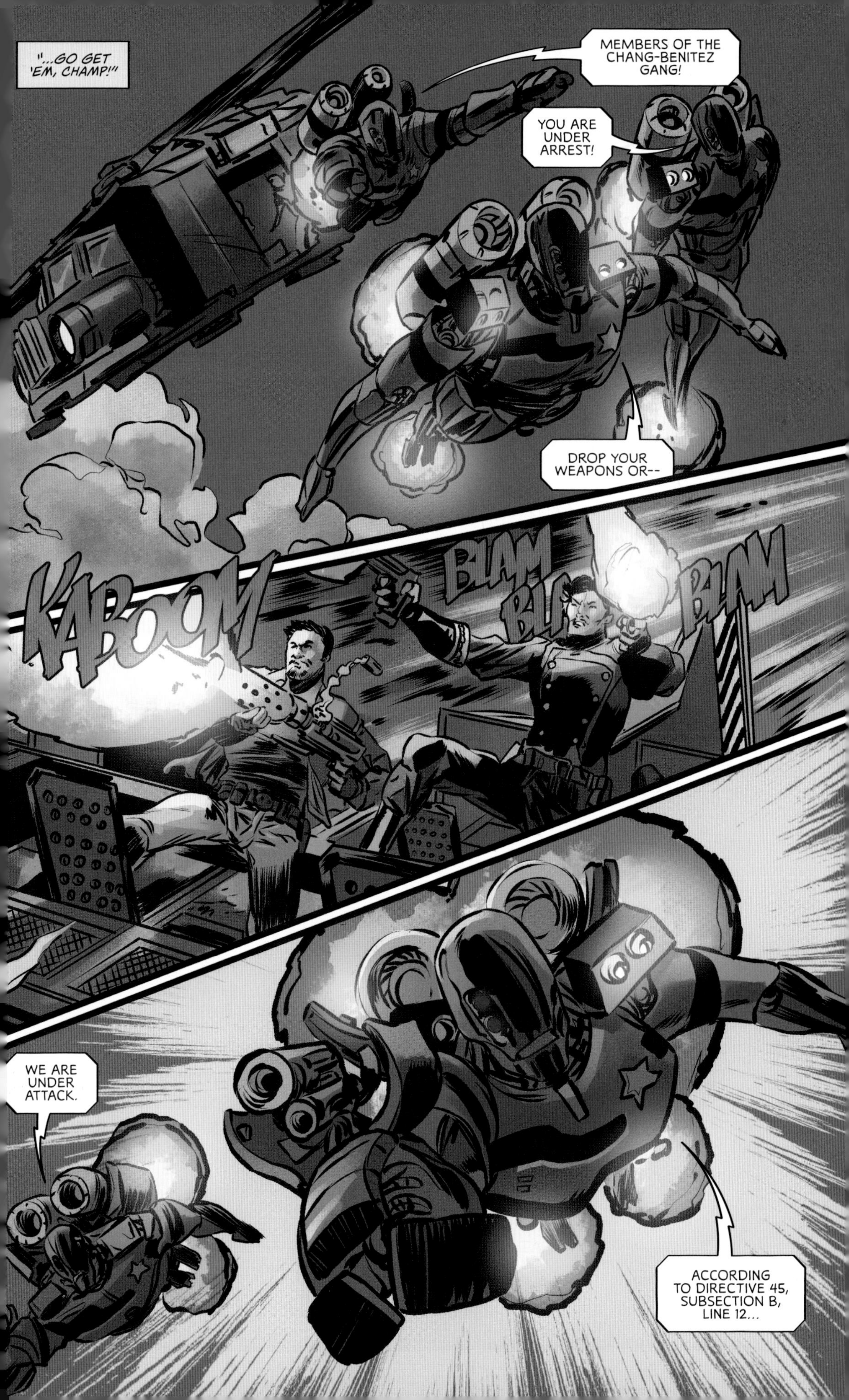
"...GO GET 'EM, CHAMP!"
MEMBERS OF THE CHANG-BENITEZ GANG!
YOU ARE UNDER ARREST!
DROP YOUR WEAPONS OR--
KABOOM
BLAM
BLA
BLAM
WE ARE UNDER ATTACK.
ACCORDING TO DIRECTIVE 45, SUBSECTION B, LINE 12...

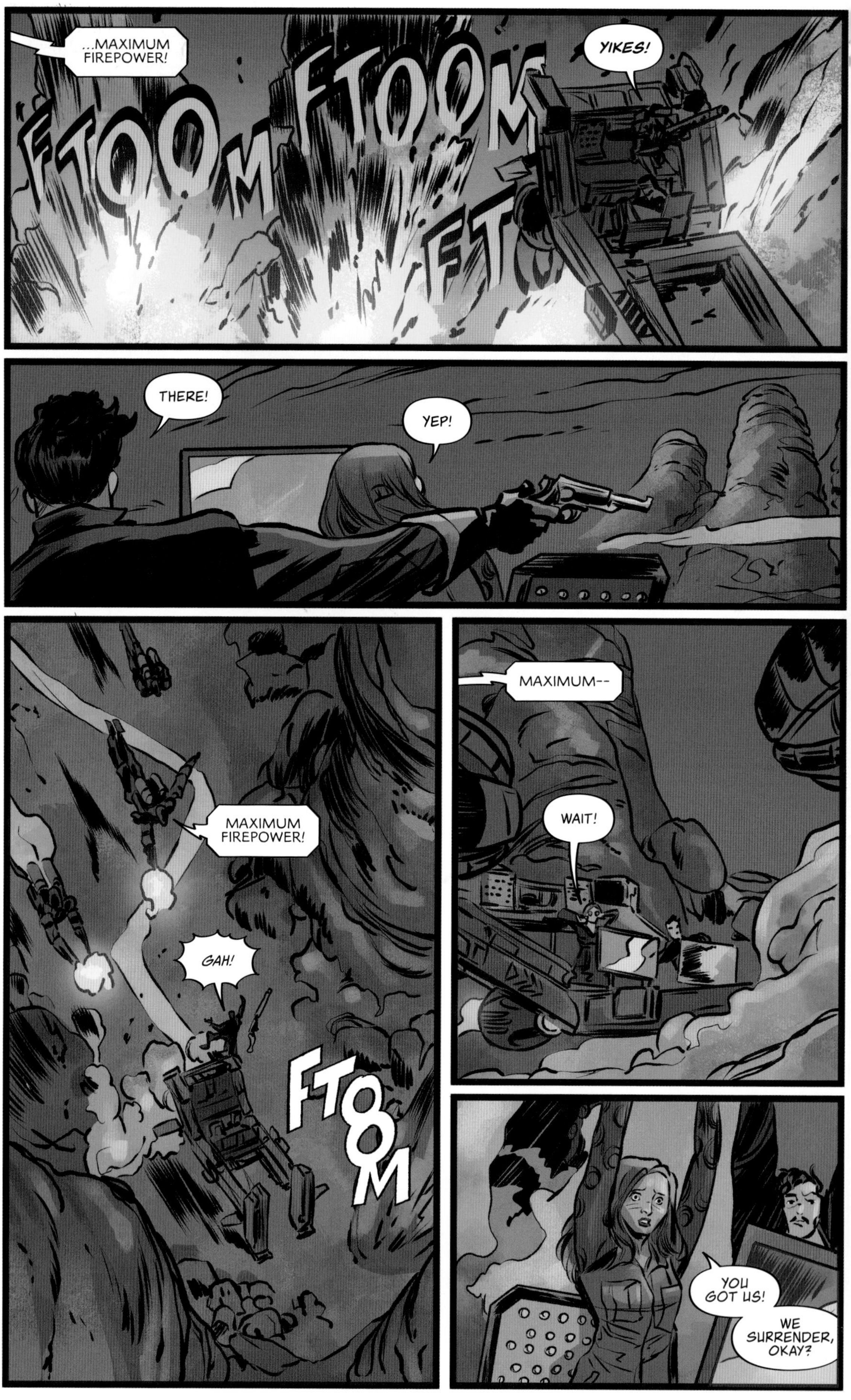
...MAXIMUM FIREPOWER!
FTOOM FTOOM FT
YIKES!
THERE!
YEP!
MAXIMUM FIREPOWER!
GAH!
FTOOM
MAXIMUM--
WAIT!
YOU GOT US!
WE SURRENDER, OKAY?

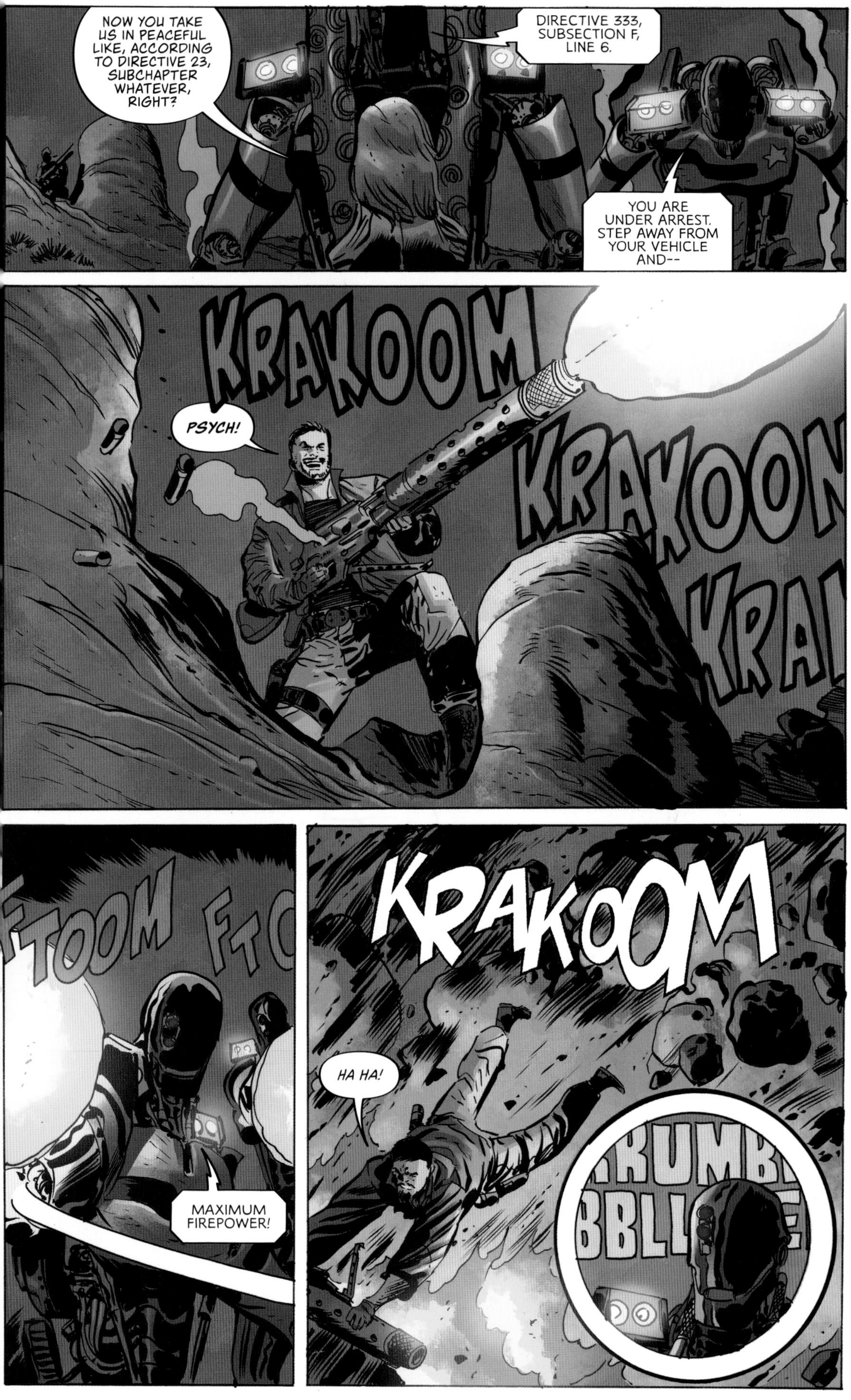
NOW YOU TAKE US IN PEACEFUL LIKE, ACCORDING TO DIRECTIVE 23, SUBCHAPTER WHATEVER, RIGHT?
DIRECTIVE 333, SUBSECTION F, LINE 6.
YOU ARE UNDER ARREST. STEP AWAY FROM YOUR VEHICLE AND--
KRAKOOM
PSYCH!
FTOOM
MAXIMUM FIREPOWER!
KRAKOOM
HA HA!

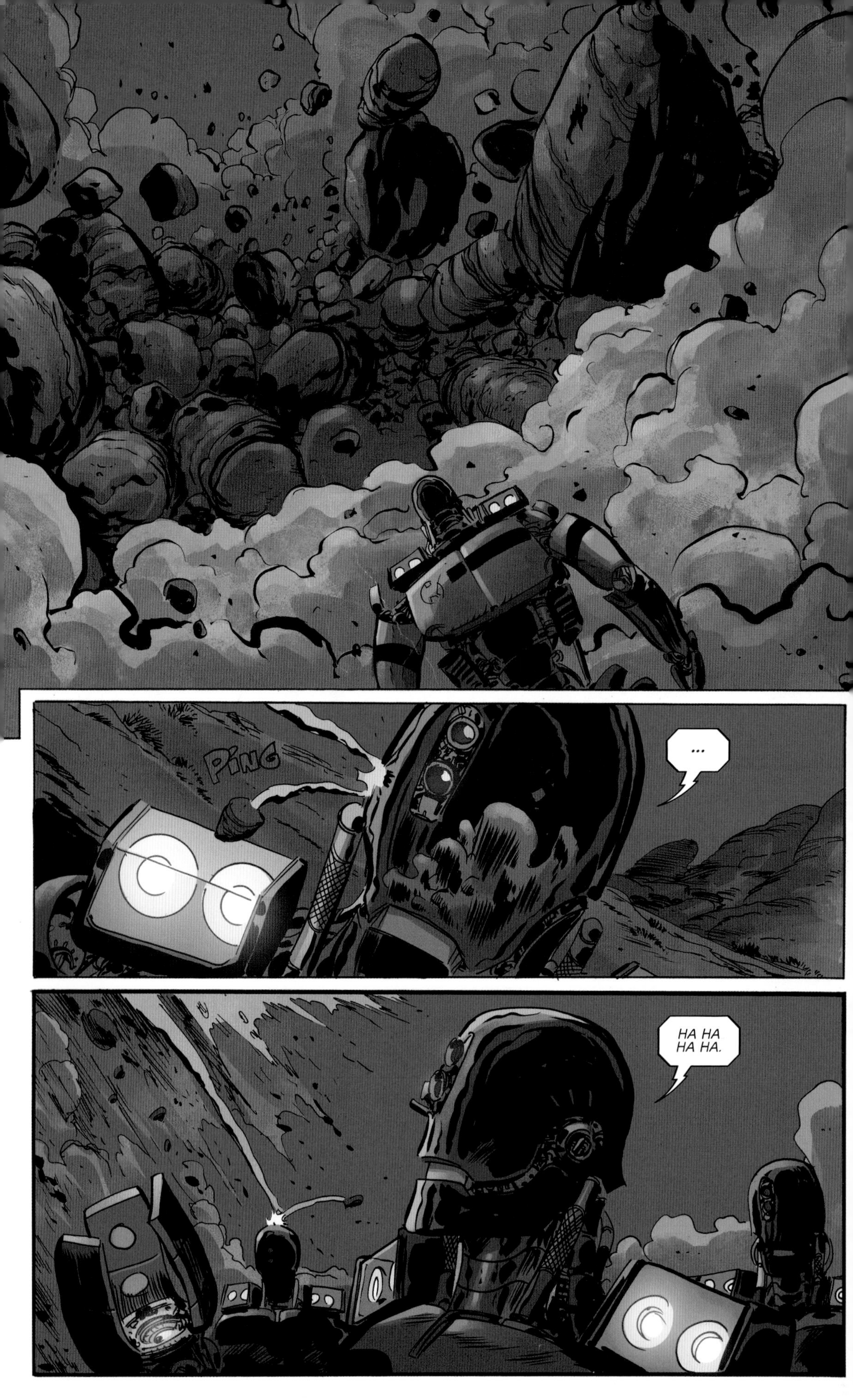
PING
...
HA HA
HA HA.

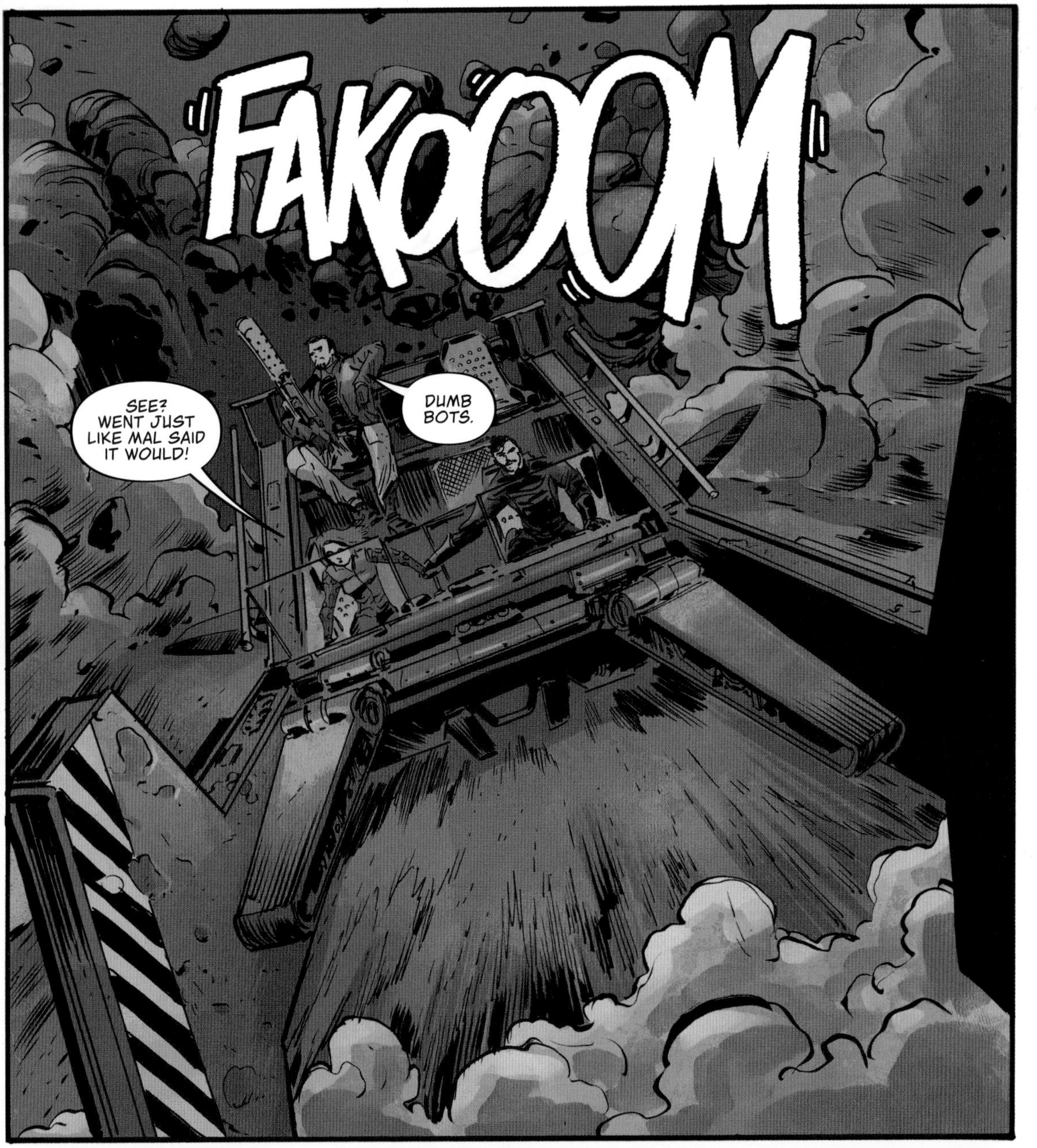
FAKOOOM
SEE? WENT JUST LIKE MAL SAID IT WOULD!
DUMB BOTS.

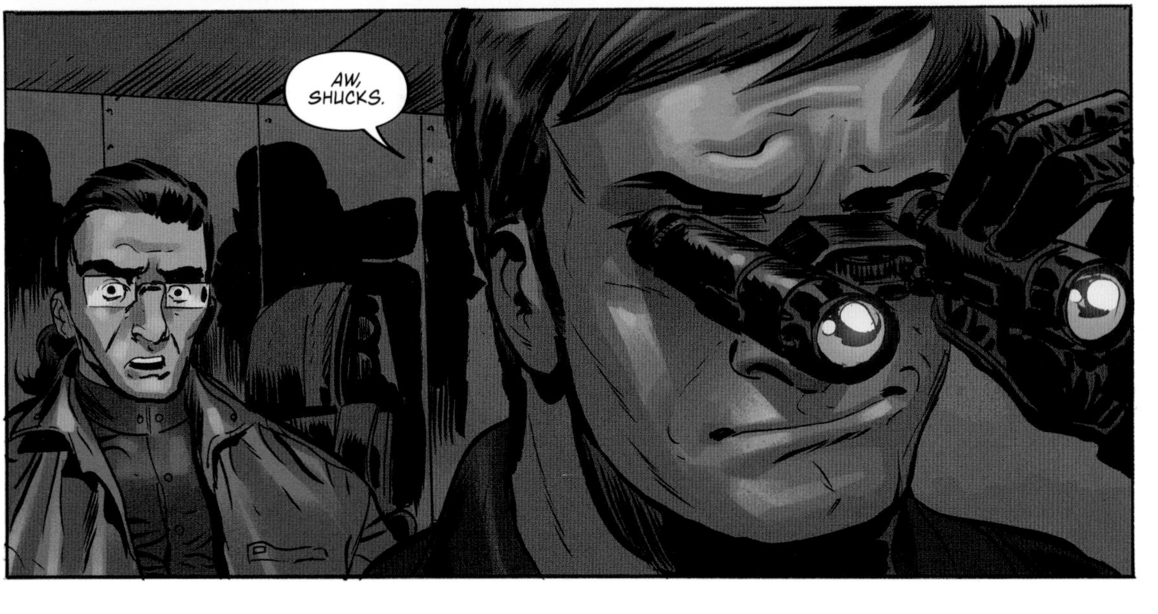
AW, SHUCKS.

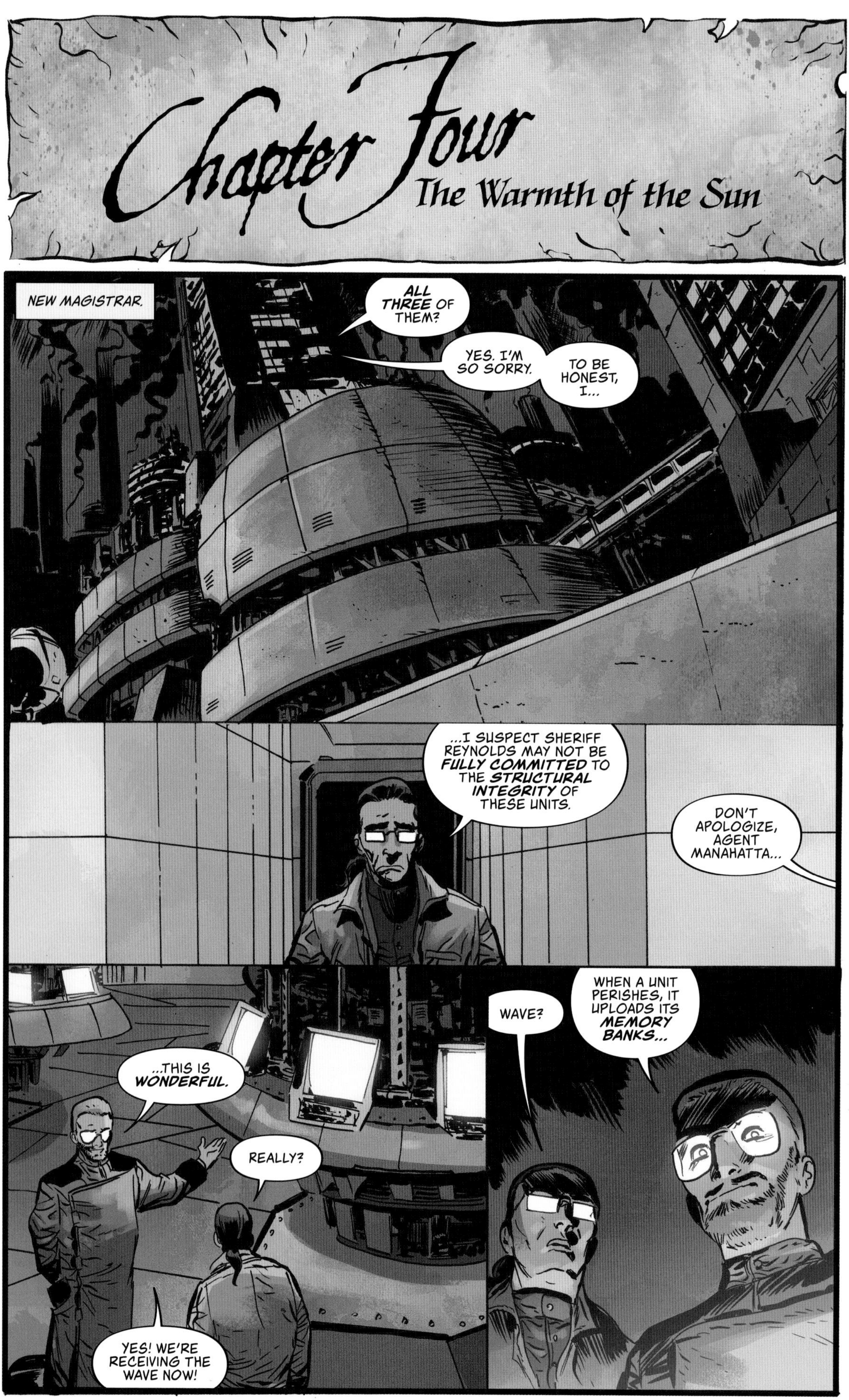
Chapter Four
The Warmth of the Sun
NEW MAGISTRAR.
ALL THREE OF THEM?
YES. I'M SO SORRY.
TO BE HONEST, I...
...I SUSPECT SHERIFF REYNOLDS MAY NOT BE FULLY COMMITTED TO THE STRUCTURAL INTEGRITY OF THESE UNITS.
DON'T APOLOGIZE, AGENT MANAHATTA...
...THIS IS WONDERFUL.
REALLY?
YES! WE'RE RECEIVING THE WAVE NOW!
WAVE?
WHEN A UNIT PERISHES, IT UPLOADS ITS MEMORY BANKS...

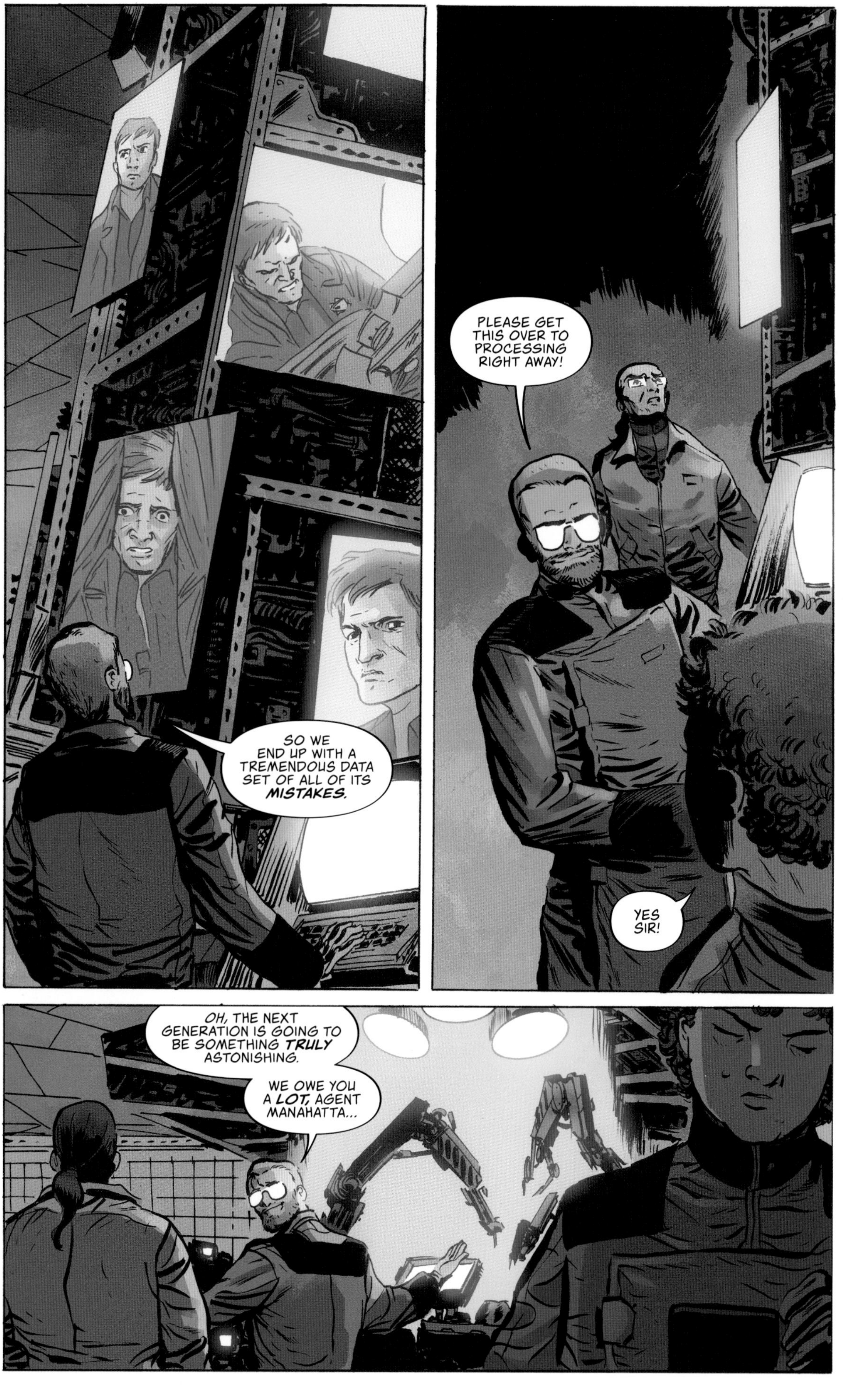
SO WE END UP WITH A TREMENDOUS DATA SET OF ALL OF ITS ***MISTAKES.***
PLEASE GET THIS OVER TO PROCESSING RIGHT AWAY!
YES SIR!
OH, THE NEXT GENERATION IS GOING TO BE SOMETHING ***TRULY*** ASTONISHING.
WE OWE YOU A ***LOT,*** AGENT MANAHATTA...

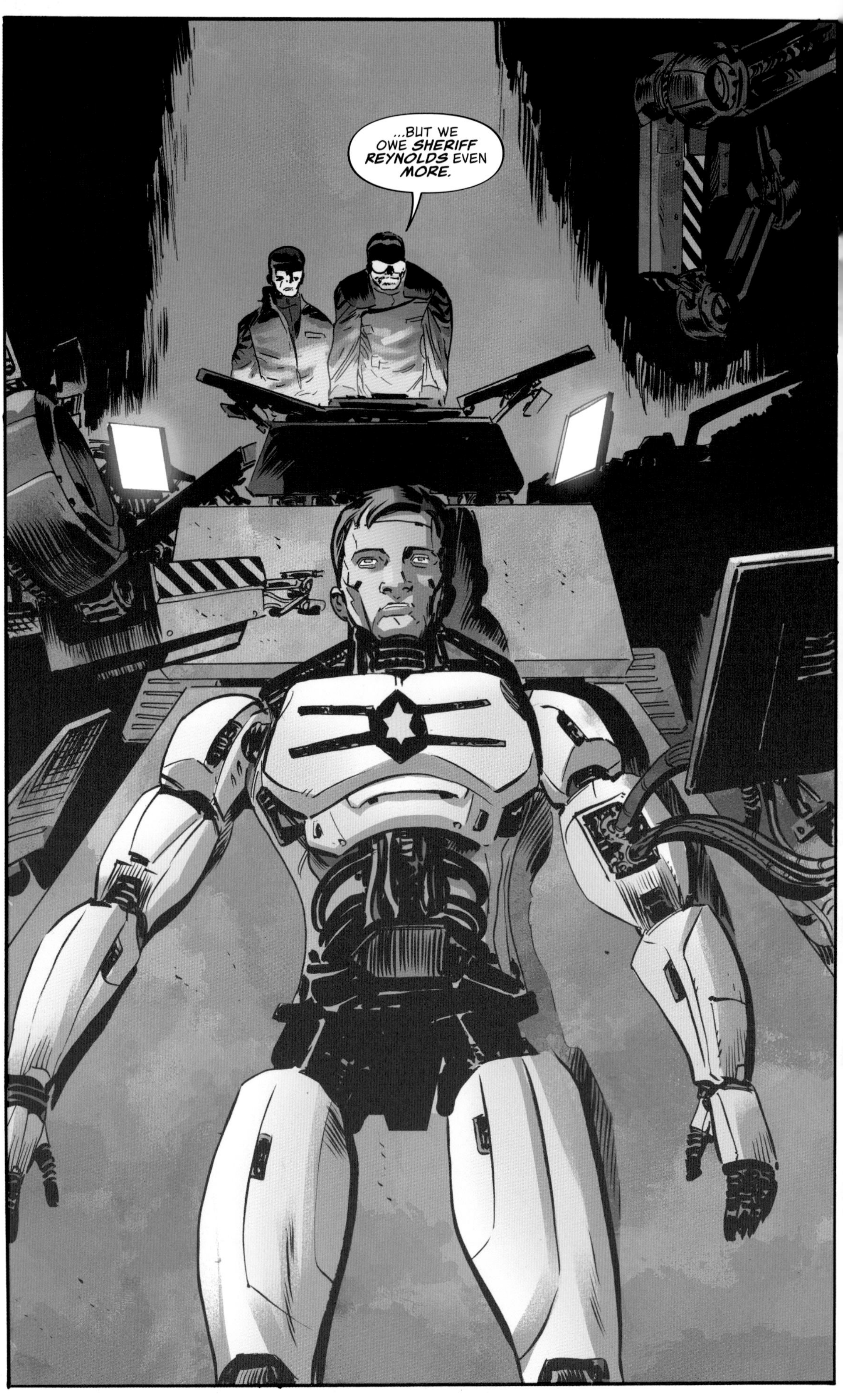
...BUT WE OWE SHERIFF REYNOLDS EVEN MORE.

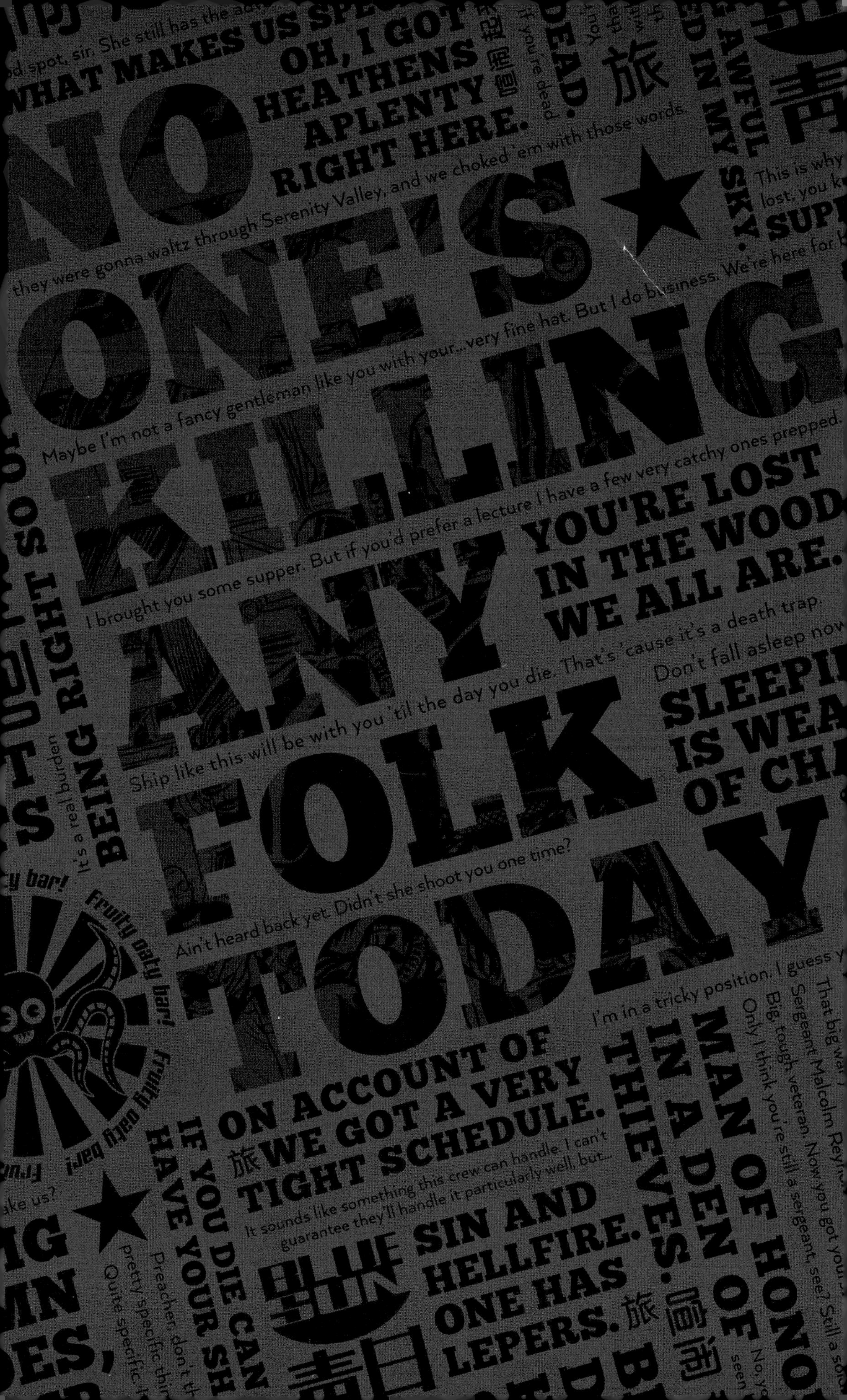

NO ONE'S KILLING ANY FOLK TODAY
WHAT MAKES US SPE
OH, I GOT HEATHENS APLENTY RIGHT HERE.
DEAD.
If you're dead
IN MY SKY.
This is why
lost, you k
SUPE
they were gonna waltz through Serenity Valley, and we choked 'em with those words.
Maybe I'm not a fancy gentleman like you with your...very fine hat. But I do business. We're here for b
I brought you some supper. But if you'd prefer a lecture I have a few very catchy ones prepped.
YOU'RE LOST IN THE WOOD WE ALL ARE.
Ship like this will be with you 'til the day you die. That's 'cause it's a death trap.
Don't fall asleep now
SLEEPI IS WEA OF CHA
BEING RIGHT
It's a real burden
Fruity oaty bar!
Ain't heard back yet. Didn't she shoot you one time?
I'm in a tricky position. I guess y
ON ACCOUNT OF WE GOT A VERY TIGHT SCHEDULE.
It sounds like something this crew can handle. I can't guarantee they'll handle it particularly well, but...
IF YOU DIE CAN HAVE YOUR SH
Preacher, don't
pretty specific thi
Quite specific
SIN AND HELLFIRE. ONE HAS LEPERS.
THIEVES.
IN A DEN OF
MAN OF HONO
That big war
Sergeant Malcolm Reyn
Big, tough veteran. Now you got yours
Only I think you're still a sergeant, see? Still a so
BLUE SUN
旅

BLUE SUN RISING

CHAPTER TWO

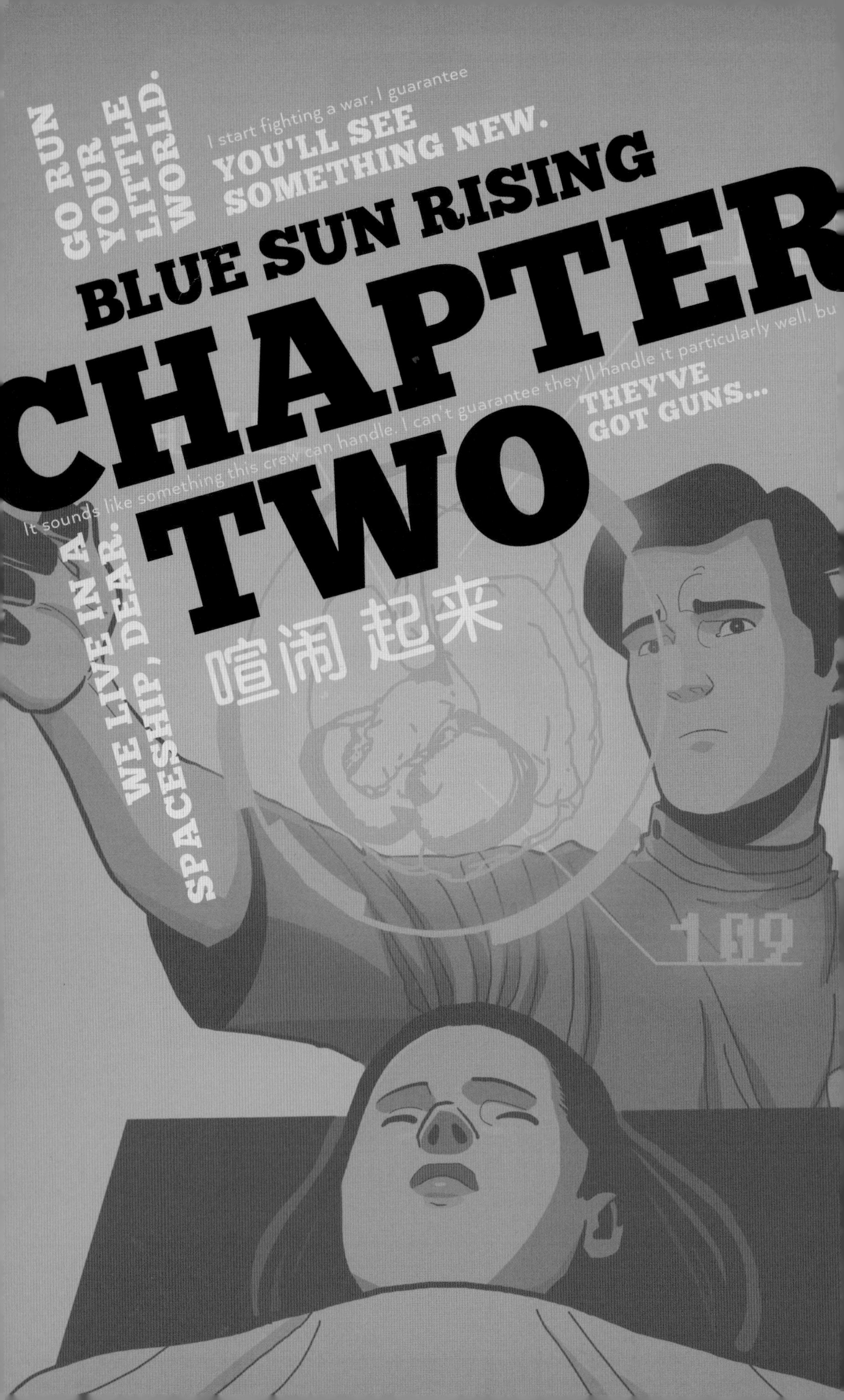

GO RUN YOUR LITTLE WORLD.
I start fighting a war, I guarantee
YOU'LL SEE SOMETHING NEW.
It sounds like something this crew can handle. I can't guarantee they'll handle it particularly well, bu
THEY'VE GOT GUNS...
WE LIVE IN A SPACESHIP, DEAR.
喧闹起来

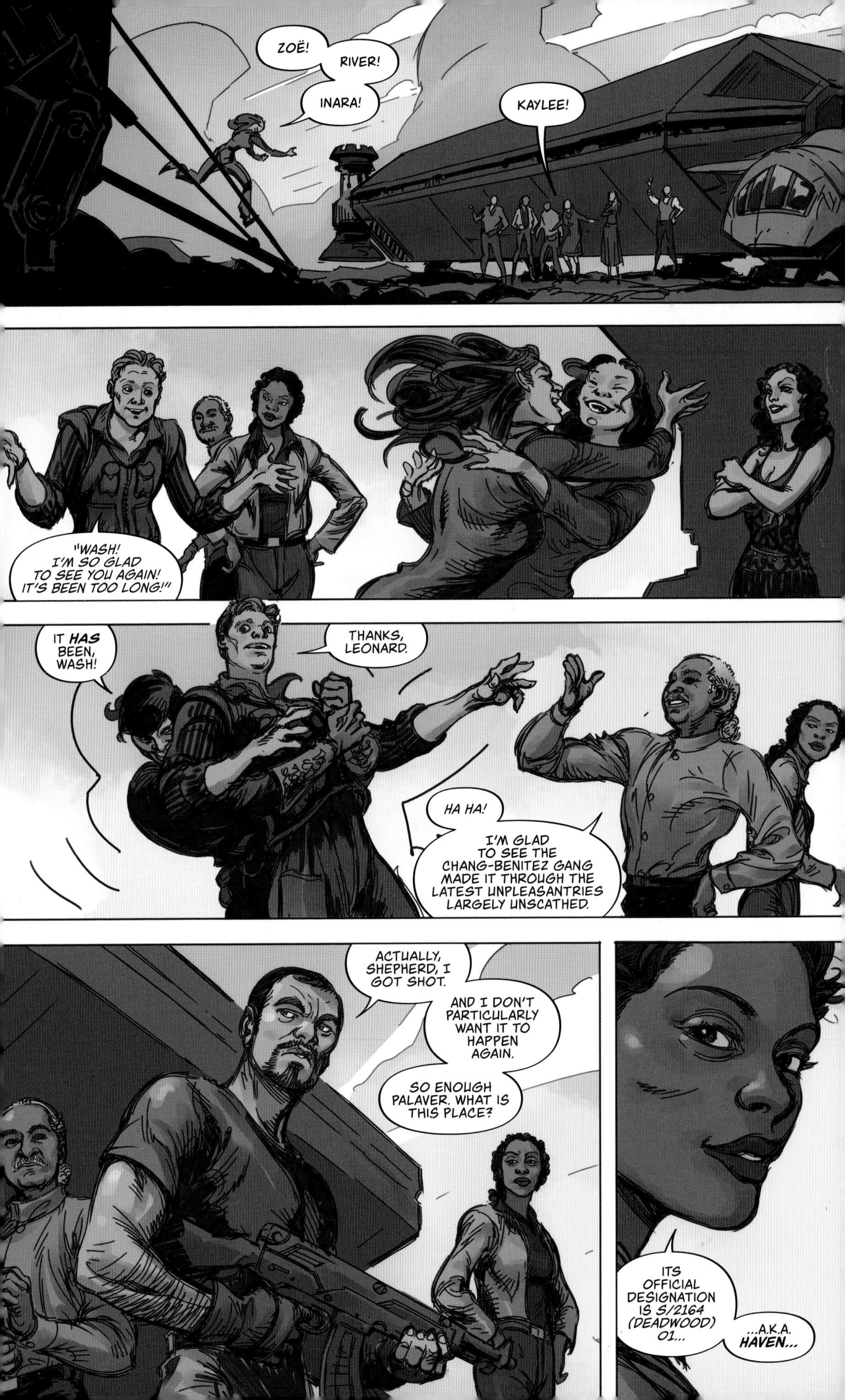

ZOË!
RIVER!
INARA!
KAYLEE!
"WASH! I'M SO GLAD TO SEE YOU AGAIN! IT'S BEEN TOO LONG!"
IT **HAS** BEEN, WASH!
THANKS, LEONARD.
HA HA!
I'M GLAD TO SEE THE CHANG-BENITEZ GANG MADE IT THROUGH THE LATEST UNPLEASANTRIES LARGELY UNSCATHED.
ACTUALLY, SHEPHERD, I GOT SHOT.
AND I DON'T PARTICULARLY WANT IT TO HAPPEN AGAIN.
SO ENOUGH PALAVER. WHAT IS THIS PLACE?
ITS OFFICIAL DESIGNATION IS S/2164 (DEADWOOD) 01...
...A.K.A. **HAVEN...**

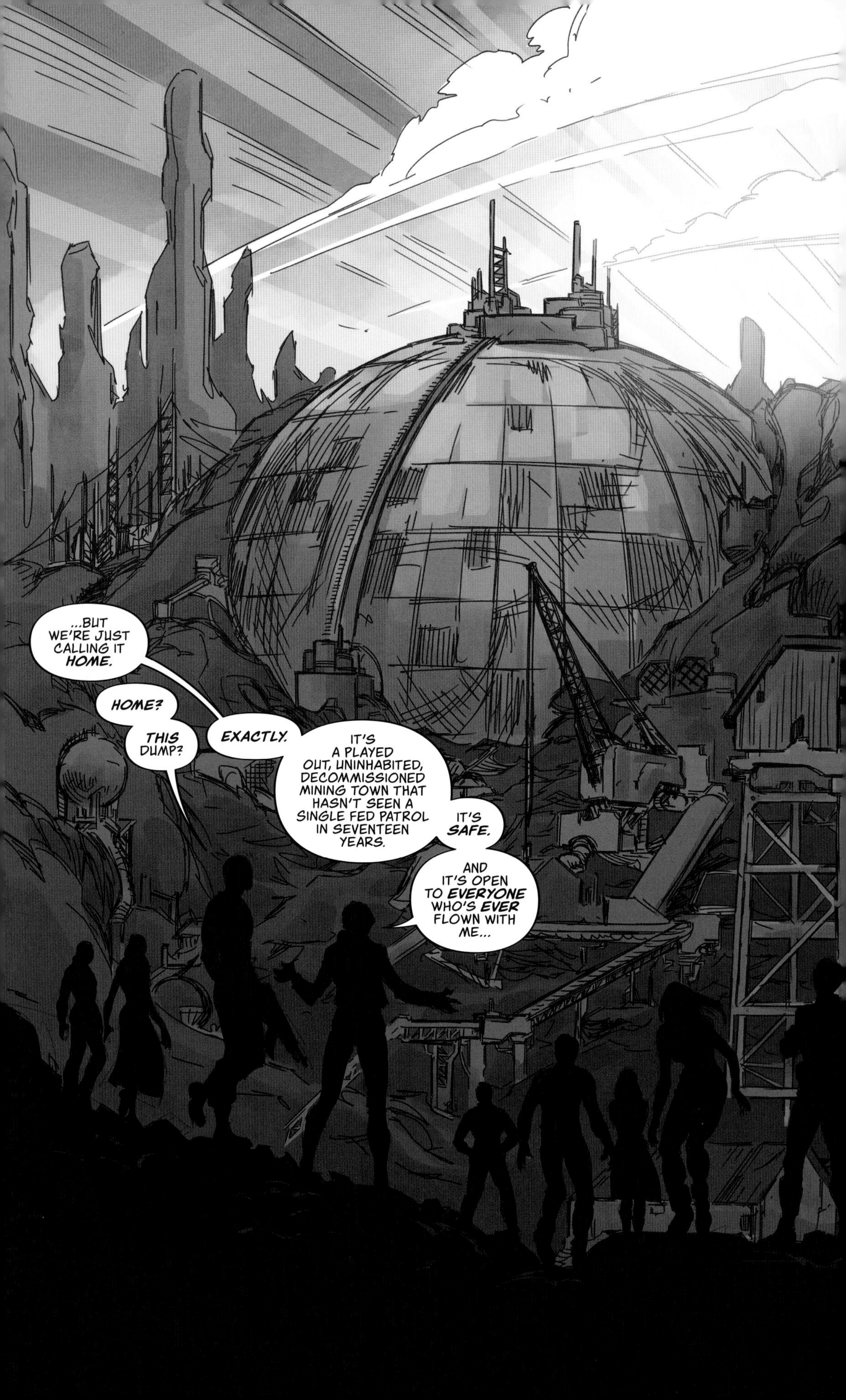
...BUT WE'RE JUST CALLING IT HOME.
HOME?
THIS DUMP?
EXACTLY.
IT'S A PLAYED OUT, UNINHABITED, DECOMMISSIONED MINING TOWN THAT HASN'T SEEN A SINGLE FED PATROL IN SEVENTEEN YEARS.
IT'S SAFE.
AND IT'S OPEN TO EVERYONE WHO'S EVER FLOWN WITH ME...

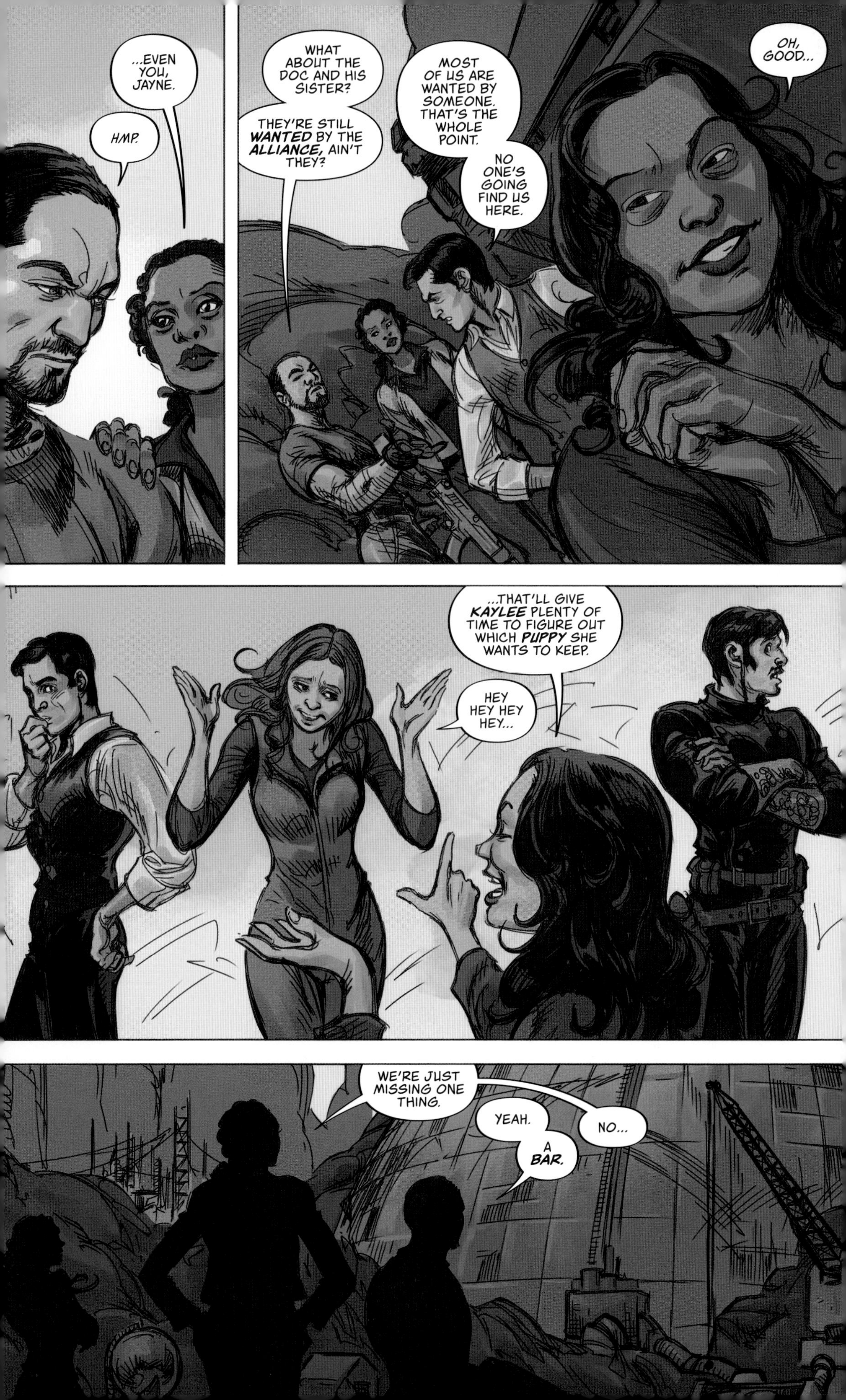

...EVEN YOU, JAYNE.
HMP.
WHAT ABOUT THE DOC AND HIS SISTER?
THEY'RE STILL **WANTED** BY THE **ALLIANCE,** AIN'T THEY?
MOST OF US ARE WANTED BY SOMEONE. THAT'S THE WHOLE POINT.
NO ONE'S GOING FIND US HERE.
OH, GOOD...
...THAT'LL GIVE **KAYLEE** PLENTY OF TIME TO FIGURE OUT WHICH **PUPPY** SHE WANTS TO KEEP.
HEY HEY HEY HEY...
WE'RE JUST MISSING ONE THING.
YEAH.
NO...
A **BAR.**

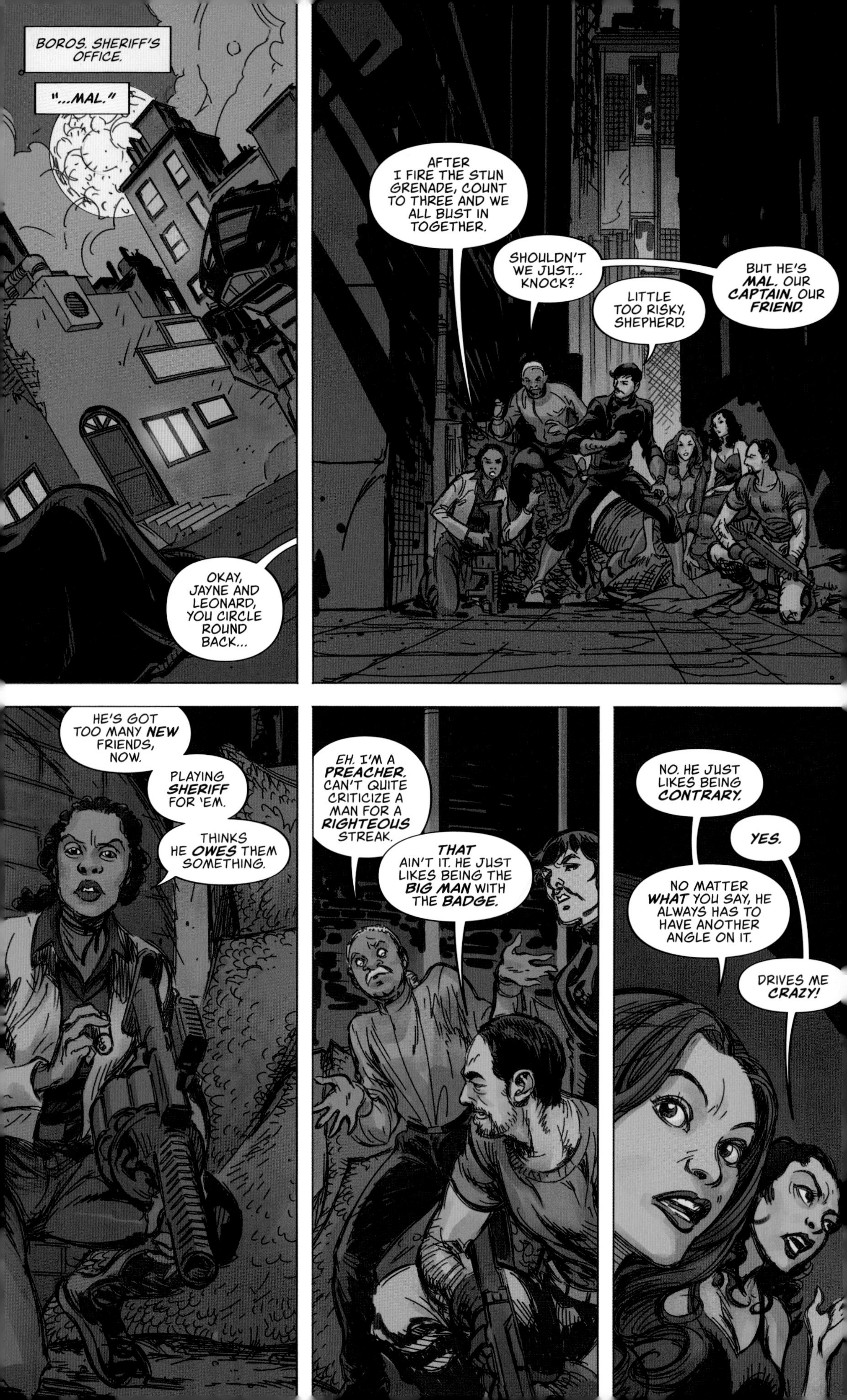
BOROS. SHERIFF'S OFFICE.
"...MAL."
OKAY, JAYNE AND LEONARD, YOU CIRCLE ROUND BACK...
AFTER I FIRE THE STUN GRENADE, COUNT TO THREE AND WE ALL BUST IN TOGETHER.
SHOULDN'T WE JUST... KNOCK?
LITTLE TOO RISKY, SHEPHERD.
BUT HE'S MAL. OUR CAPTAIN. OUR FRIEND.
HE'S GOT TOO MANY NEW FRIENDS, NOW.
PLAYING SHERIFF FOR 'EM.
THINKS HE OWES THEM SOMETHING.
EH. I'M A PREACHER. CAN'T QUITE CRITICIZE A MAN FOR A RIGHTEOUS STREAK.
THAT AIN'T IT. HE JUST LIKES BEING THE BIG MAN WITH THE BADGE.
NO. HE JUST LIKES BEING CONTRARY.
YES.
NO MATTER WHAT YOU SAY, HE ALWAYS HAS TO HAVE ANOTHER ANGLE ON IT.
DRIVES ME CRAZY!

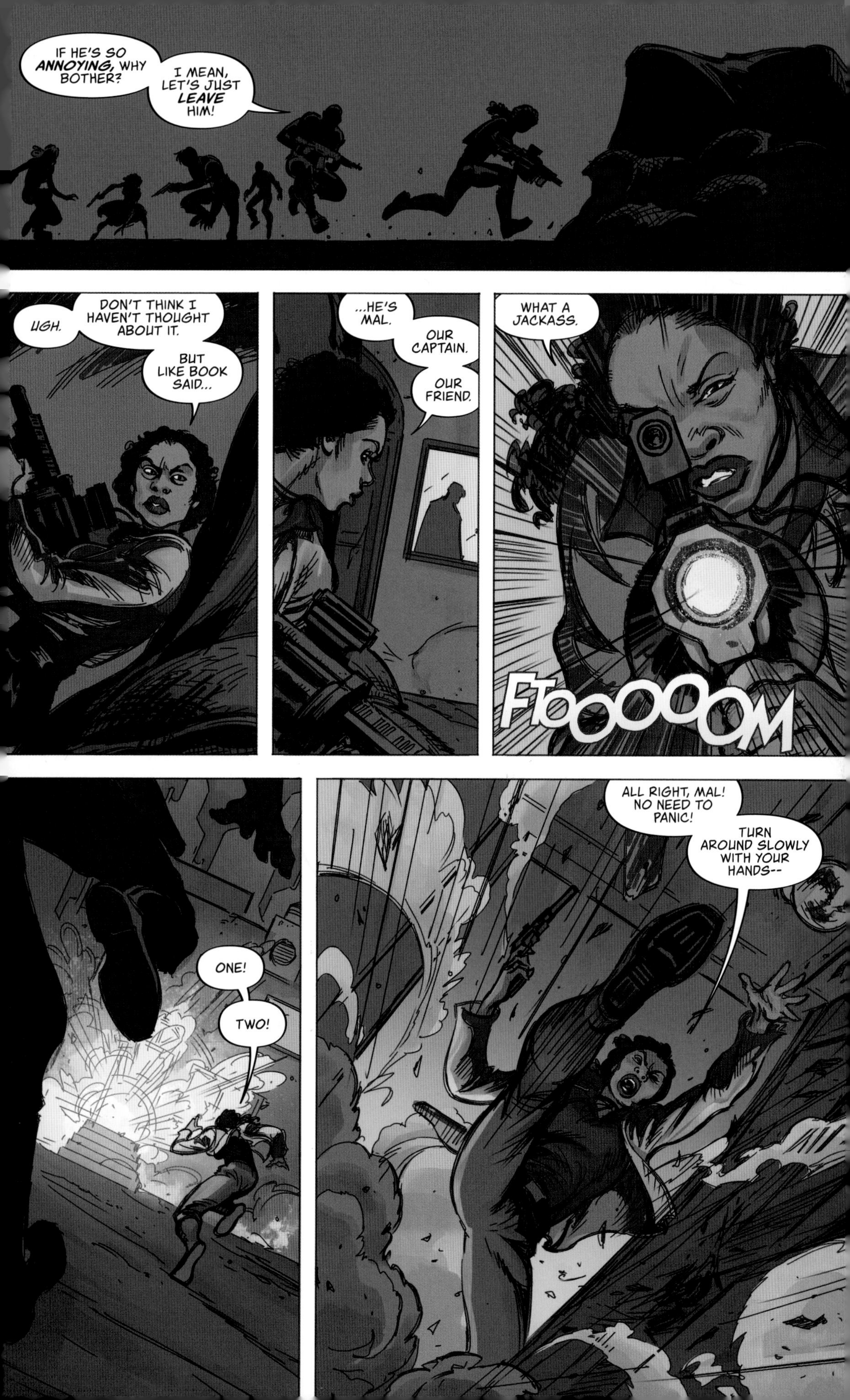
IF HE'S SO ANNOYING, WHY BOTHER?
I MEAN, LET'S JUST LEAVE HIM!
UGH.
DON'T THINK I HAVEN'T THOUGHT ABOUT IT.
BUT LIKE BOOK SAID...
...HE'S MAL.
OUR CAPTAIN.
OUR FRIEND.
WHAT A JACKASS.
FTOOOOOM
ONE!
TWO!
ALL RIGHT, MAL! NO NEED TO PANIC!
TURN AROUND SLOWLY WITH YOUR HANDS--

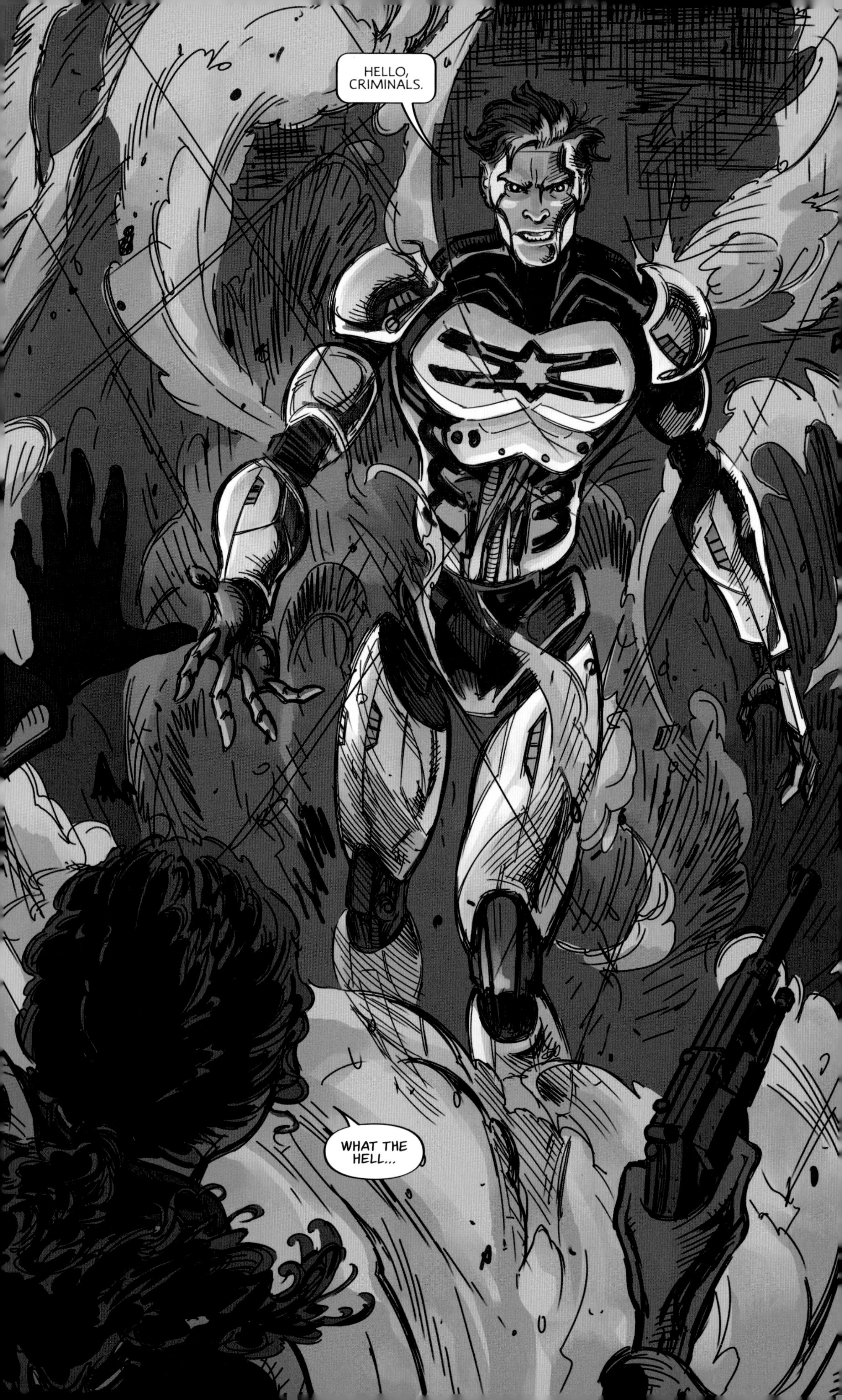
HELLO, CRIMINALS.
WHAT THE HELL...

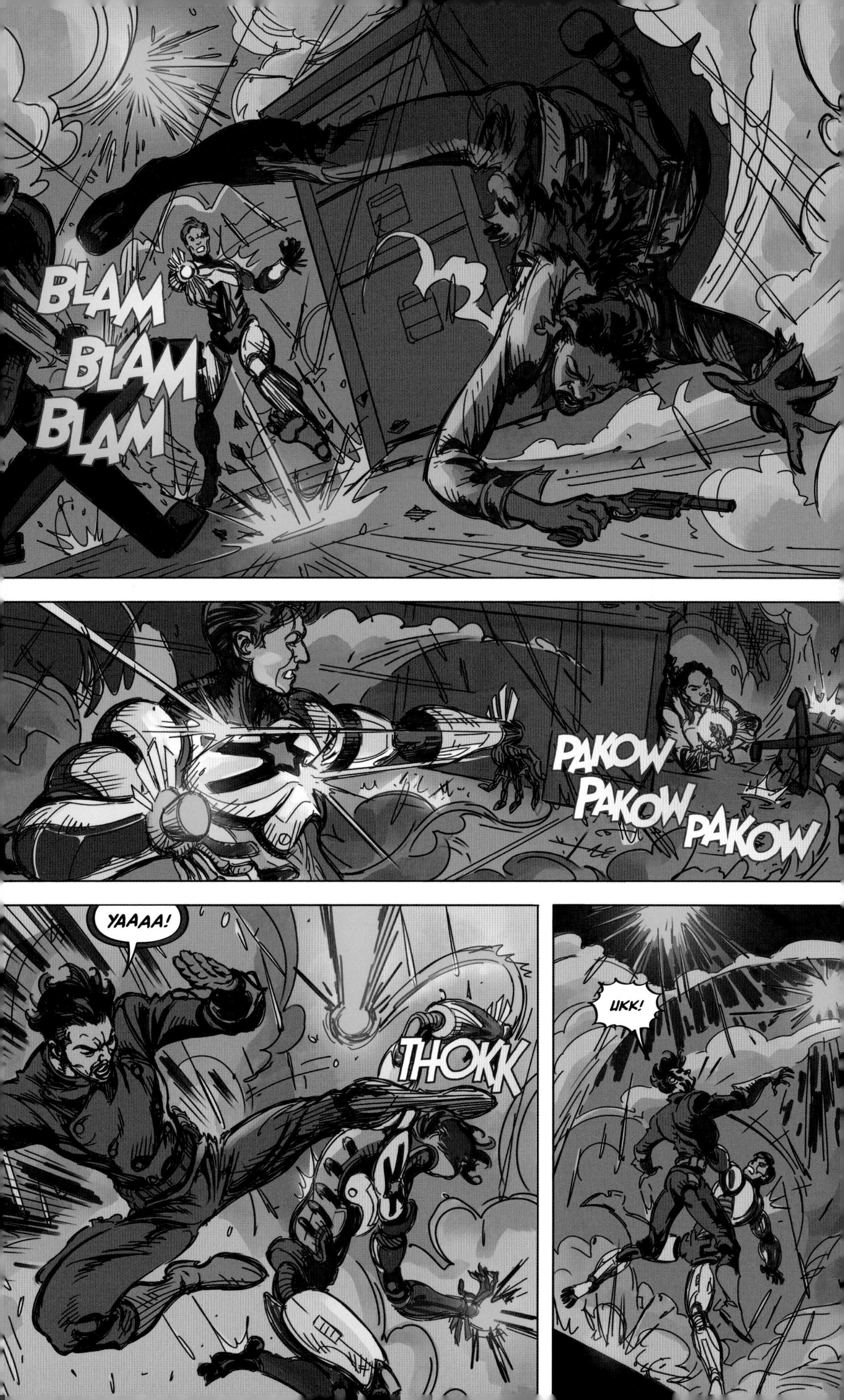
BLAM
BLAM
BLAM
PAKOW
PAKOW
PAKOW
YAAAA!
THOKK
UKK!

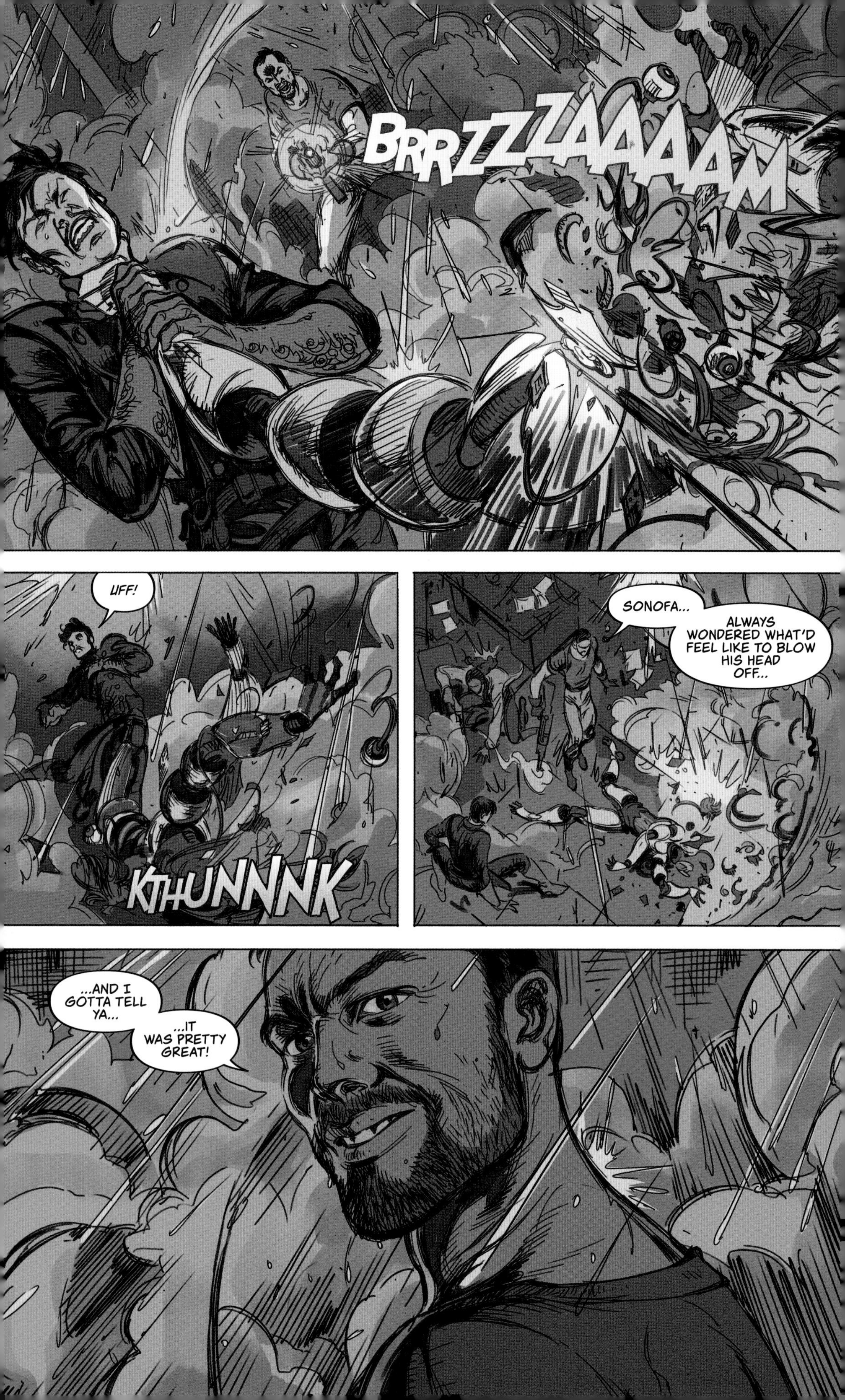
BRRZZZAAAAAM
UFF!
KTHUNNNK
SONOFA...
ALWAYS WONDERED WHAT'D FEEL LIKE TO BLOW HIS HEAD OFF...
...AND I GOTTA TELL YA...
...IT WAS PRETTY GREAT!

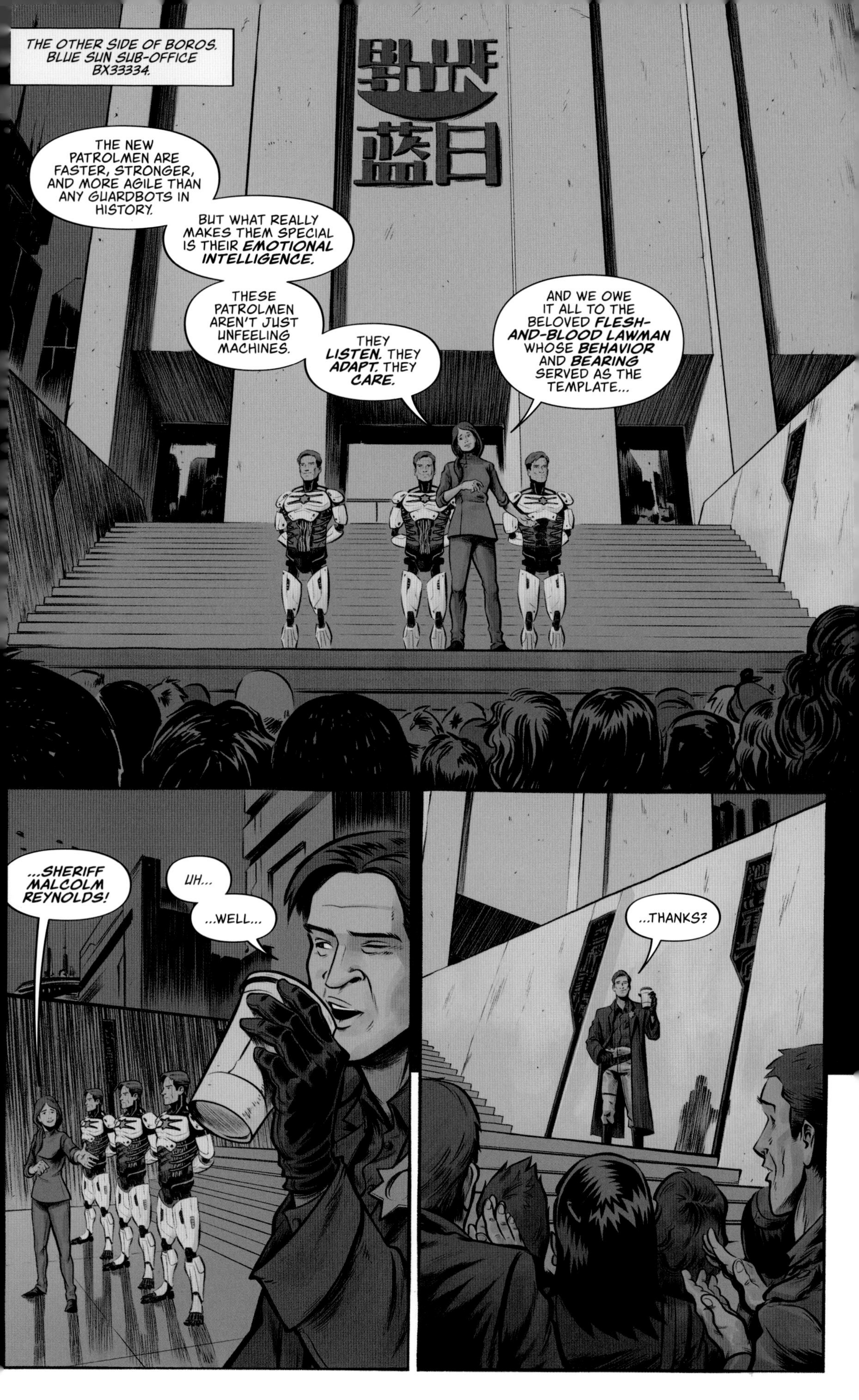
THE OTHER SIDE OF BOROS. BLUE SUN SUB-OFFICE BX33334.
BLUE SUN
蓝日
THE NEW PATROLMEN ARE FASTER, STRONGER, AND MORE AGILE THAN ANY GUARDBOTS IN HISTORY.
BUT WHAT REALLY MAKES THEM SPECIAL IS THEIR EMOTIONAL INTELLIGENCE.
THESE PATROLMEN AREN'T JUST UNFEELING MACHINES.
THEY LISTEN. THEY ADAPT. THEY CARE.
AND WE OWE IT ALL TO THE BELOVED FLESH-AND-BLOOD LAWMAN WHOSE BEHAVIOR AND BEARING SERVED AS THE TEMPLATE...
...SHERIFF MALCOLM REYNOLDS!
UH...
...WELL...
...THANKS?

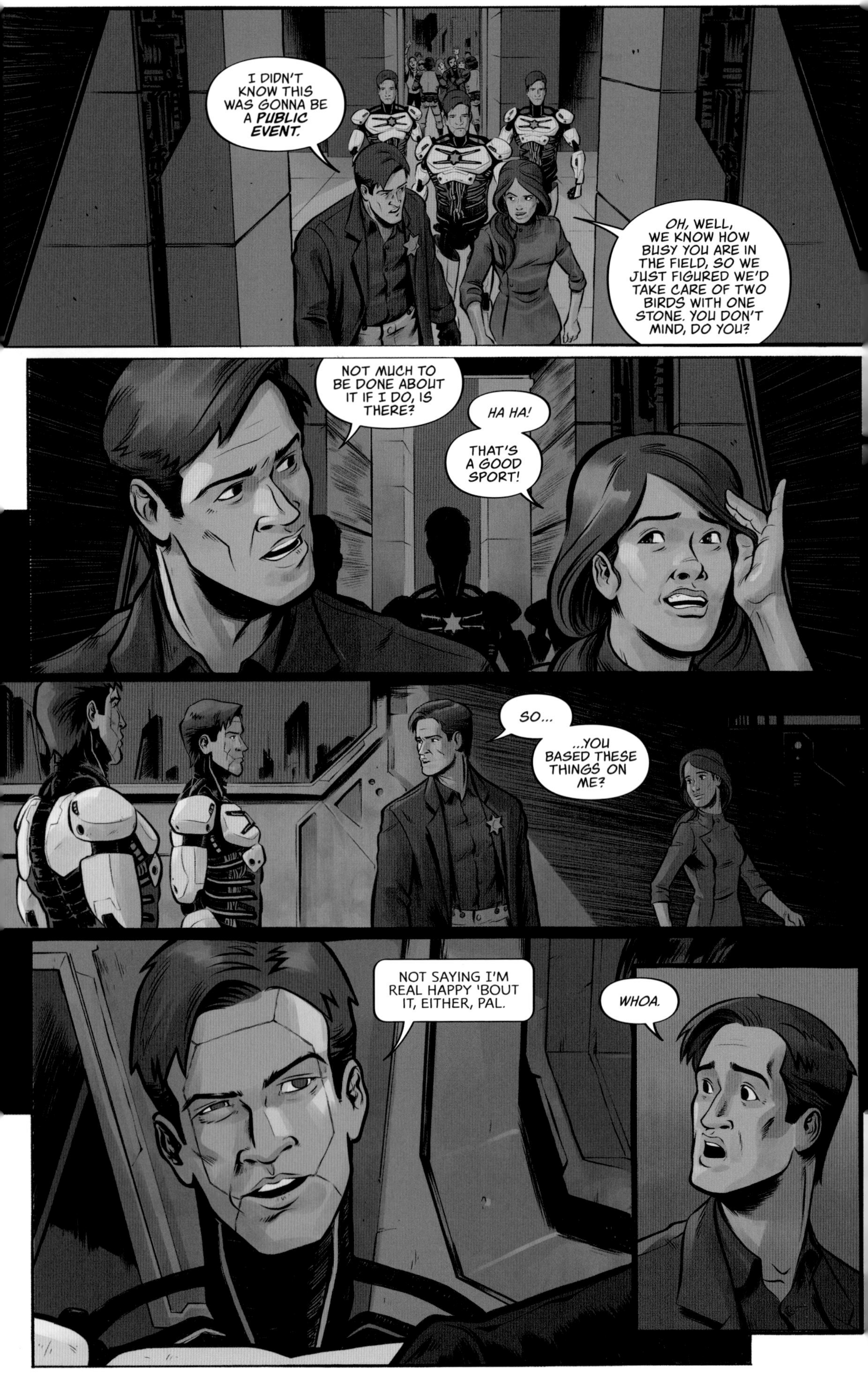
I DIDN'T KNOW THIS WAS GONNA BE A *PUBLIC EVENT.*
OH, WELL, WE KNOW HOW BUSY YOU ARE IN THE FIELD, SO WE JUST FIGURED WE'D TAKE CARE OF TWO BIRDS WITH ONE STONE. YOU DON'T MIND, DO YOU?
NOT MUCH TO BE DONE ABOUT IT IF I DO, IS THERE?
HA HA!
THAT'S A GOOD SPORT!
SO...
...YOU BASED THESE THINGS ON ME?
NOT SAYING I'M REAL HAPPY 'BOUT IT, EITHER, PAL.
WHOA.

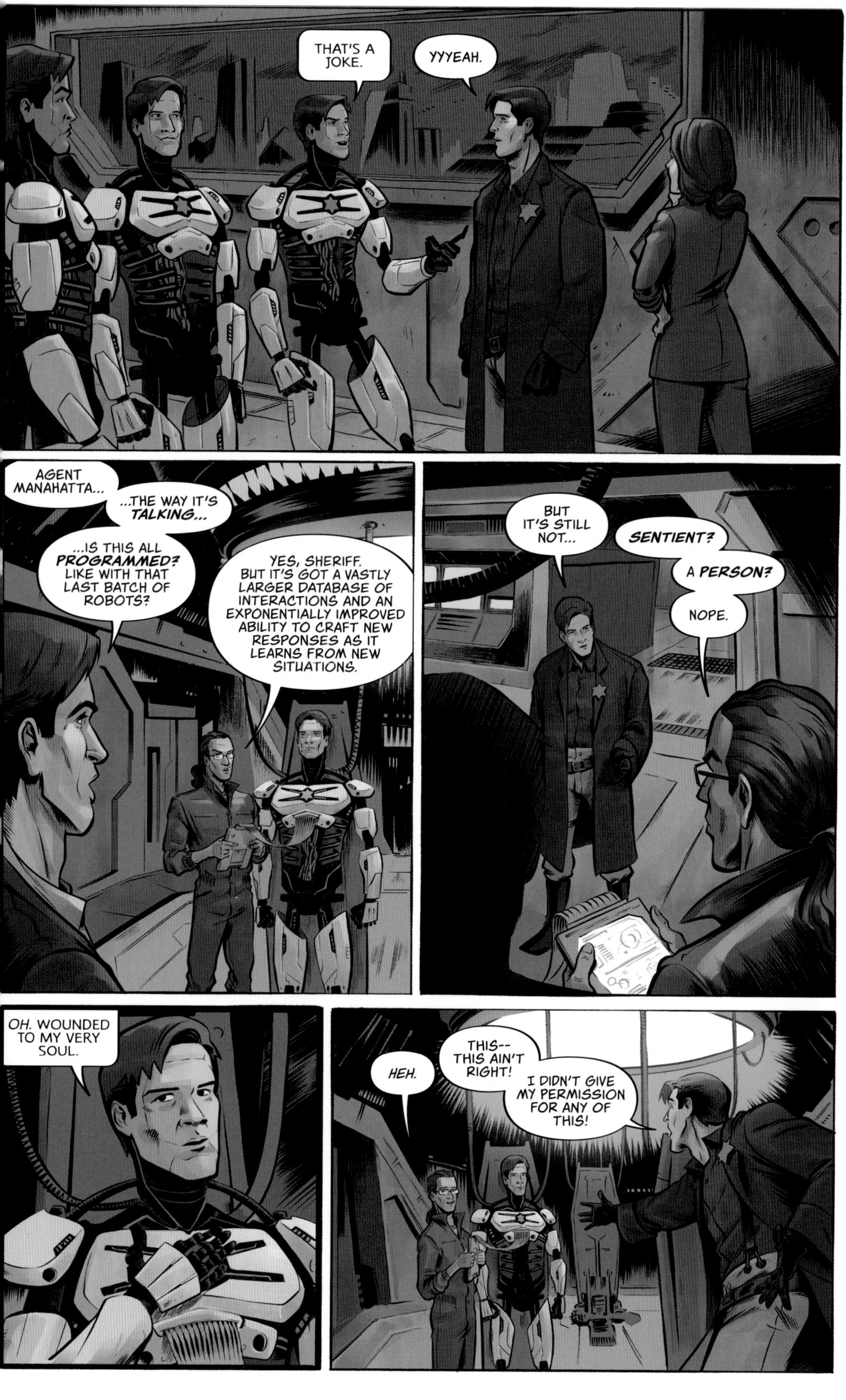
THAT'S A JOKE.
YYYEAH.
AGENT MANAHATTA...
...THE WAY IT'S *TALKING...*
...IS THIS ALL ***PROGRAMMED?*** LIKE WITH THAT LAST BATCH OF ROBOTS?
YES, SHERIFF. BUT IT'S GOT A VASTLY LARGER DATABASE OF INTERACTIONS AND AN EXPONENTIALLY IMPROVED ABILITY TO CRAFT NEW RESPONSES AS IT LEARNS FROM NEW SITUATIONS.
BUT IT'S STILL NOT...
SENTIENT?
A ***PERSON?***
NOPE.
OH. WOUNDED TO MY VERY SOUL.
HEH.
THIS-- THIS AIN'T RIGHT!
I DIDN'T GIVE MY PERMISSION FOR ANY OF THIS!

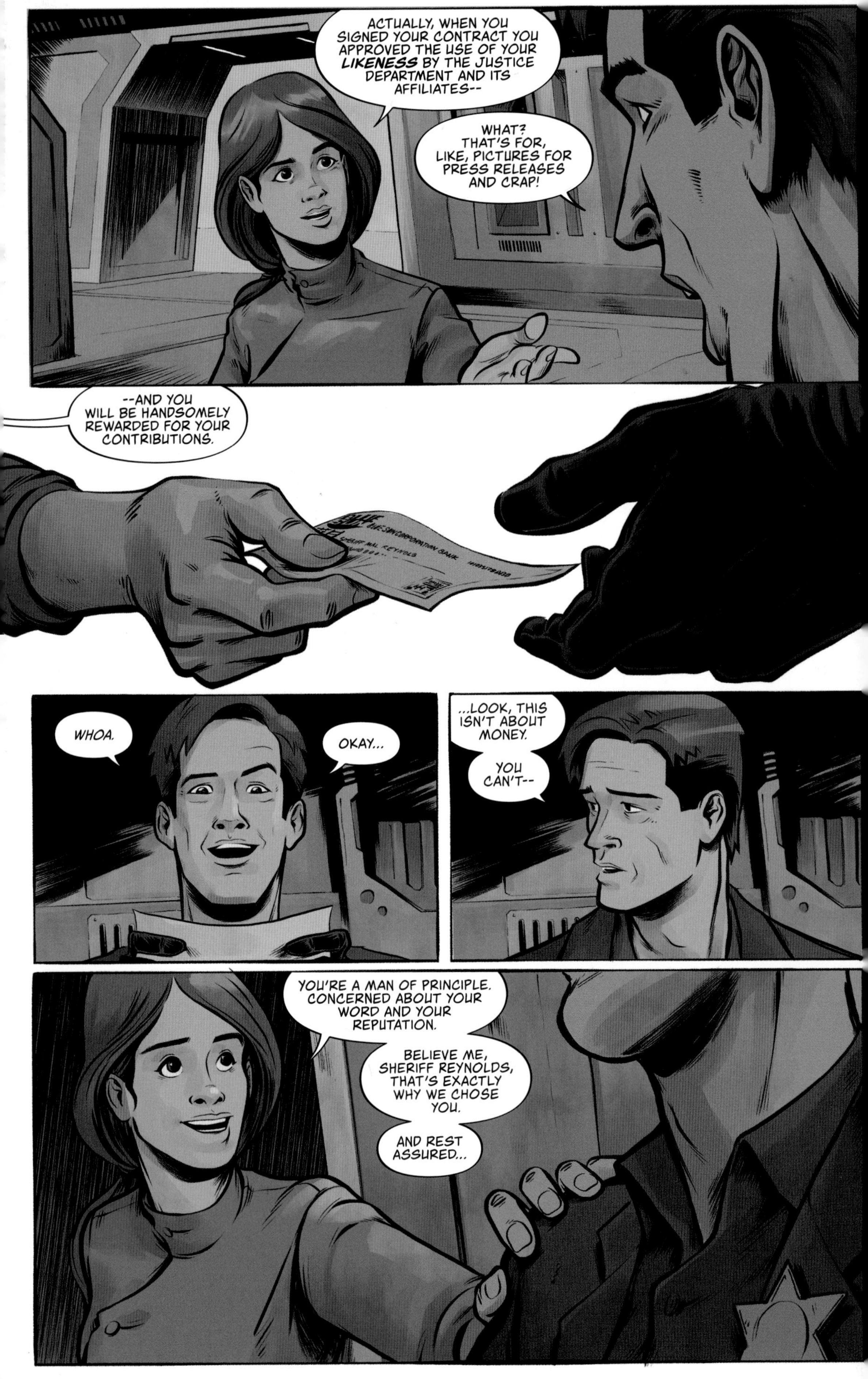
ACTUALLY, WHEN YOU SIGNED YOUR CONTRACT YOU APPROVED THE USE OF YOUR ***LIKENESS*** BY THE JUSTICE DEPARTMENT AND ITS AFFILIATES--
WHAT? THAT'S FOR, LIKE, PICTURES FOR PRESS RELEASES AND CRAP!
--AND YOU WILL BE HANDSOMELY REWARDED FOR YOUR CONTRIBUTIONS.
WHOA.
OKAY...
...LOOK, THIS ISN'T ABOUT MONEY.
YOU CAN'T--
YOU'RE A MAN OF PRINCIPLE. CONCERNED ABOUT YOUR WORD AND YOUR REPUTATION.
BELIEVE ME, SHERIFF REYNOLDS, THAT'S EXACTLY WHY WE CHOSE YOU.
AND REST ASSURED...

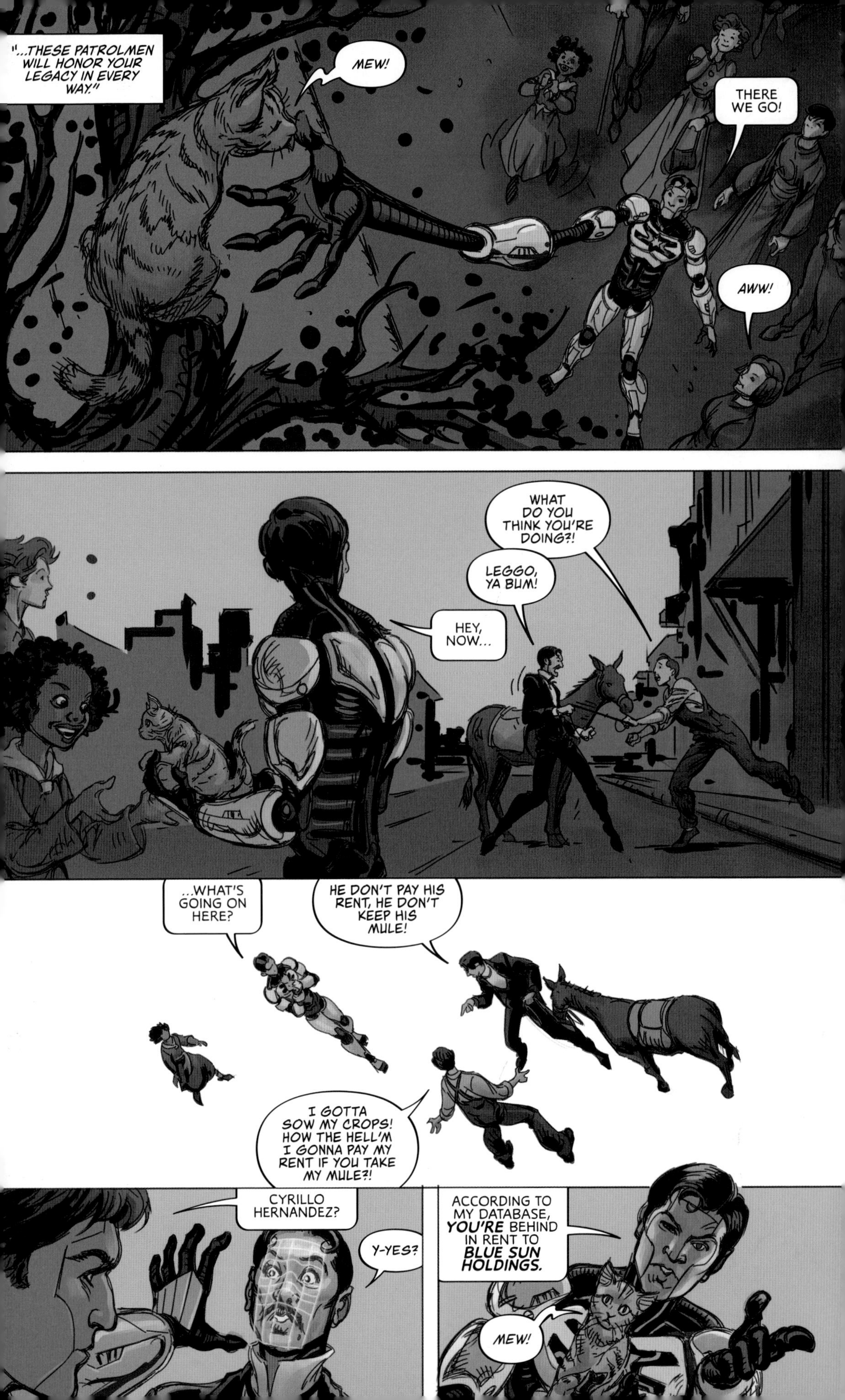
"...THESE PATROLMEN WILL HONOR YOUR LEGACY IN EVERY WAY."
MEW!
THERE WE GO!
AWW!
HEY, NOW...
LEGGO, YA BUM!
WHAT DO YOU THINK YOU'RE DOING?!
...WHAT'S GOING ON HERE?
HE DON'T PAY HIS RENT, HE DON'T KEEP HIS MULE!
I GOTTA SOW MY CROPS! HOW THE HELL'M I GONNA PAY MY RENT IF YOU TAKE MY MULE?!
CYRILLO HERNANDEZ?
Y-YES?
ACCORDING TO MY DATABASE, ***YOU'RE*** BEHIND IN RENT TO ***BLUE SUN HOLDINGS.***
MEW!

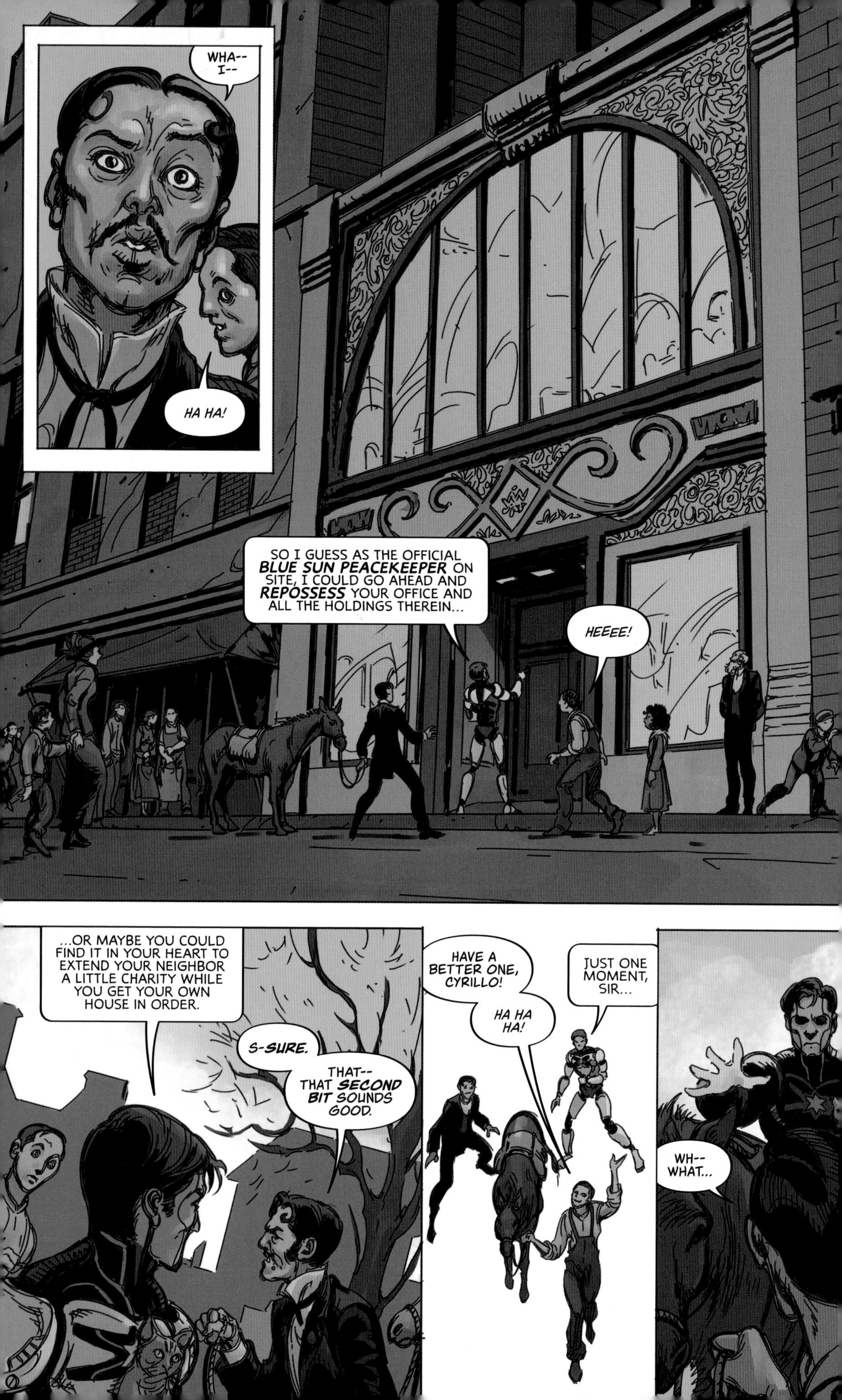
WHA-- I--
HA HA!
SO I GUESS AS THE OFFICIAL BLUE SUN PEACEKEEPER ON SITE, I COULD GO AHEAD AND REPOSSESS YOUR OFFICE AND ALL THE HOLDINGS THEREIN...
HEEEE!
...OR MAYBE YOU COULD FIND IT IN YOUR HEART TO EXTEND YOUR NEIGHBOR A LITTLE CHARITY WHILE YOU GET YOUR OWN HOUSE IN ORDER.
S-SURE.
THAT-- THAT SECOND BIT SOUNDS GOOD.
HAVE A BETTER ONE, CYRILLO!
HA HA HA!
JUST ONE MOMENT, SIR...
WH-- WHAT...

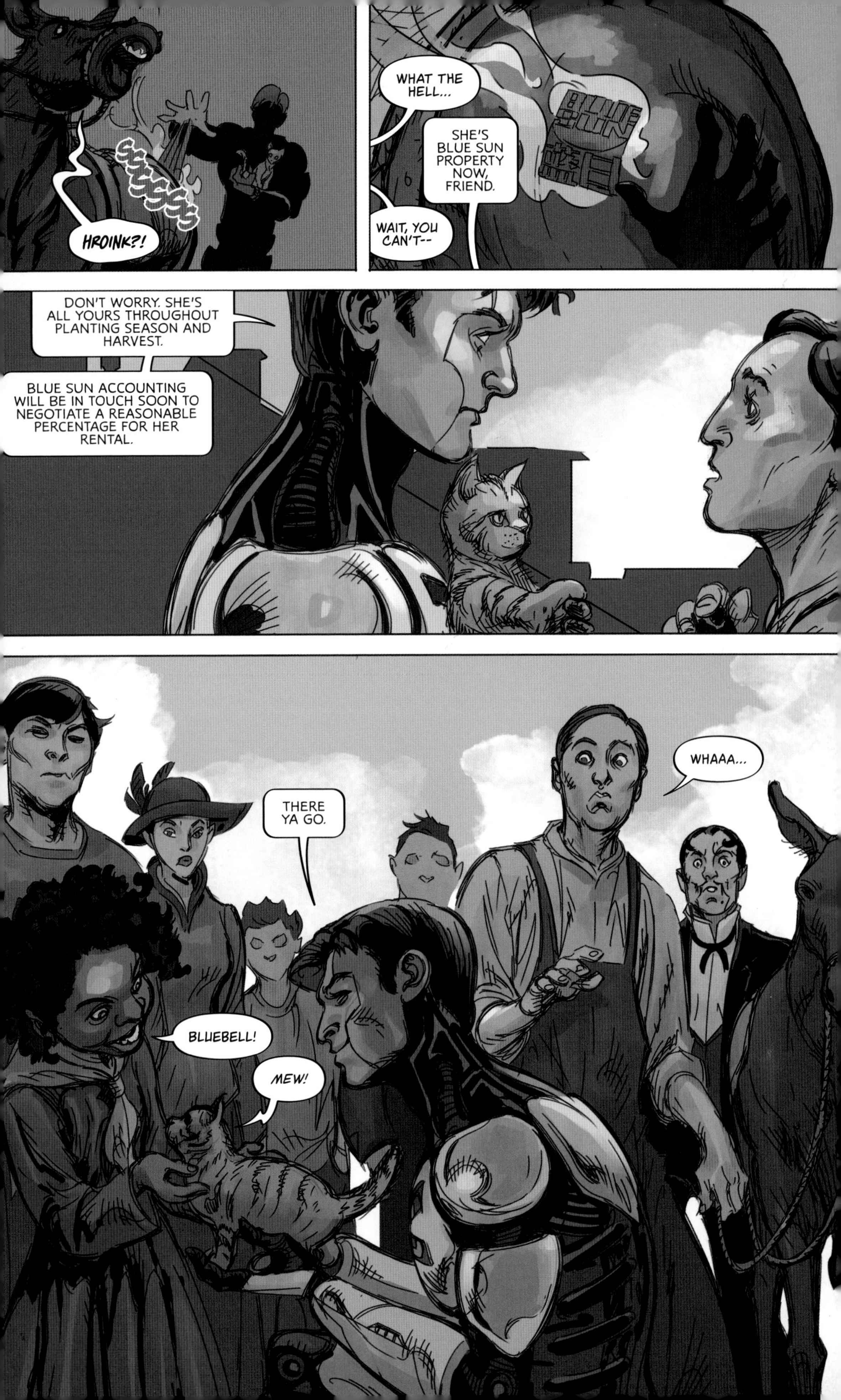
SSSSSSS
HROINK?!
WHAT THE HELL...
BLUE SUN
SHE'S BLUE SUN PROPERTY NOW, FRIEND.
WAIT, YOU CAN'T--
DON'T WORRY. SHE'S ALL YOURS THROUGHOUT PLANTING SEASON AND HARVEST.
BLUE SUN ACCOUNTING WILL BE IN TOUCH SOON TO NEGOTIATE A REASONABLE PERCENTAGE FOR HER RENTAL.
THERE YA GO.
WHAAA...
BLUEBELL!
MEW!

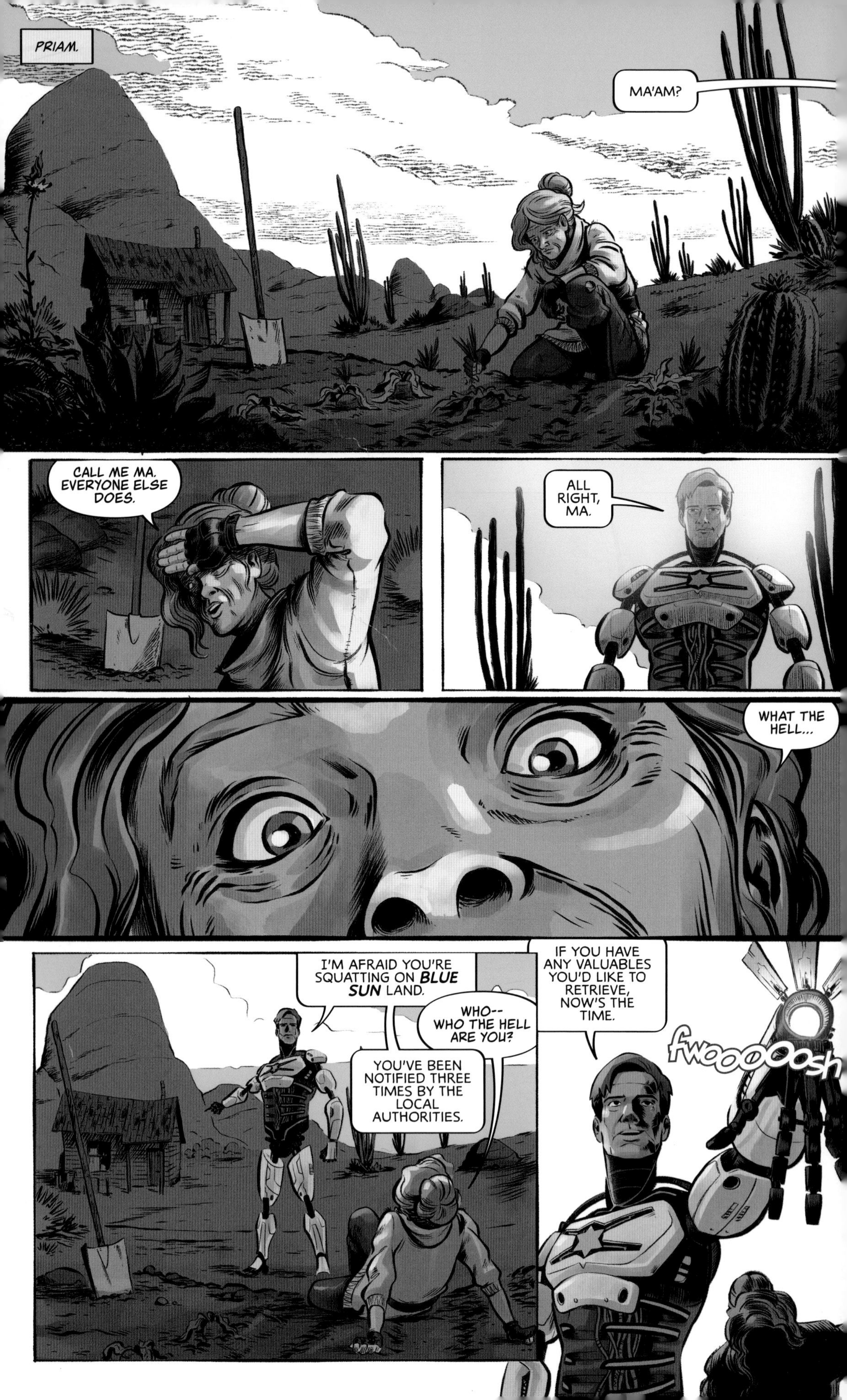
PRIAM.
MA'AM?
CALL ME MA. EVERYONE ELSE DOES.
ALL RIGHT, MA.
WHAT THE HELL...
I'M AFRAID YOU'RE SQUATTING ON **BLUE SUN** LAND.
YOU'VE BEEN NOTIFIED THREE TIMES BY THE LOCAL AUTHORITIES.
WHO-- WHO THE HELL ARE YOU?
IF YOU HAVE ANY VALUABLES YOU'D LIKE TO RETRIEVE, NOW'S THE TIME.
fwoooOOsh

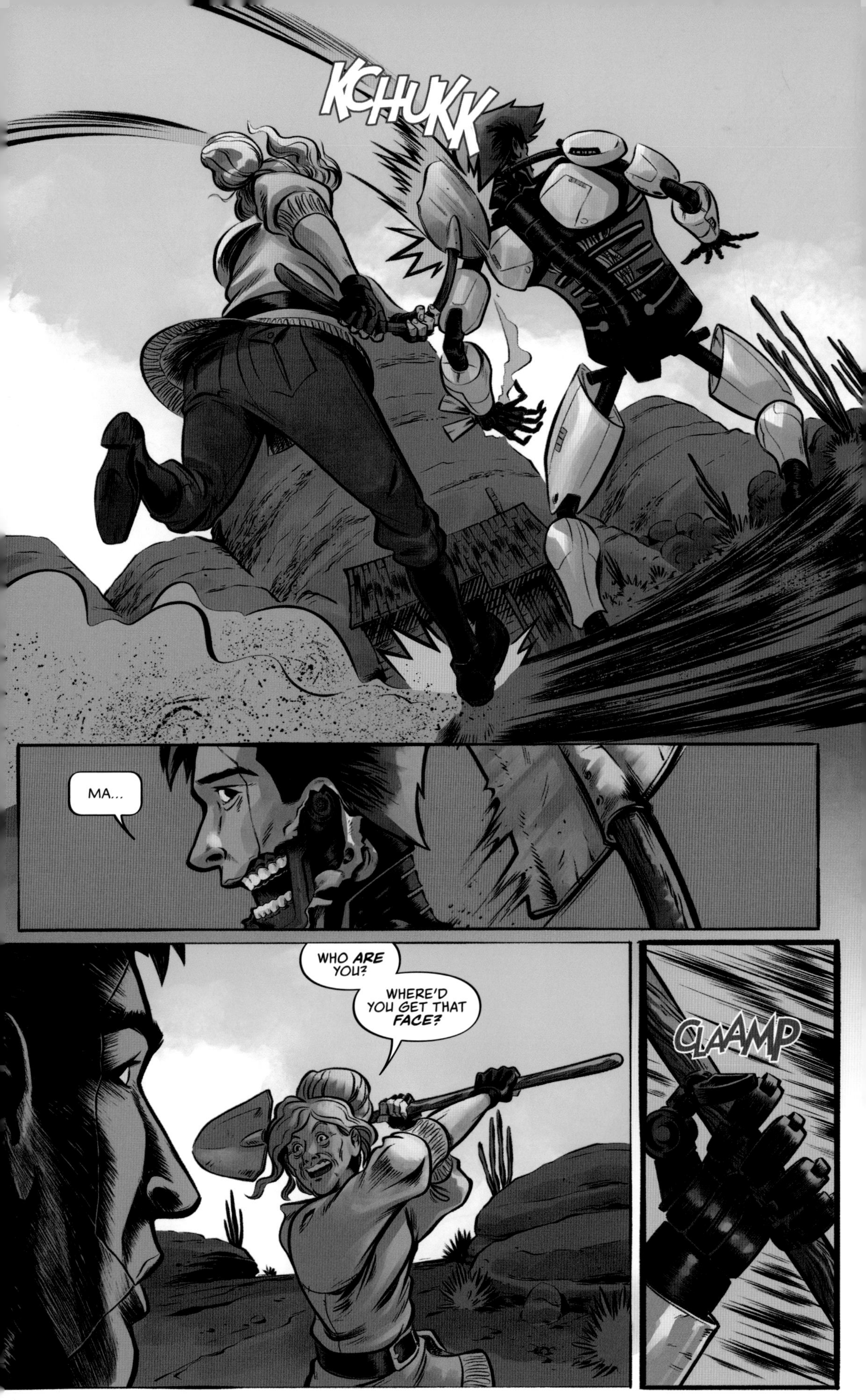
KCHUKK
MA...
WHO ARE YOU?
WHERE'D YOU GET THAT FACE?
CLAAMP

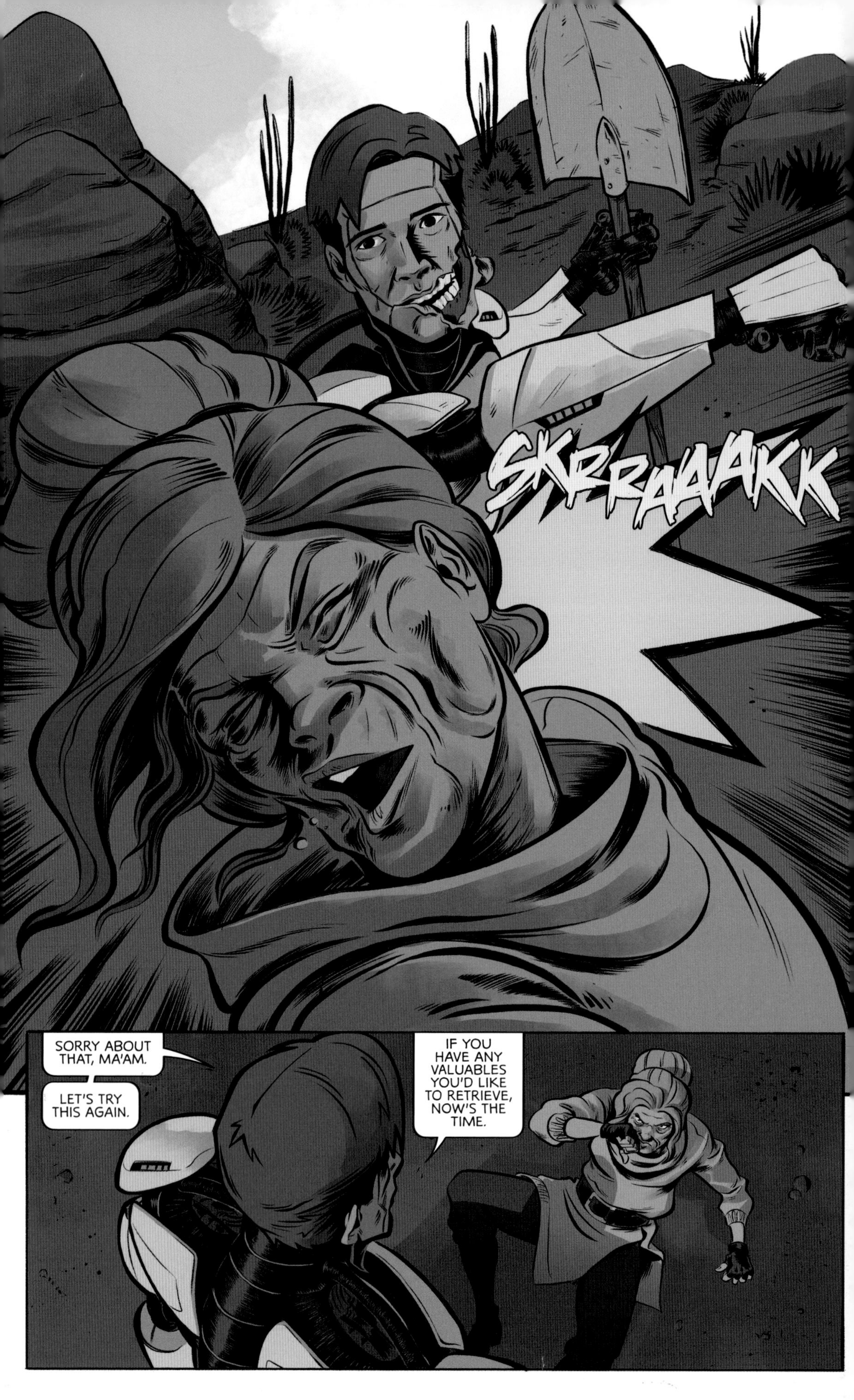
SKRRAAAKK
SORRY ABOUT THAT, MA'AM.
LET'S TRY THIS AGAIN.
IF YOU HAVE ANY VALUABLES YOU'D LIKE TO RETRIEVE, NOW'S THE TIME.

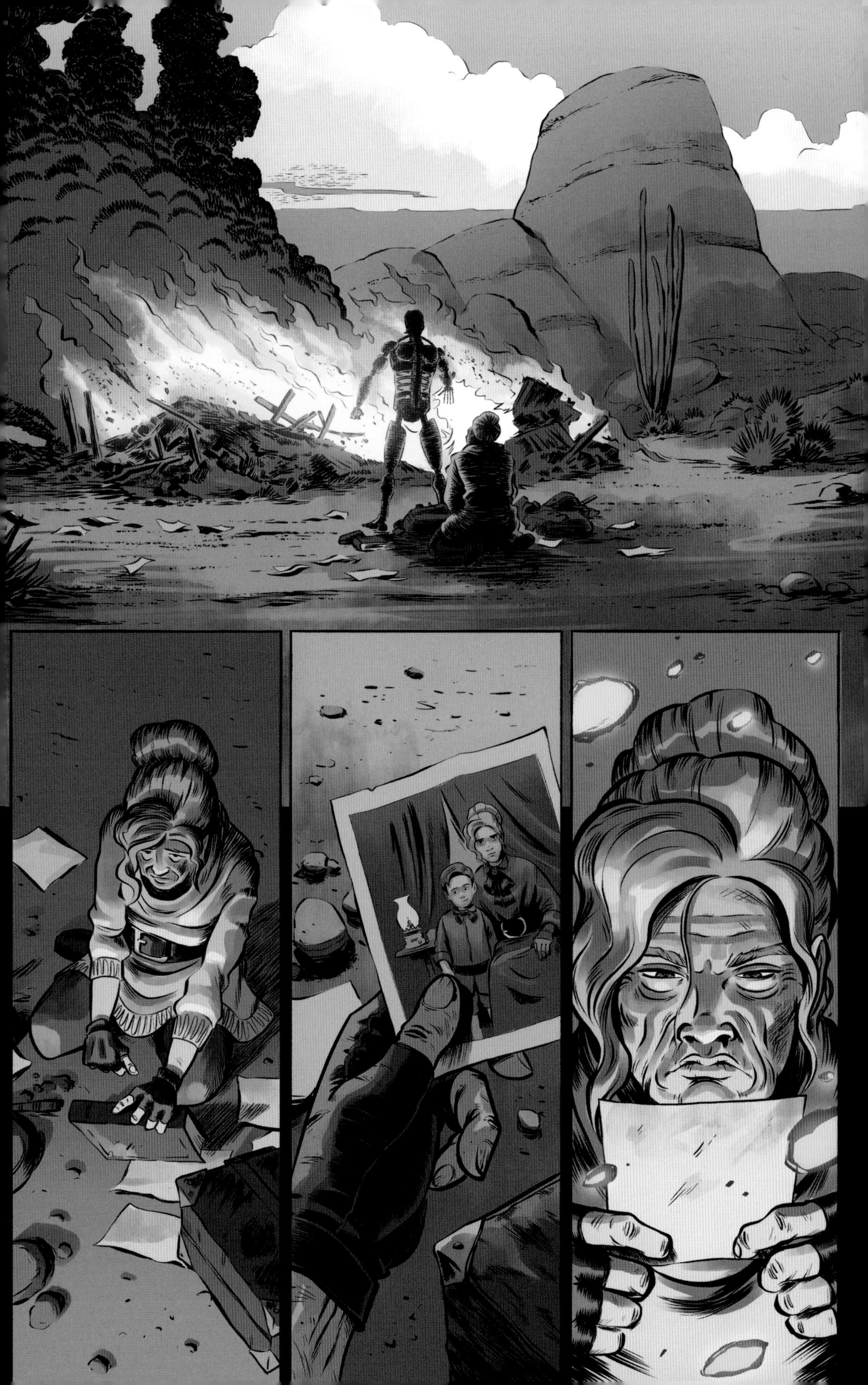

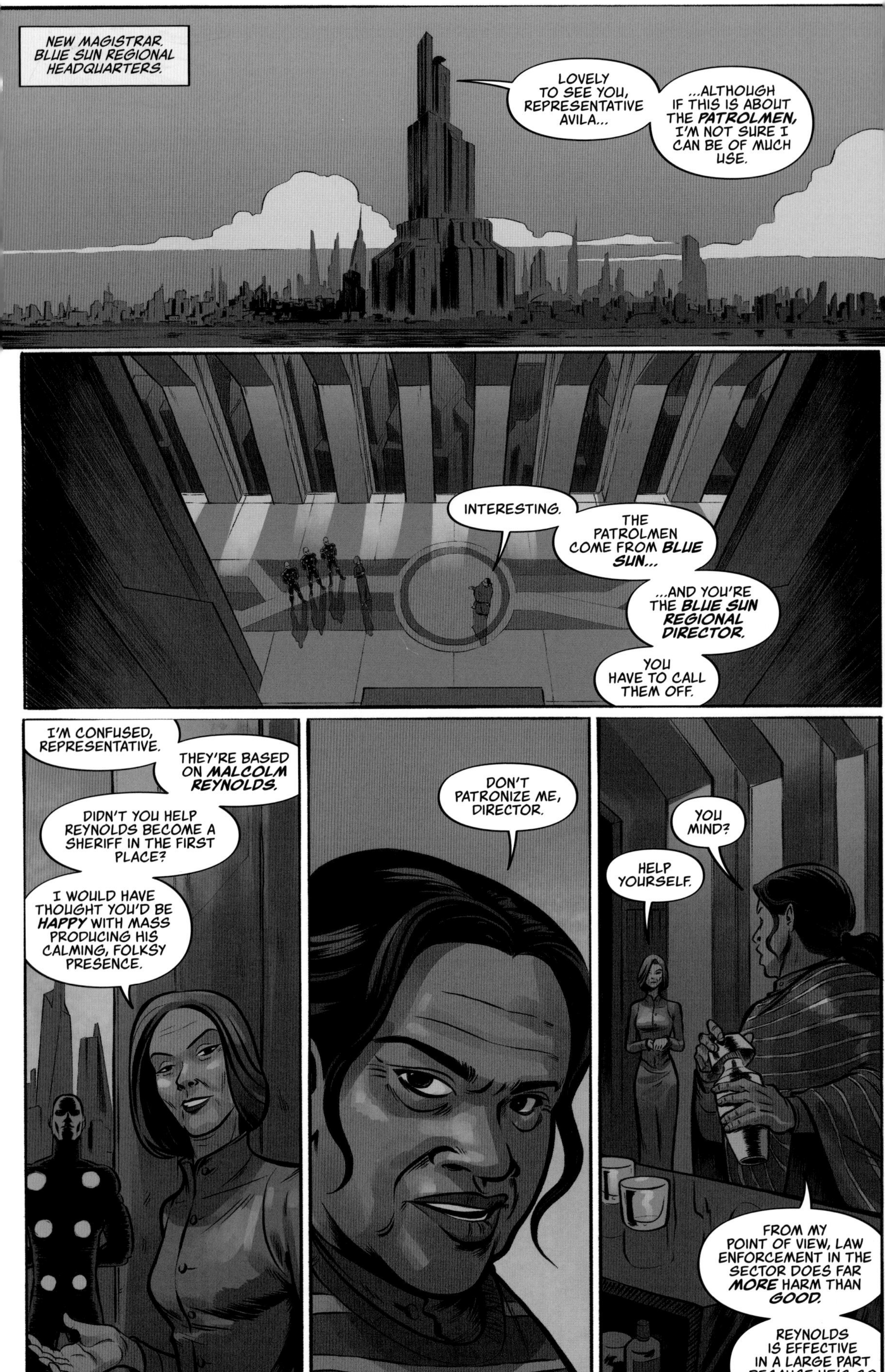
NEW MAGISTRAR. BLUE SUN REGIONAL HEADQUARTERS.
LOVELY TO SEE YOU, REPRESENTATIVE AVILA...
...ALTHOUGH IF THIS IS ABOUT THE PATROLMEN, I'M NOT SURE I CAN BE OF MUCH USE.
INTERESTING.
THE PATROLMEN COME FROM BLUE SUN...
...AND YOU'RE THE BLUE SUN REGIONAL DIRECTOR.
YOU HAVE TO CALL THEM OFF.
I'M CONFUSED, REPRESENTATIVE.
THEY'RE BASED ON MALCOLM REYNOLDS.
DIDN'T YOU HELP REYNOLDS BECOME A SHERIFF IN THE FIRST PLACE?
I WOULD HAVE THOUGHT YOU'D BE HAPPY WITH MASS PRODUCING HIS CALMING, FOLKSY PRESENCE.
DON'T PATRONIZE ME, DIRECTOR.
YOU MIND?
HELP YOURSELF.
FROM MY POINT OF VIEW, LAW ENFORCEMENT IN THE SECTOR DOES FAR MORE HARM THAN GOOD.
REYNOLDS IS EFFECTIVE IN A LARGE PART BECAUSE HE'S SO INEFFECTIVE.

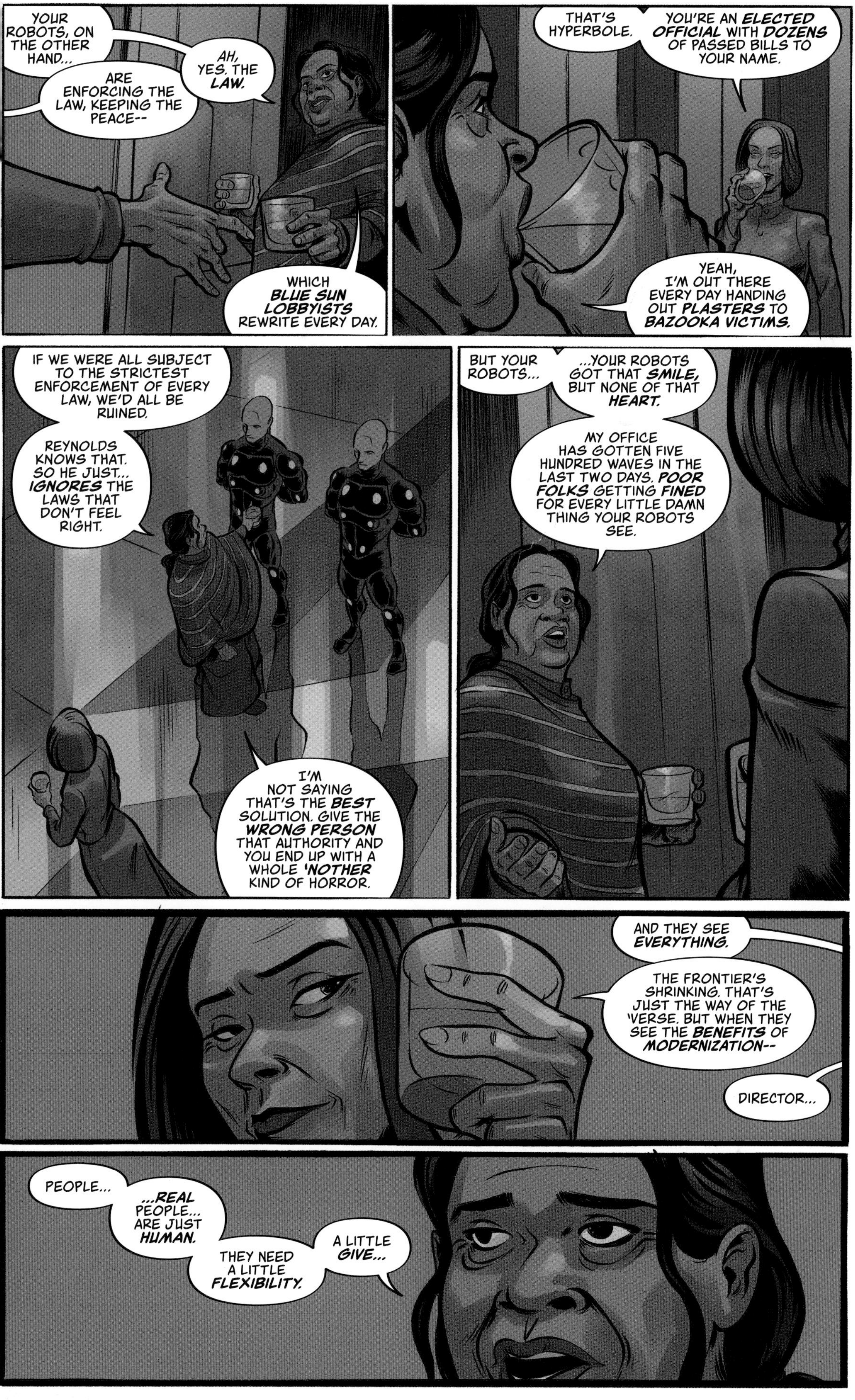
YOUR ROBOTS, ON THE OTHER HAND...
ARE ENFORCING THE LAW, KEEPING THE PEACE--
AH, YES. THE LAW.
WHICH BLUE SUN LOBBYISTS REWRITE EVERY DAY.
THAT'S HYPERBOLE.
YOU'RE AN ELECTED OFFICIAL WITH DOZENS OF PASSED BILLS TO YOUR NAME.
YEAH, I'M OUT THERE EVERY DAY HANDING OUT PLASTERS TO BAZOOKA VICTIMS.
IF WE WERE ALL SUBJECT TO THE STRICTEST ENFORCEMENT OF EVERY LAW, WE'D ALL BE RUINED.
REYNOLDS KNOWS THAT. SO HE JUST... IGNORES THE LAWS THAT DON'T FEEL RIGHT.
I'M NOT SAYING THAT'S THE BEST SOLUTION. GIVE THE WRONG PERSON THAT AUTHORITY AND YOU END UP WITH A WHOLE 'NOTHER KIND OF HORROR.
BUT YOUR ROBOTS...
...YOUR ROBOTS GOT THAT SMILE, BUT NONE OF THAT HEART.
MY OFFICE HAS GOTTEN FIVE HUNDRED WAVES IN THE LAST TWO DAYS. POOR FOLKS GETTING FINED FOR EVERY LITTLE DAMN THING YOUR ROBOTS SEE.
AND THEY SEE EVERYTHING.
THE FRONTIER'S SHRINKING. THAT'S JUST THE WAY OF THE 'VERSE. BUT WHEN THEY SEE THE BENEFITS OF MODERNIZATION--
DIRECTOR...
PEOPLE...
...REAL PEOPLE... ARE JUST HUMAN.
THEY NEED A LITTLE FLEXIBILITY.
A LITTLE GIVE...

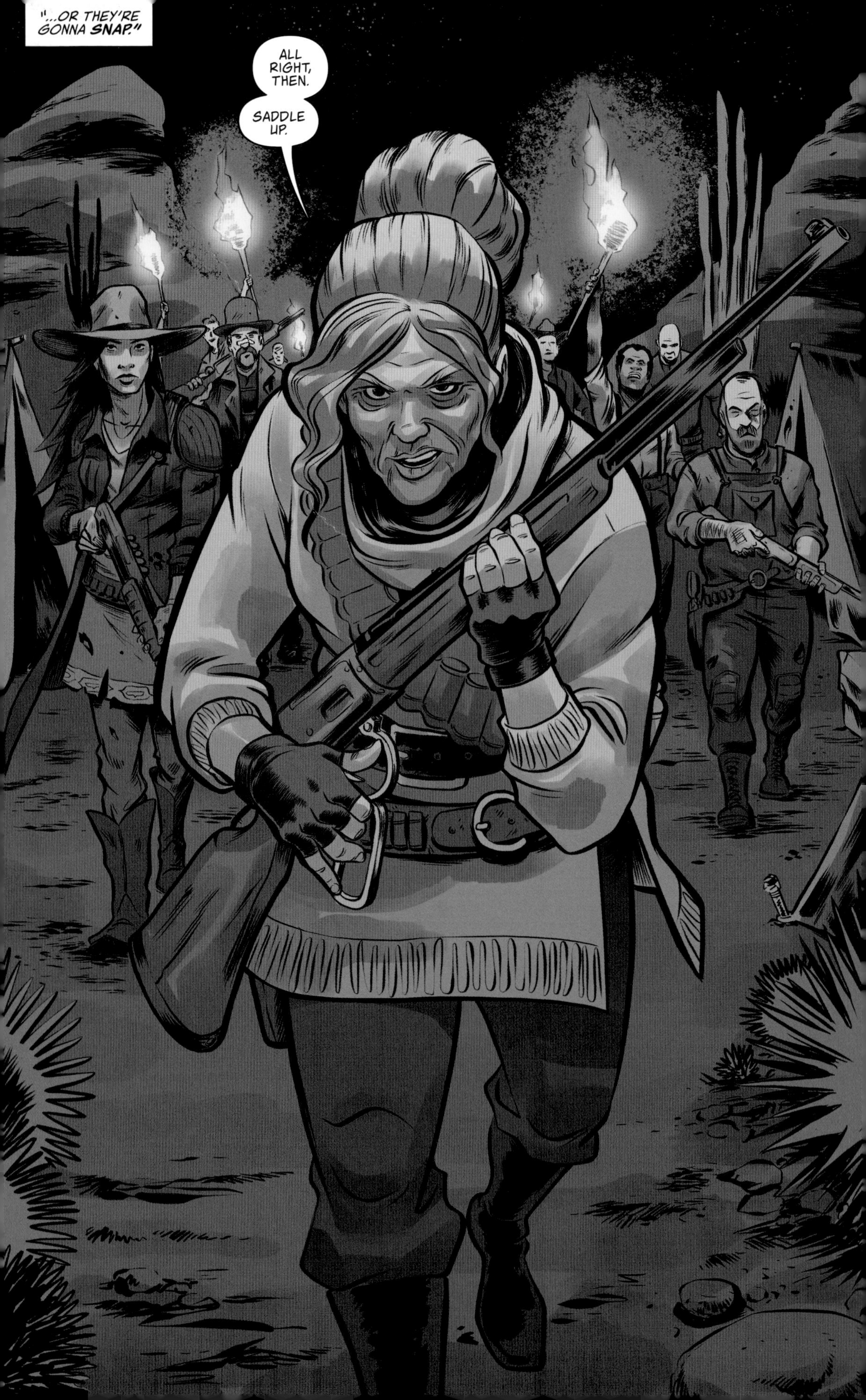
"...OR THEY'RE GONNA **SNAP.**"
ALL RIGHT, THEN.
SADDLE UP.

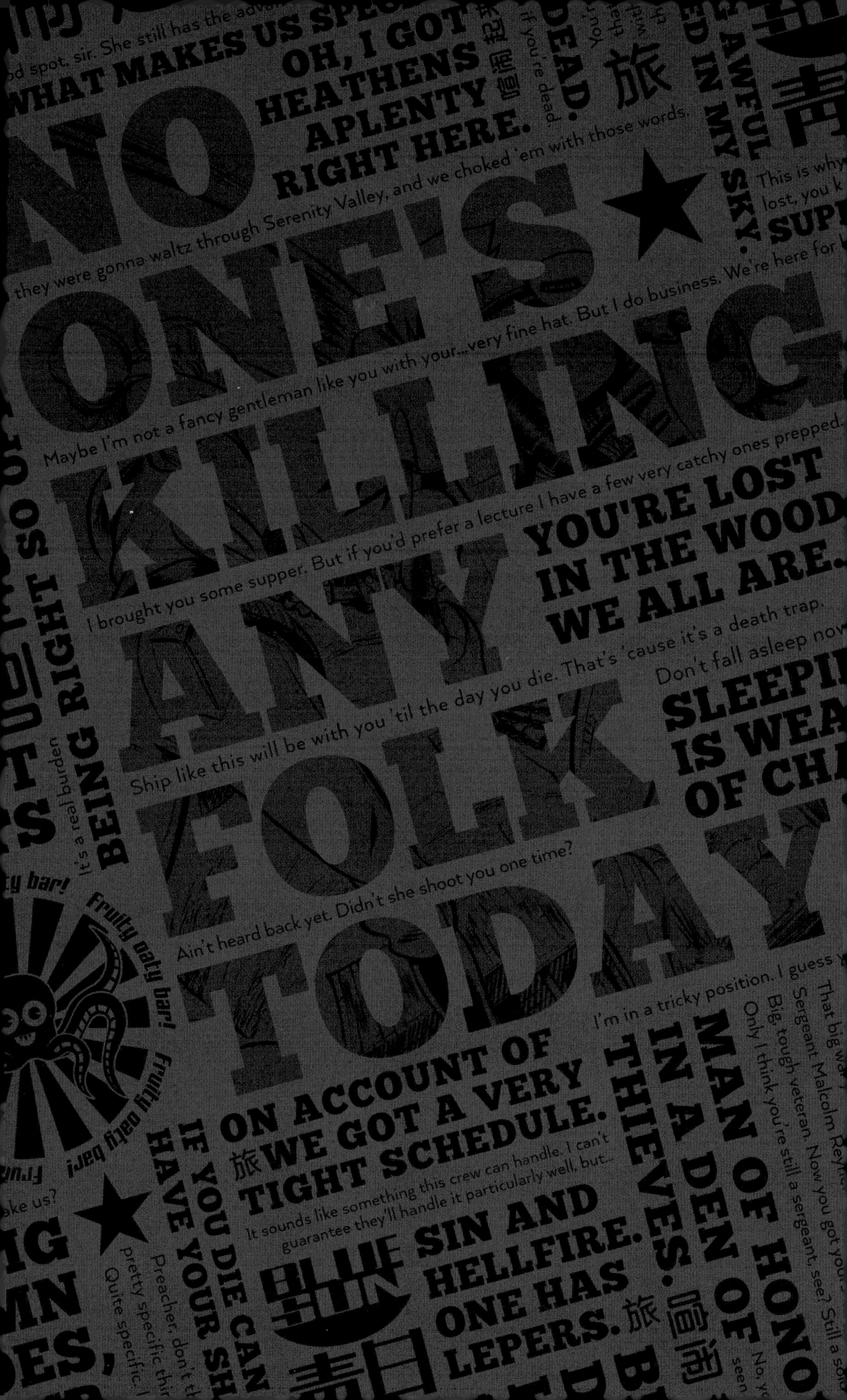
WHAT MAKES US SPE
od spot, sir. She still has the adv
OH, I GOT
HEATHENS
APLENTY
RIGHT HERE.
if you're dead
DEAD.
旅
AWFUL
IN MY SKY.
This is why
lost, you k
SUP
NO
ONE'S
KILLING
ANY
FOLK
TODAY
they were gonna waltz through Serenity Valley, and we choked 'em with those words.
We're here for
Maybe I'm not a fancy gentleman like you with your...very fine hat. But I do business.
I brought you some supper. But if you'd prefer a lecture I have a few very catchy ones prepped.
YOU'RE LOST
IN THE WOOD
WE ALL ARE.
Ship like this will be with you 'til the day you die. That's 'cause it's a death trap.
Don't fall asleep now
SLEEPI
IS WEA
OF CH
Ain't heard back yet. Didn't she shoot you one time?
It's a real burden
BEING RIGHT SO OF
Fruity oaty bar!
I'm in a tricky position. I guess
That big wa
Sergeant Malcolm Reyn
Big, tough veteran. Now you got your
Only I think you're still a sergeant, see? Still a sol
ON ACCOUNT OF
旅 WE GOT A VERY
TIGHT SCHEDULE.
It sounds like something this crew can handle. I can't
guarantee they'll handle it particularly well, but...
IF YOU DIE CAN
HAVE YOUR SH
Preacher, don't
pretty specific thi
Quite specific
SIN AND
HELLFIRE.
ONE HAS
LEPERS.
IN A DEN OF
THIEVES.
MAN OF HONO
BLUE SUN

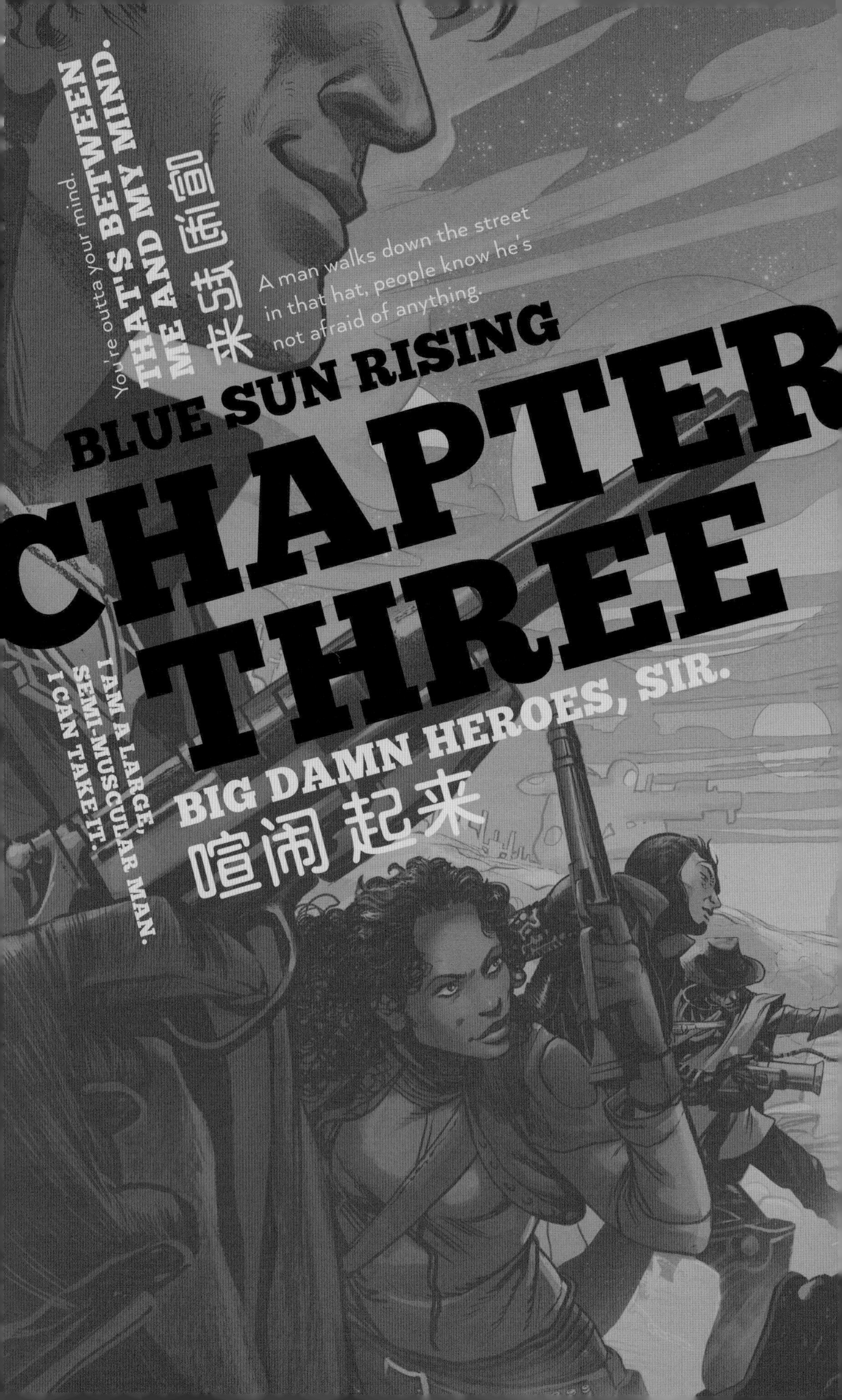
You're outta your mind.
THAT'S BETWEEN
ME AND MY MIND.
A man walks down the street
in that hat, people know he's
not afraid of anything.
BLUE SUN RISING
CHAPTER
THREE
I AM A LARGE,
SEMI-MUSCULAR MAN.
I CAN TAKE IT.
BIG DAMN HEROES, SIR.
喧闹起来

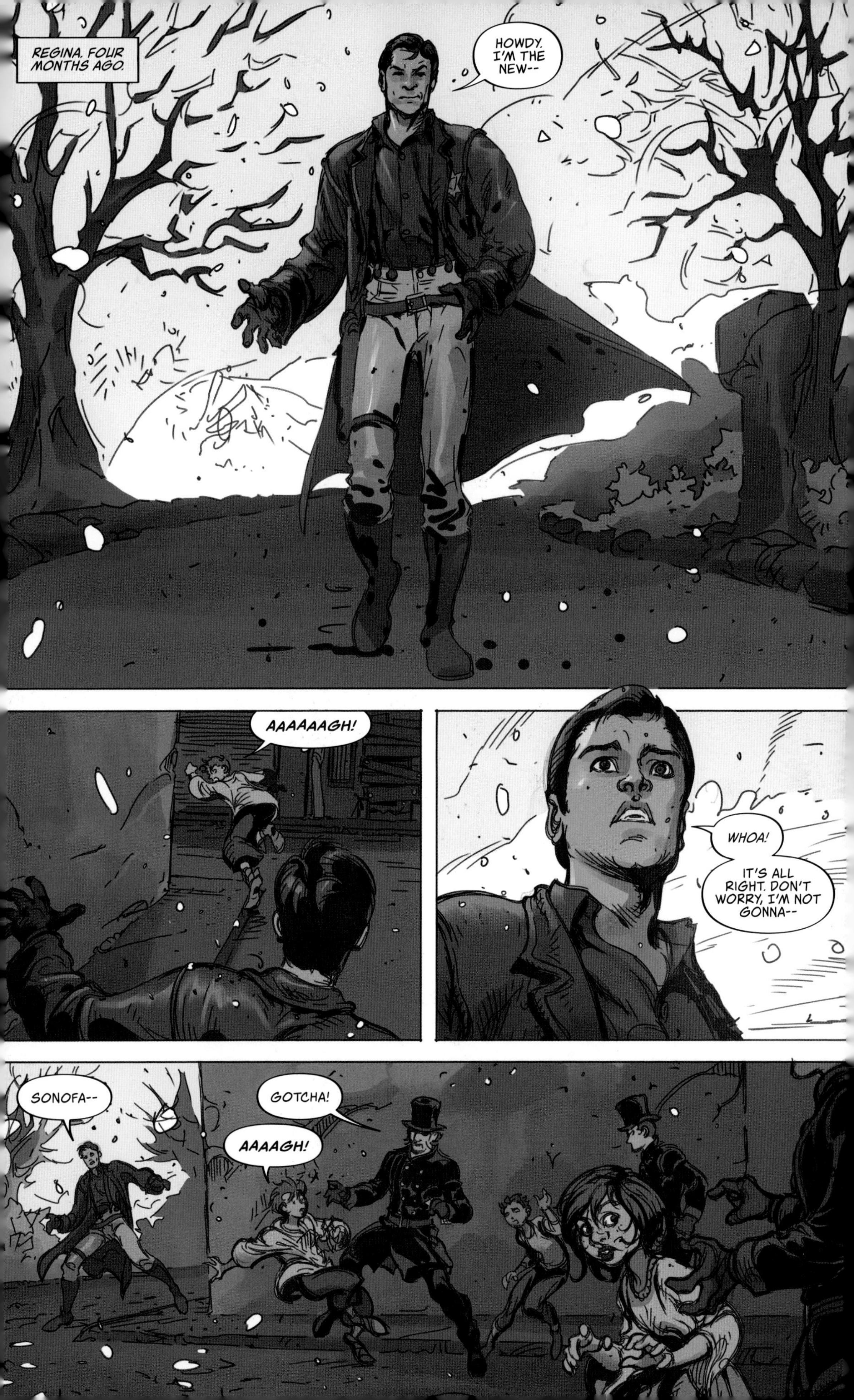
REGINA. FOUR MONTHS AGO.
HOWDY. I'M THE NEW--
AAAAAAGH!
WHOA!
IT'S ALL RIGHT. DON'T WORRY, I'M NOT GONNA--
SONOFA--
GOTCHA!
AAAAGH!

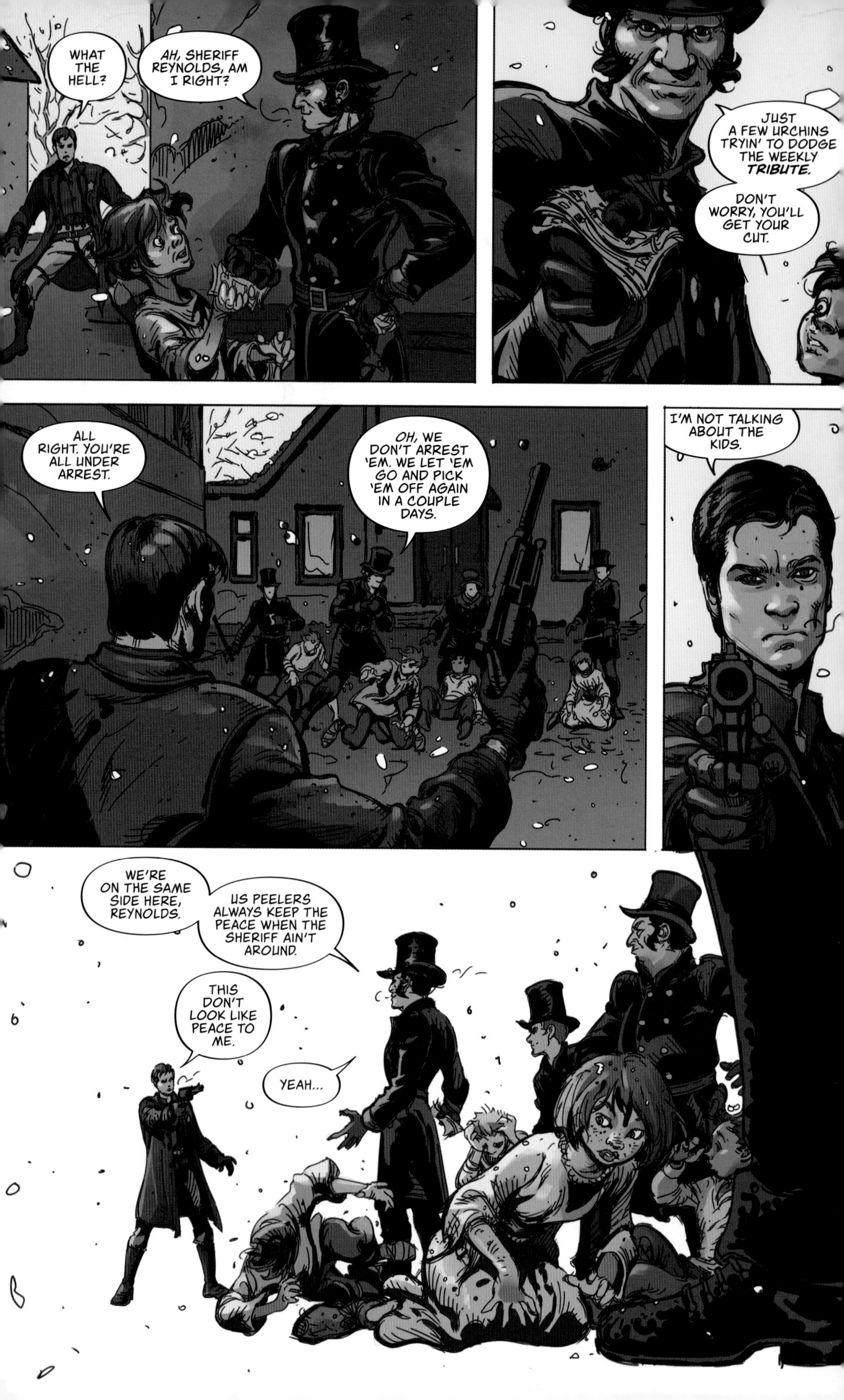
WHAT THE HELL?
AH, SHERIFF REYNOLDS, AM I RIGHT?
JUST A FEW URCHINS TRYIN' TO DODGE THE WEEKLY *TRIBUTE.*
DON'T WORRY, YOU'LL GET YOUR CUT.
ALL RIGHT. YOU'RE ALL UNDER ARREST.
OH, WE DON'T ARREST 'EM. WE LET 'EM GO AND PICK 'EM OFF AGAIN IN A COUPLE DAYS.
I'M NOT TALKING ABOUT THE KIDS.
WE'RE ON THE SAME SIDE HERE, REYNOLDS.
US PEELERS ALWAYS KEEP THE PEACE WHEN THE SHERIFF AIN'T AROUND.
THIS DON'T LOOK LIKE PEACE TO ME.
YEAH...

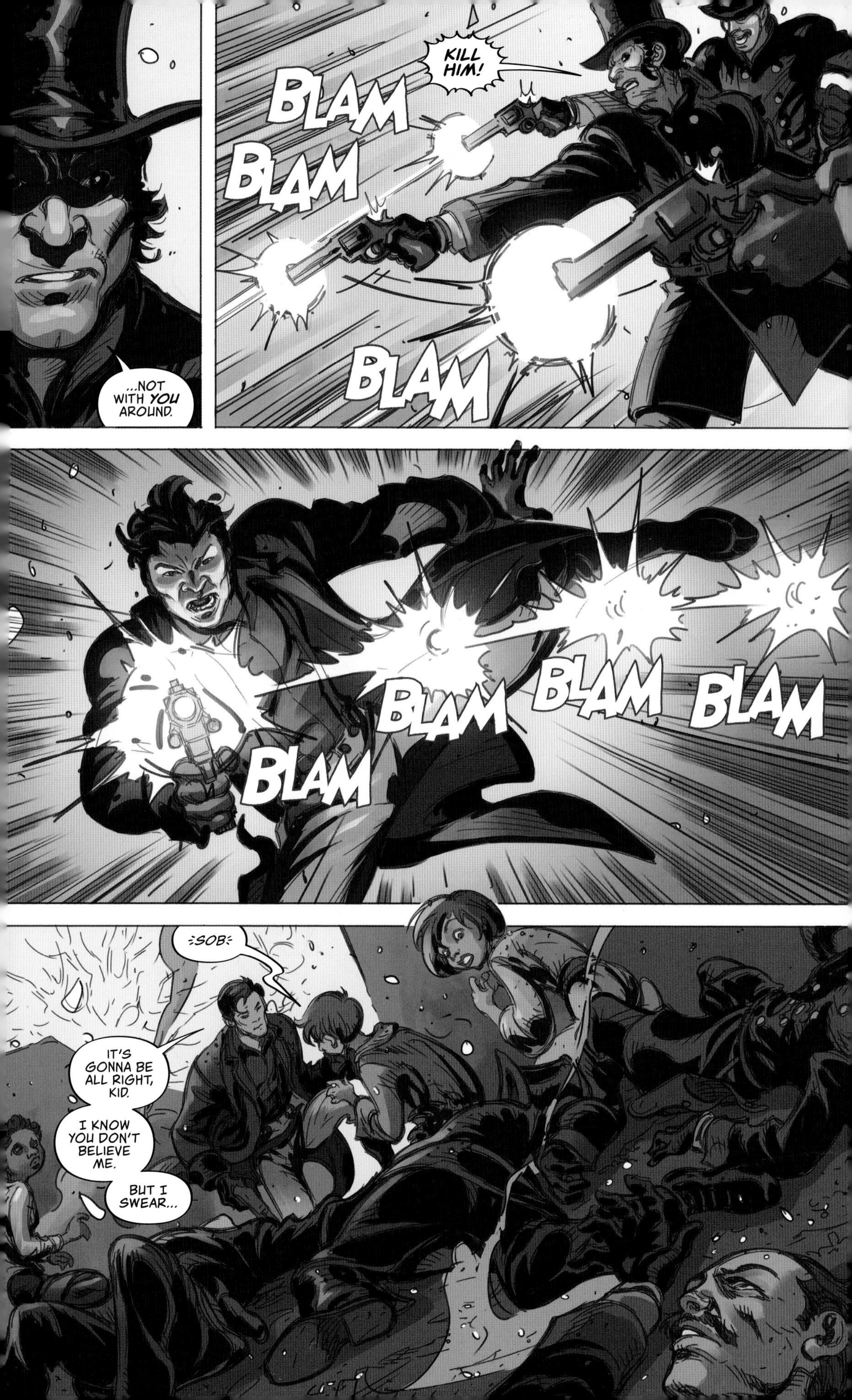
...NOT WITH YOU AROUND.
KILL HIM!
BLAM
BLAM
BLAM
BLAM
BLAM
BLAM
BLAM
:SOB:
IT'S GONNA BE ALL RIGHT, KID.
I KNOW YOU DON'T BELIEVE ME.
BUT I SWEAR...

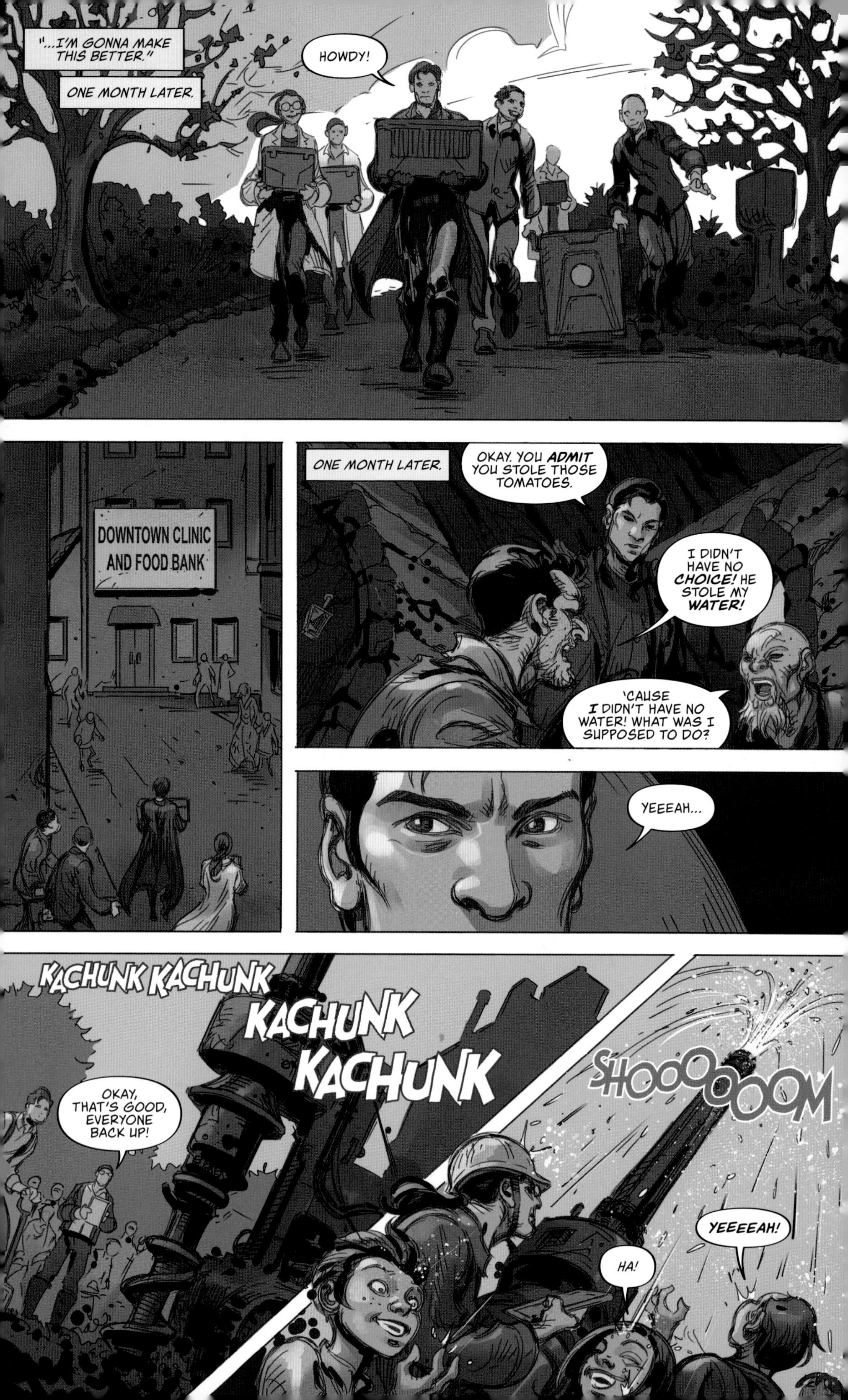
"...I'M GONNA MAKE THIS BETTER."
ONE MONTH LATER.
HOWDY!
DOWNTOWN CLINIC AND FOOD BANK
ONE MONTH LATER.
OKAY. YOU ADMIT YOU STOLE THOSE TOMATOES.
I DIDN'T HAVE NO CHOICE! HE STOLE MY WATER!
'CAUSE I DIDN'T HAVE NO WATER! WHAT WAS I SUPPOSED TO DO?
YEEEAH...
KACHUNK KACHUNK
KACHUNK
KACHUNK
OKAY, THAT'S GOOD, EVERYONE BACK UP!
SHOOOOOOM
YEEEEAH!
HA!

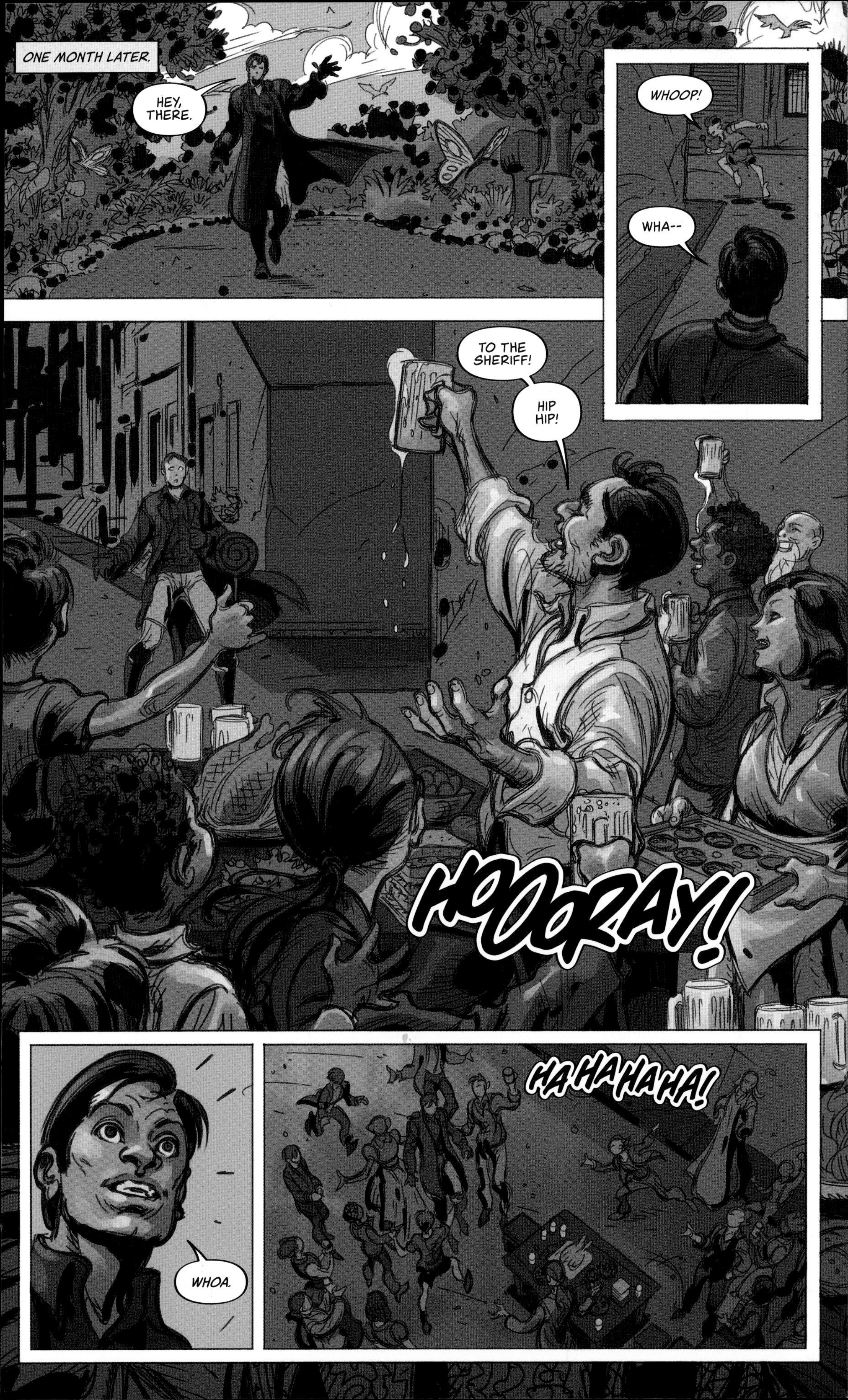
ONE MONTH LATER.
HEY, THERE.
WHOOP!
WHA--
TO THE SHERIFF!
HIP HIP!
HOORAY!
WHOA.
HA HA HA HA!

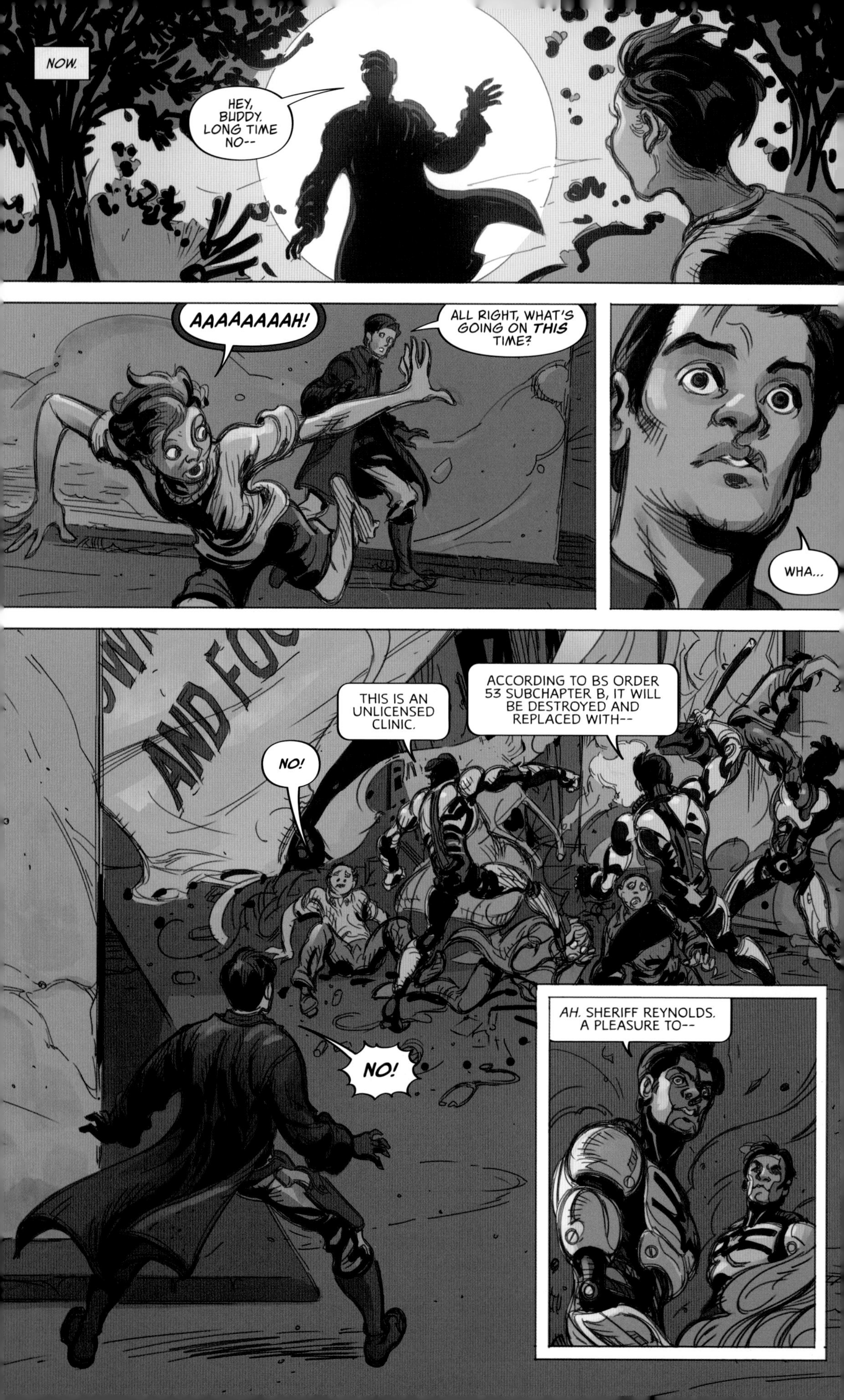
NOW.
HEY, BUDDY. LONG TIME NO--
AAAAAAAAH!
ALL RIGHT, WHAT'S GOING ON THIS TIME?
WHA...
NO!
THIS IS AN UNLICENSED CLINIC.
ACCORDING TO BS ORDER 53 SUBCHAPTER B, IT WILL BE DESTROYED AND REPLACED WITH--
NO!
AH. SHERIFF REYNOLDS. A PLEASURE TO--

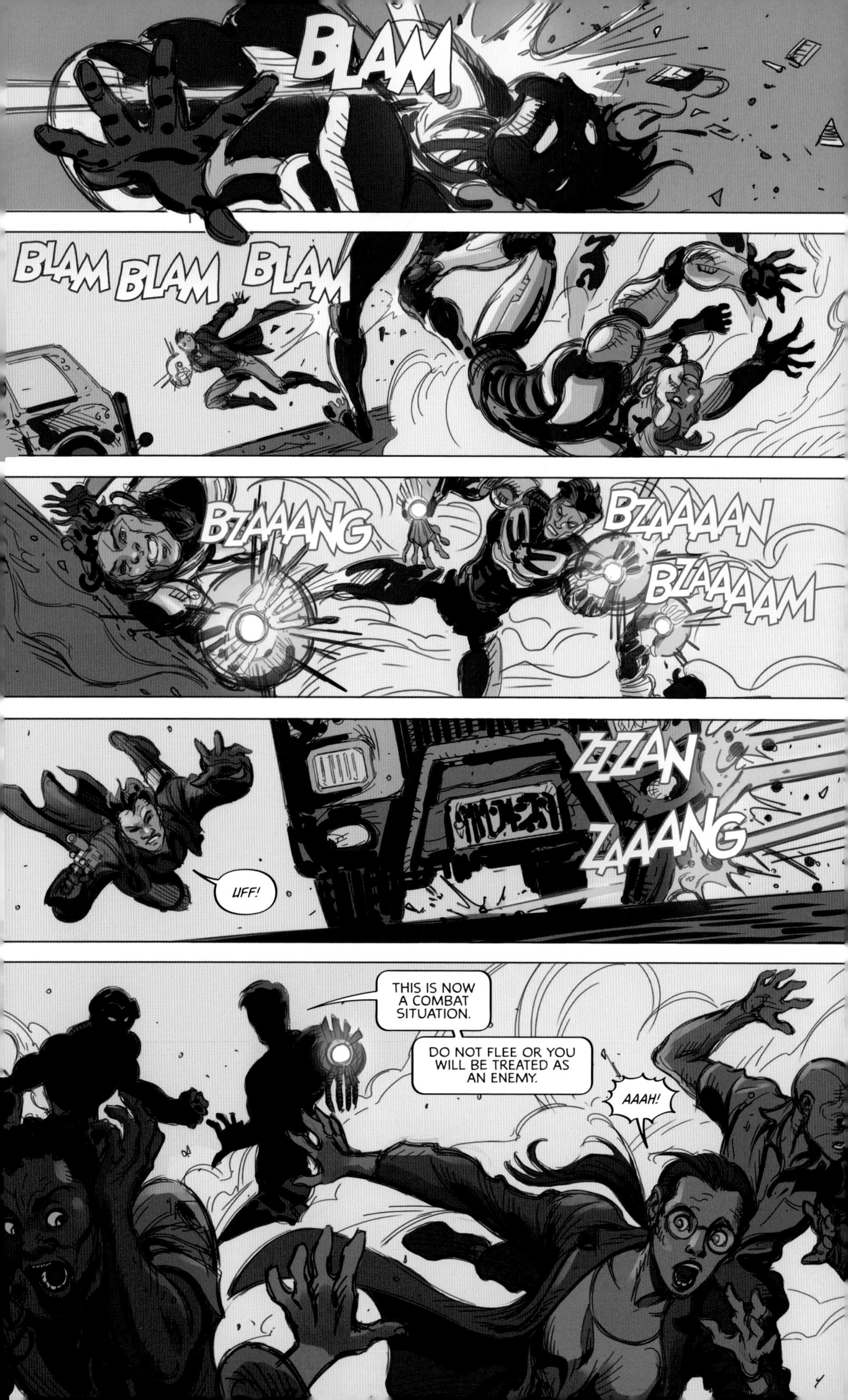
BLAM
BLAM BLAM BLAM
BZAAANG
BZAAAAN
BZAAAAM
ZZZAN
ZAAANG
UFF!
THIS IS NOW A COMBAT SITUATION.
DO NOT FLEE OR YOU WILL BE TREATED AS AN ENEMY.
AAAH!

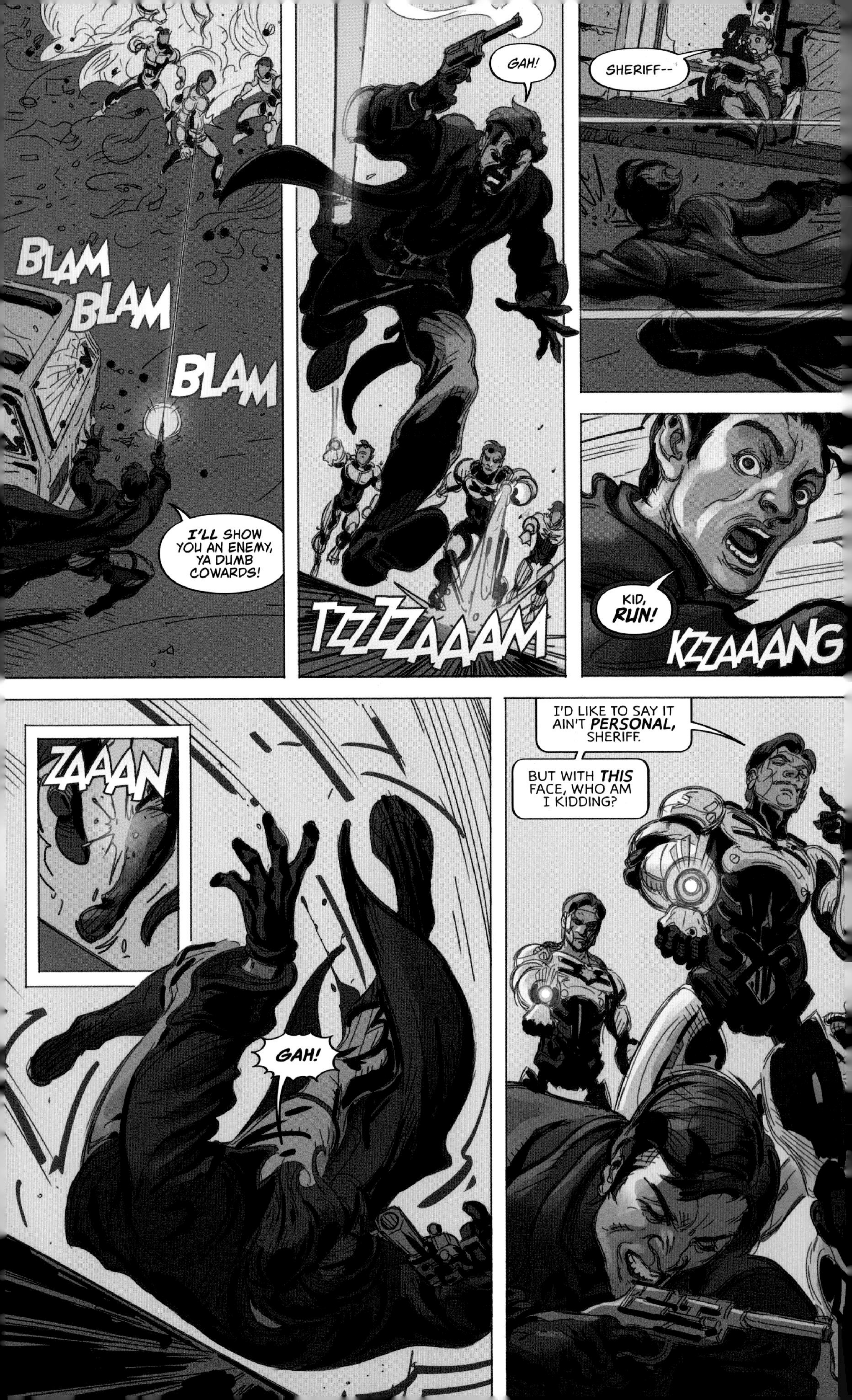
BLAM
BLAM
BLAM
I'LL SHOW YOU AN ENEMY, YA DUMB COWARDS!
GAH!
TZZZZAAAAM
SHERIFF--
KID, RUN!
KZZAAANG
ZAAAN
GAH!
I'D LIKE TO SAY IT AIN'T PERSONAL, SHERIFF.
BUT WITH THIS FACE, WHO AM I KIDDING?

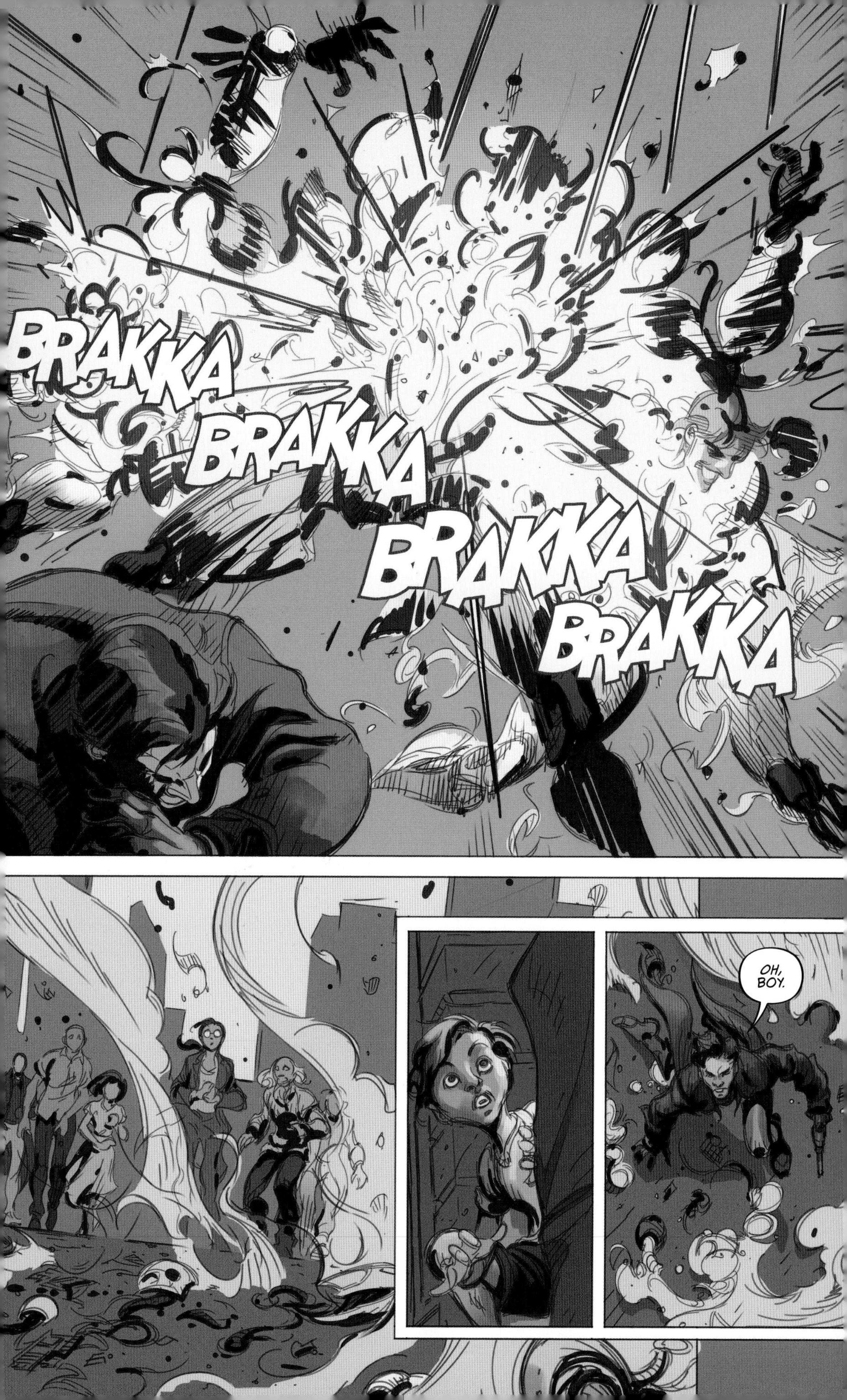
BRAKKA
BRAKKA
BRAKKA
BRAKKA
OH, BOY.

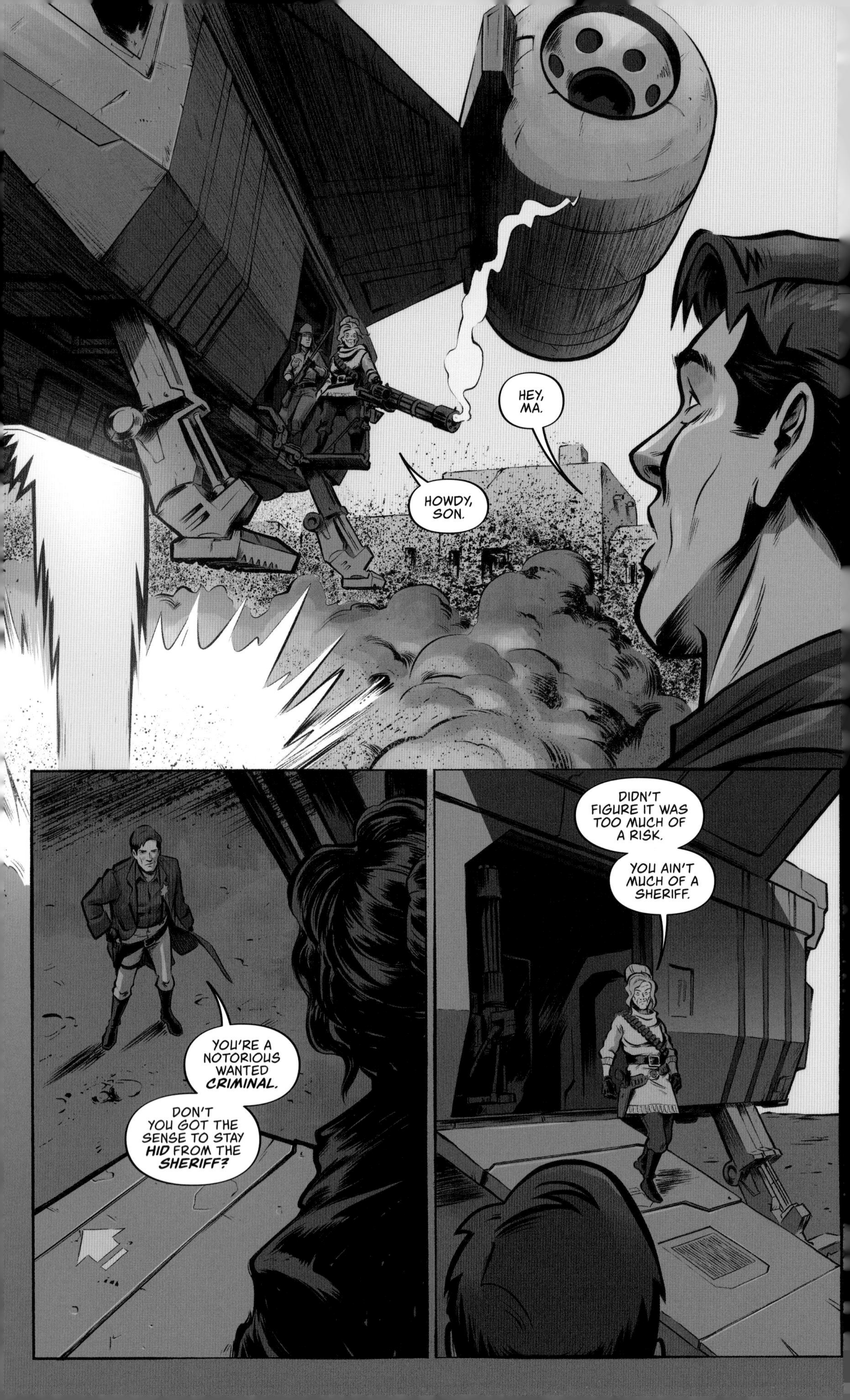
HEY, MA.
HOWDY, SON.
YOU'RE A NOTORIOUS WANTED CRIMINAL.
DON'T YOU GOT THE SENSE TO STAY HID FROM THE SHERIFF?
DIDN'T FIGURE IT WAS TOO MUCH OF A RISK.
YOU AIN'T MUCH OF A SHERIFF.

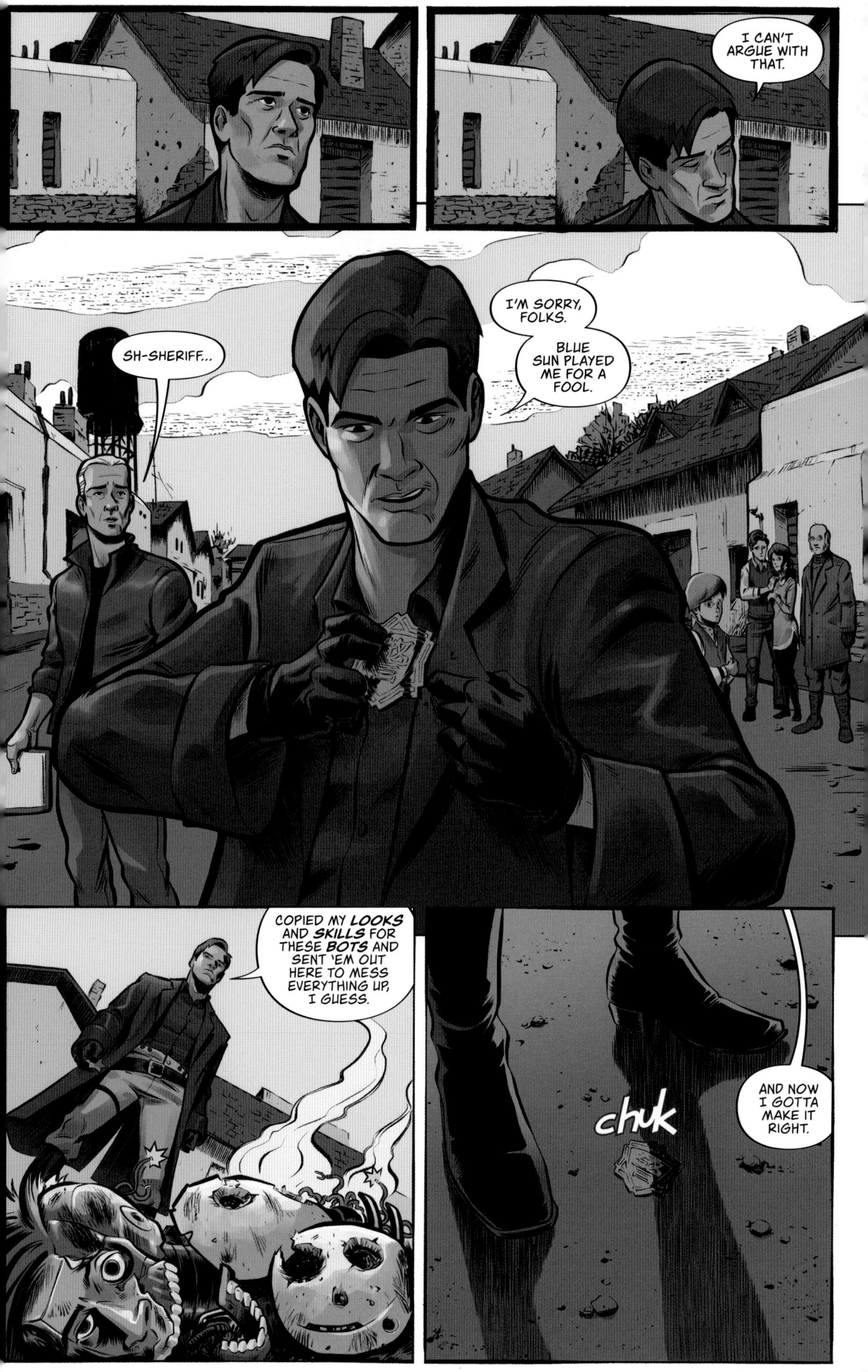
I CAN'T ARGUE WITH THAT.
SH-SHERIFF...
I'M SORRY, FOLKS.
BLUE SUN PLAYED ME FOR A FOOL.
COPIED MY LOOKS AND SKILLS FOR THESE BOTS AND SENT 'EM OUT HERE TO MESS EVERYTHING UP, I GUESS.
chuk
AND NOW I GOTTA MAKE IT RIGHT.

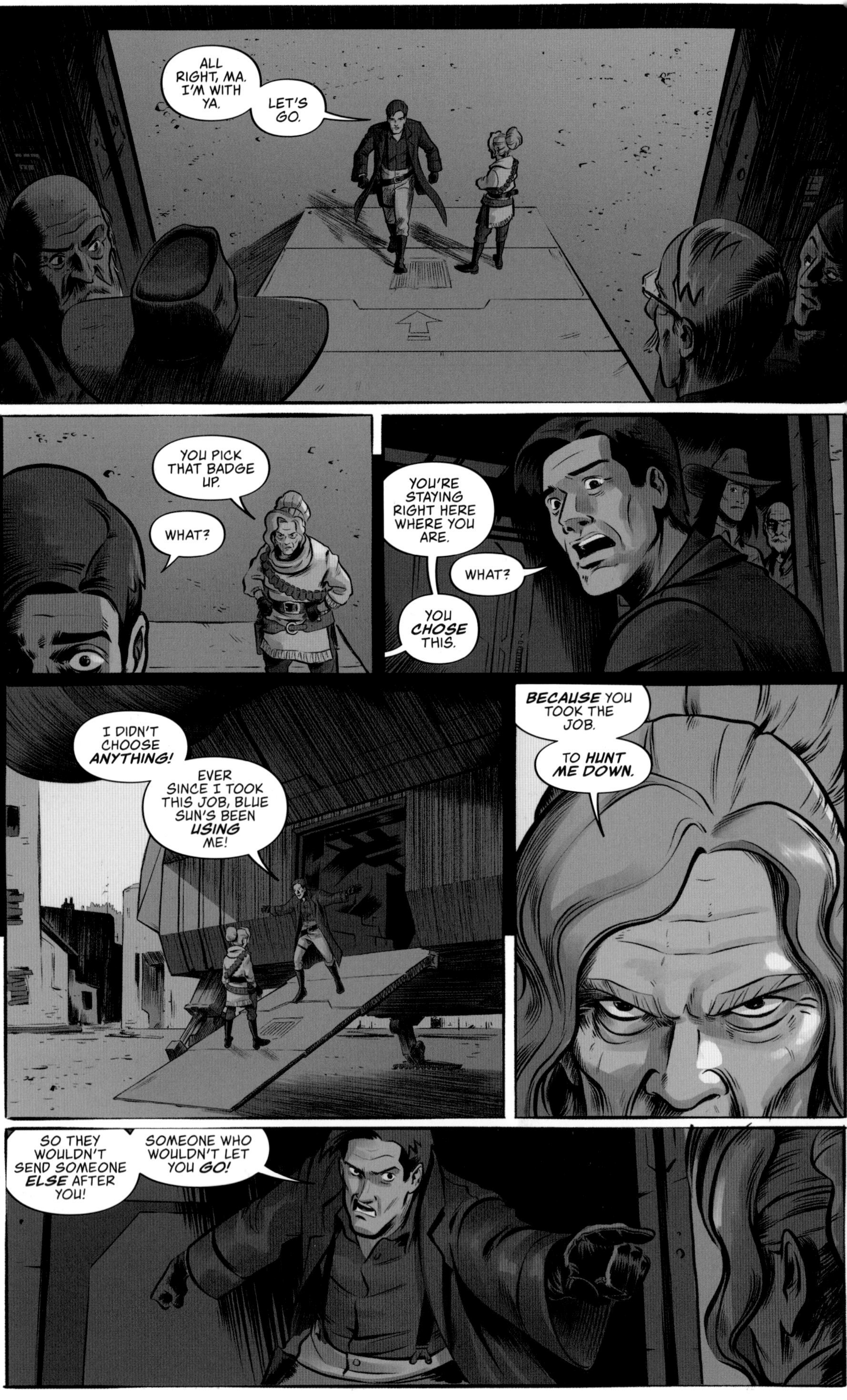
ALL RIGHT, MA. I'M WITH YA.
LET'S GO.
YOU PICK THAT BADGE UP.
WHAT?
YOU'RE STAYING RIGHT HERE WHERE YOU ARE.
WHAT?
YOU CHOSE THIS.
I DIDN'T CHOOSE ANYTHING!
EVER SINCE I TOOK THIS JOB, BLUE SUN'S BEEN USING ME!
BECAUSE YOU TOOK THE JOB.
TO HUNT ME DOWN.
SO THEY WOULDN'T SEND SOMEONE ELSE AFTER YOU!
SOMEONE WHO WOULDN'T LET YOU GO!

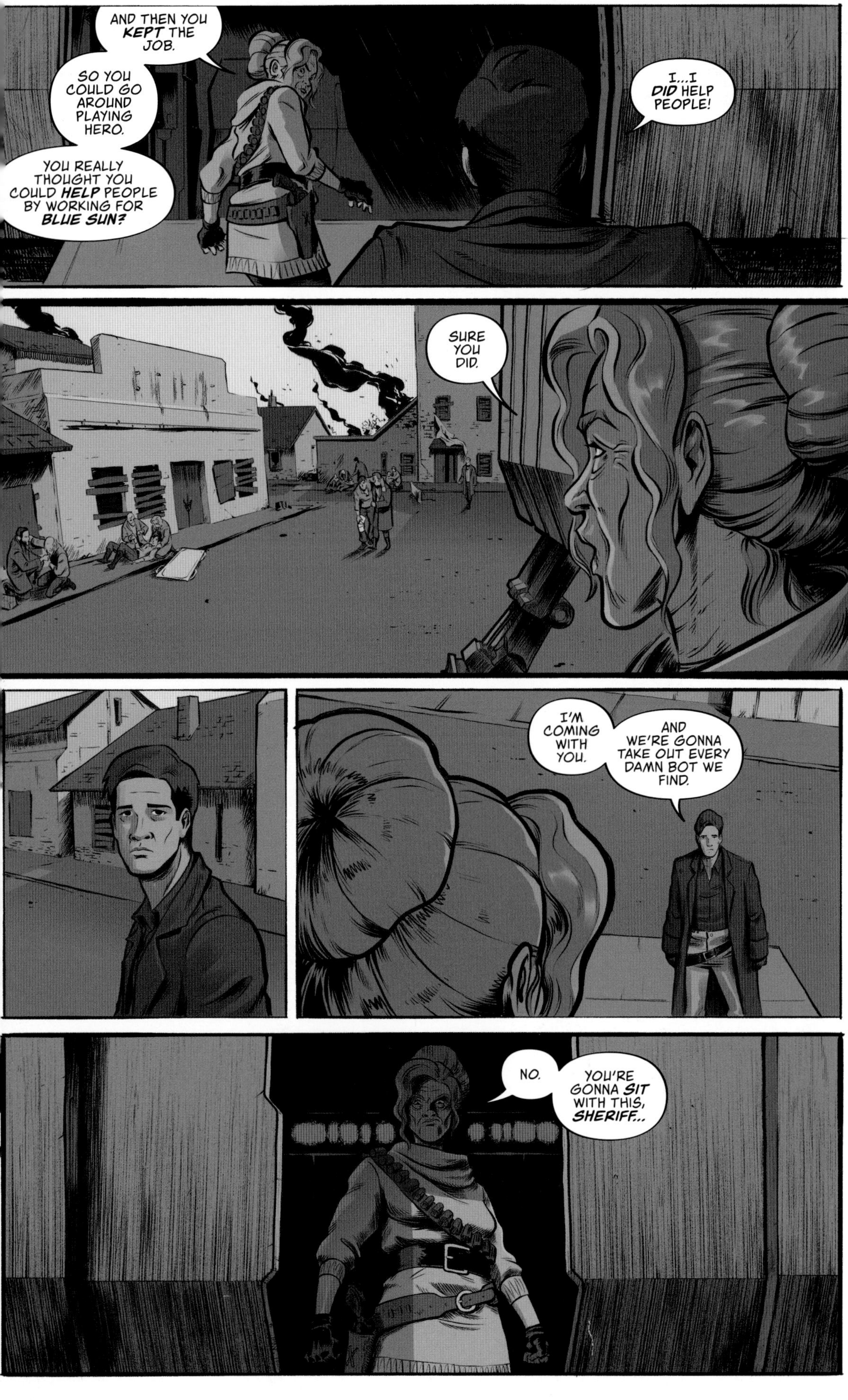
AND THEN YOU KEPT THE JOB.
SO YOU COULD GO AROUND PLAYING HERO.
YOU REALLY THOUGHT YOU COULD HELP PEOPLE BY WORKING FOR BLUE SUN?
I...I DID HELP PEOPLE!
SURE YOU DID.
I'M COMING WITH YOU.
AND WE'RE GONNA TAKE OUT EVERY DAMN BOT WE FIND.
NO.
YOU'RE GONNA SIT WITH THIS, SHERIFF...

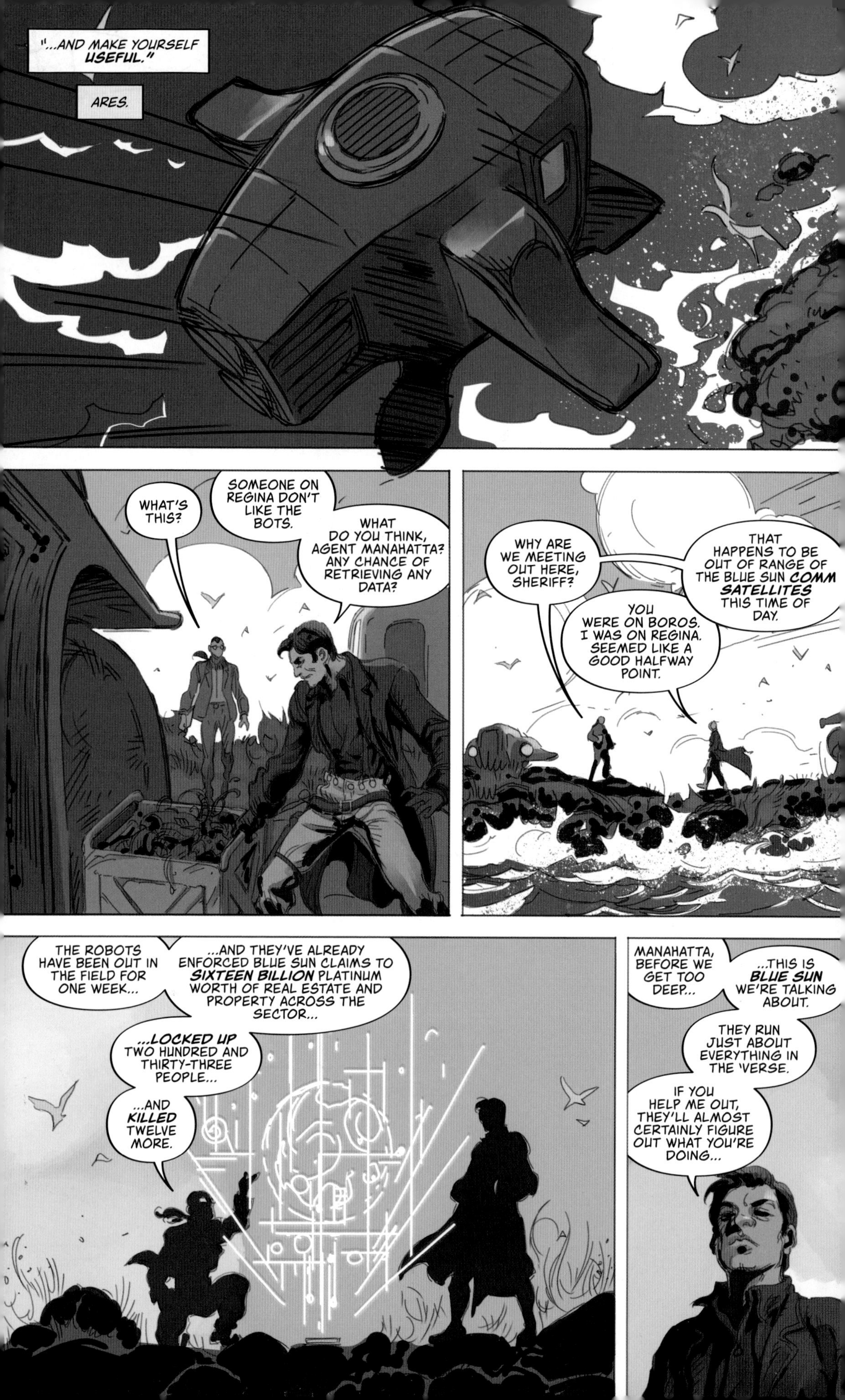
"...AND MAKE YOURSELF USEFUL."
ARES.
WHAT'S THIS?
SOMEONE ON REGINA DON'T LIKE THE BOTS.
WHAT DO YOU THINK, AGENT MANAHATTA? ANY CHANCE OF RETRIEVING ANY DATA?
WHY ARE WE MEETING OUT HERE, SHERIFF?
THAT HAPPENS TO BE OUT OF RANGE OF THE BLUE SUN COMM SATELLITES THIS TIME OF DAY.
YOU WERE ON BOROS. I WAS ON REGINA. SEEMED LIKE A GOOD HALFWAY POINT.
THE ROBOTS HAVE BEEN OUT IN THE FIELD FOR ONE WEEK...
...AND THEY'VE ALREADY ENFORCED BLUE SUN CLAIMS TO SIXTEEN BILLION PLATINUM WORTH OF REAL ESTATE AND PROPERTY ACROSS THE SECTOR...
...LOCKED UP TWO HUNDRED AND THIRTY-THREE PEOPLE...
...AND KILLED TWELVE MORE.
MANAHATTA, BEFORE WE GET TOO DEEP...
...THIS IS BLUE SUN WE'RE TALKING ABOUT.
THEY RUN JUST ABOUT EVERYTHING IN THE 'VERSE.
IF YOU HELP ME OUT, THEY'LL ALMOST CERTAINLY FIGURE OUT WHAT YOU'RE DOING...

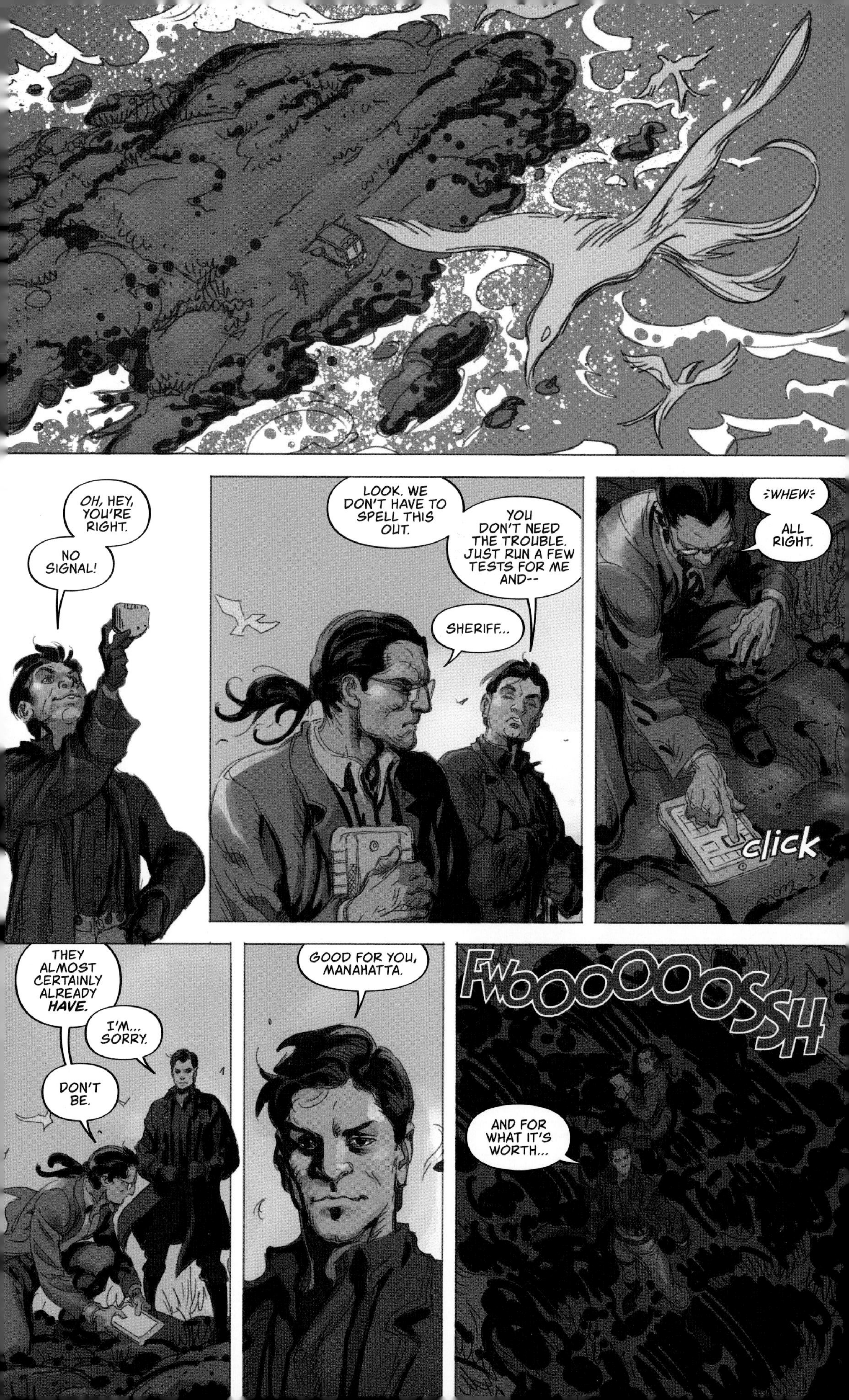
OH, HEY, YOU'RE RIGHT.
NO SIGNAL!
LOOK. WE DON'T HAVE TO SPELL THIS OUT.
YOU DON'T NEED THE TROUBLE. JUST RUN A FEW TESTS FOR ME AND--
SHERIFF...
WHEW
ALL RIGHT.
click
THEY ALMOST CERTAINLY ALREADY HAVE.
I'M... SORRY.
DON'T BE.
GOOD FOR YOU, MANAHATTA.
FWOOOOOOSSH
AND FOR WHAT IT'S WORTH...

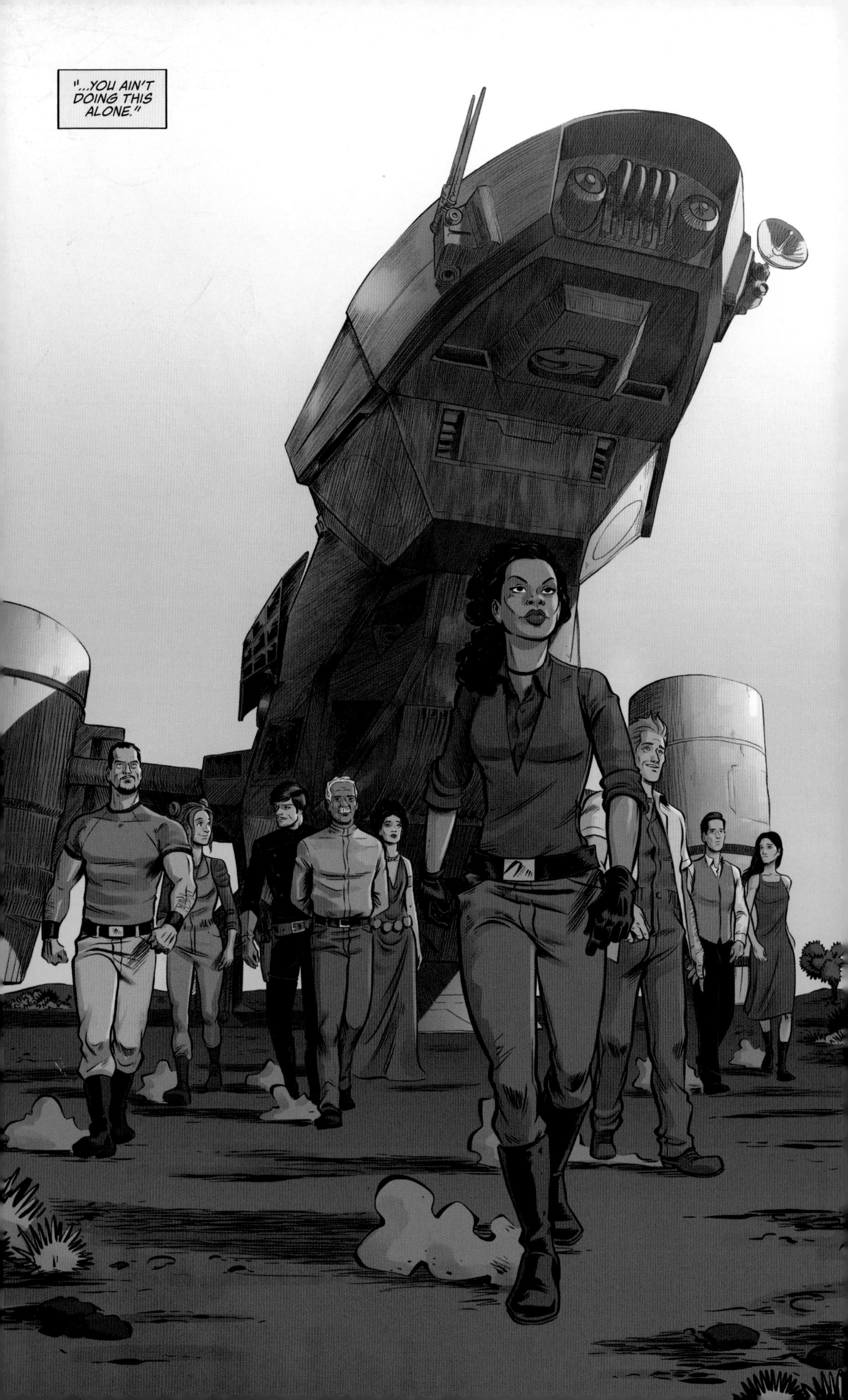
"...YOU AIN'T DOING THIS ALONE."

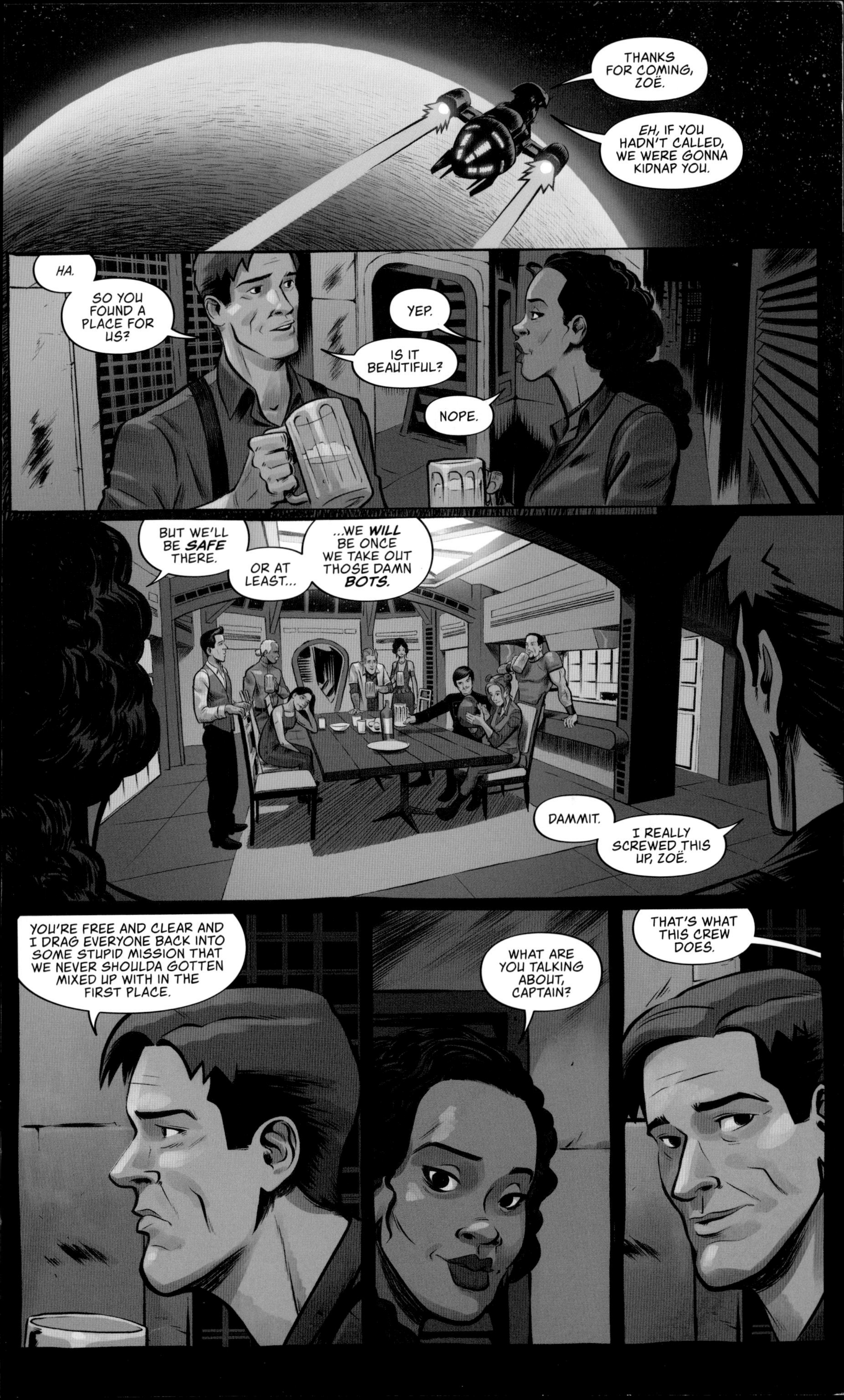
THANKS FOR COMING, ZOË.
EH, IF YOU HADN'T CALLED, WE WERE GONNA KIDNAP YOU.
HA.
SO YOU FOUND A PLACE FOR US?
YEP.
IS IT BEAUTIFUL?
NOPE.
BUT WE'LL BE *SAFE* THERE.
OR AT LEAST...
...WE *WILL* BE ONCE WE TAKE OUT THOSE DAMN *BOTS*.
DAMMIT.
I REALLY SCREWED THIS UP, ZOË.
YOU'RE FREE AND CLEAR AND I DRAG EVERYONE BACK INTO SOME STUPID MISSION THAT WE NEVER SHOULDA GOTTEN MIXED UP WITH IN THE FIRST PLACE.
WHAT ARE YOU TALKING ABOUT, CAPTAIN?
THAT'S WHAT THIS CREW DOES.

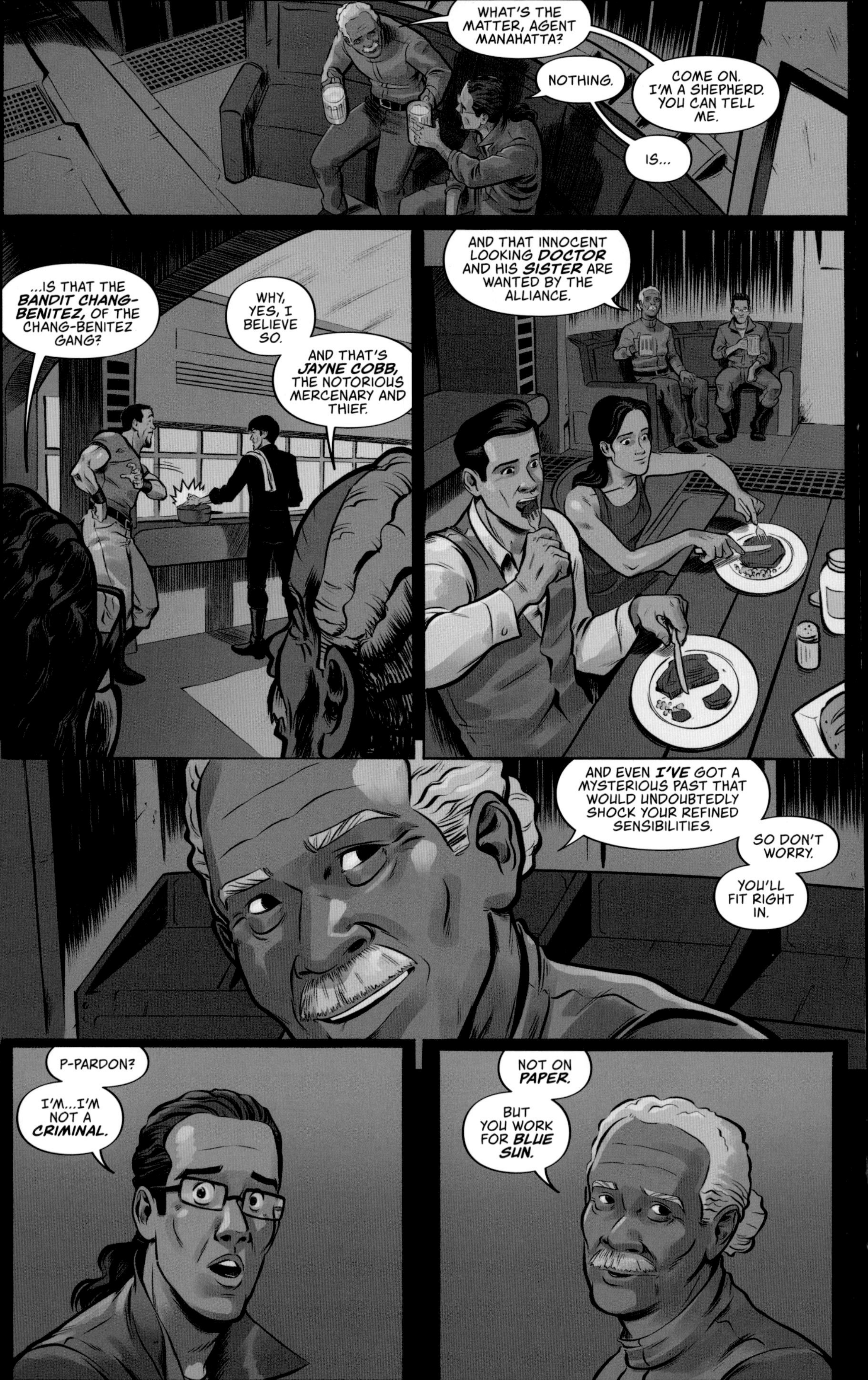
WHAT'S THE MATTER, AGENT MANAHATTA?
NOTHING.
COME ON. I'M A SHEPHERD. YOU CAN TELL ME.
IS...
...IS THAT THE BANDIT CHANG-BENITEZ, OF THE CHANG-BENITEZ GANG?
WHY, YES, I BELIEVE SO.
AND THAT'S JAYNE COBB, THE NOTORIOUS MERCENARY AND THIEF.
AND THAT INNOCENT LOOKING DOCTOR AND HIS SISTER ARE WANTED BY THE ALLIANCE.
AND EVEN I'VE GOT A MYSTERIOUS PAST THAT WOULD UNDOUBTEDLY SHOCK YOUR REFINED SENSIBILITIES.
SO DON'T WORRY.
YOU'LL FIT RIGHT IN.
P-PARDON?
I'M...I'M NOT A CRIMINAL.
NOT ON PAPER.
BUT YOU WORK FOR BLUE SUN.

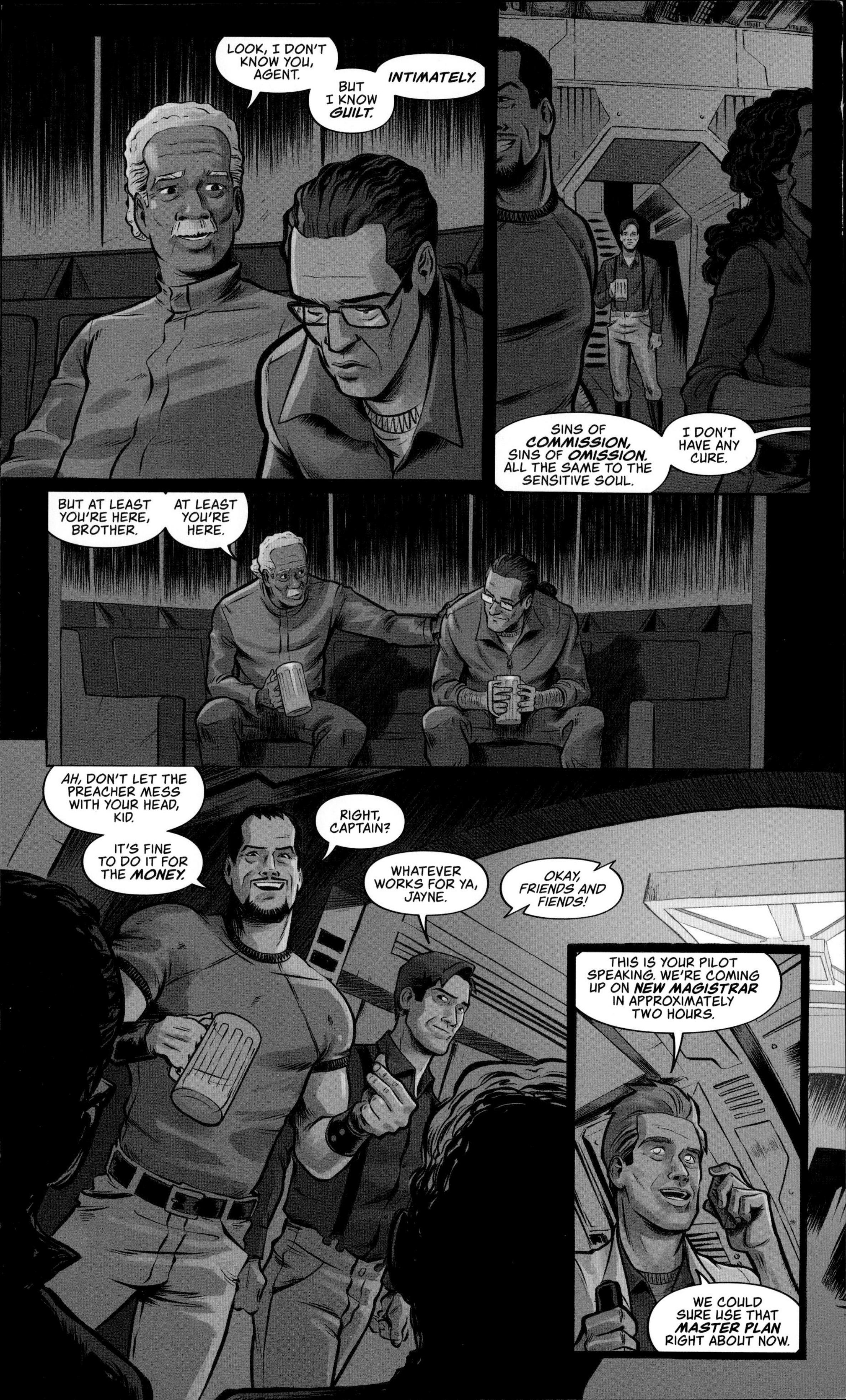
LOOK, I DON'T KNOW YOU, AGENT.
BUT I KNOW GUILT.
INTIMATELY.
SINS OF COMMISSION, SINS OF OMISSION. ALL THE SAME TO THE SENSITIVE SOUL.
I DON'T HAVE ANY CURE.
BUT AT LEAST YOU'RE HERE, BROTHER.
AT LEAST YOU'RE HERE.
AH, DON'T LET THE PREACHER MESS WITH YOUR HEAD, KID.
IT'S FINE TO DO IT FOR THE MONEY.
RIGHT, CAPTAIN?
WHATEVER WORKS FOR YA, JAYNE.
OKAY, FRIENDS AND FIENDS!
THIS IS YOUR PILOT SPEAKING. WE'RE COMING UP ON NEW MAGISTRAR IN APPROXIMATELY TWO HOURS.
WE COULD SURE USE THAT MASTER PLAN RIGHT ABOUT NOW.

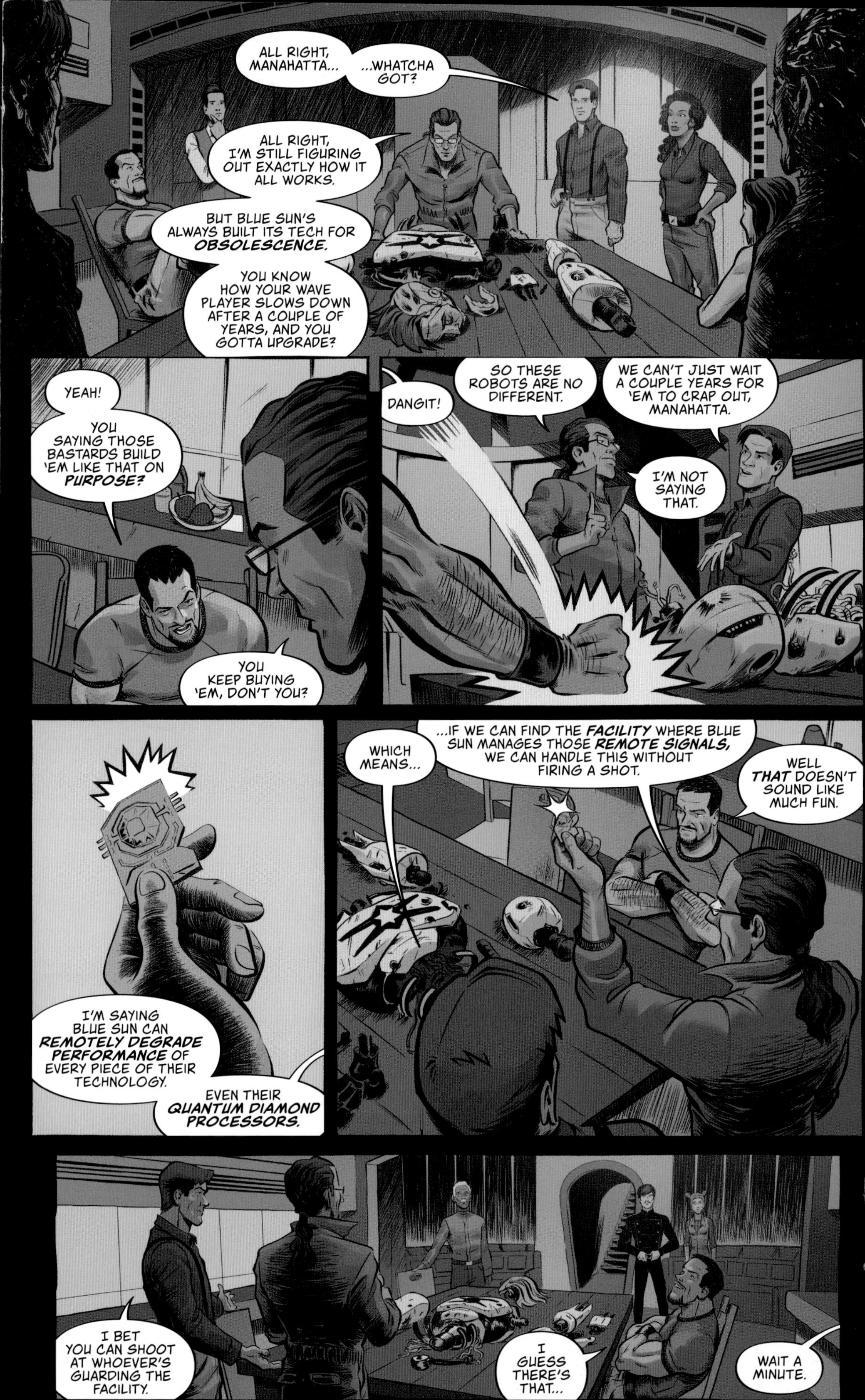
ALL RIGHT, MANAHATTA...
...WHATCHA GOT?
ALL RIGHT, I'M STILL FIGURING OUT EXACTLY HOW IT ALL WORKS.
BUT BLUE SUN'S ALWAYS BUILT ITS TECH FOR OBSOLESCENCE.
YOU KNOW HOW YOUR WAVE PLAYER SLOWS DOWN AFTER A COUPLE OF YEARS, AND YOU GOTTA UPGRADE?
YEAH!
YOU SAYING THOSE BASTARDS BUILD 'EM LIKE THAT ON PURPOSE?
YOU KEEP BUYING 'EM, DON'T YOU?
DANGIT!
SO THESE ROBOTS ARE NO DIFFERENT.
WE CAN'T JUST WAIT A COUPLE YEARS FOR 'EM TO CRAP OUT, MANAHATTA.
I'M NOT SAYING THAT.
I'M SAYING BLUE SUN CAN REMOTELY DEGRADE PERFORMANCE OF EVERY PIECE OF THEIR TECHNOLOGY.
EVEN THEIR QUANTUM DIAMOND PROCESSORS.
WHICH MEANS...
...IF WE CAN FIND THE FACILITY WHERE BLUE SUN MANAGES THOSE REMOTE SIGNALS, WE CAN HANDLE THIS WITHOUT FIRING A SHOT.
WELL THAT DOESN'T SOUND LIKE MUCH FUN.
I BET YOU CAN SHOOT AT WHOEVER'S GUARDING THE FACILITY.
I GUESS THERE'S THAT...
WAIT A MINUTE.

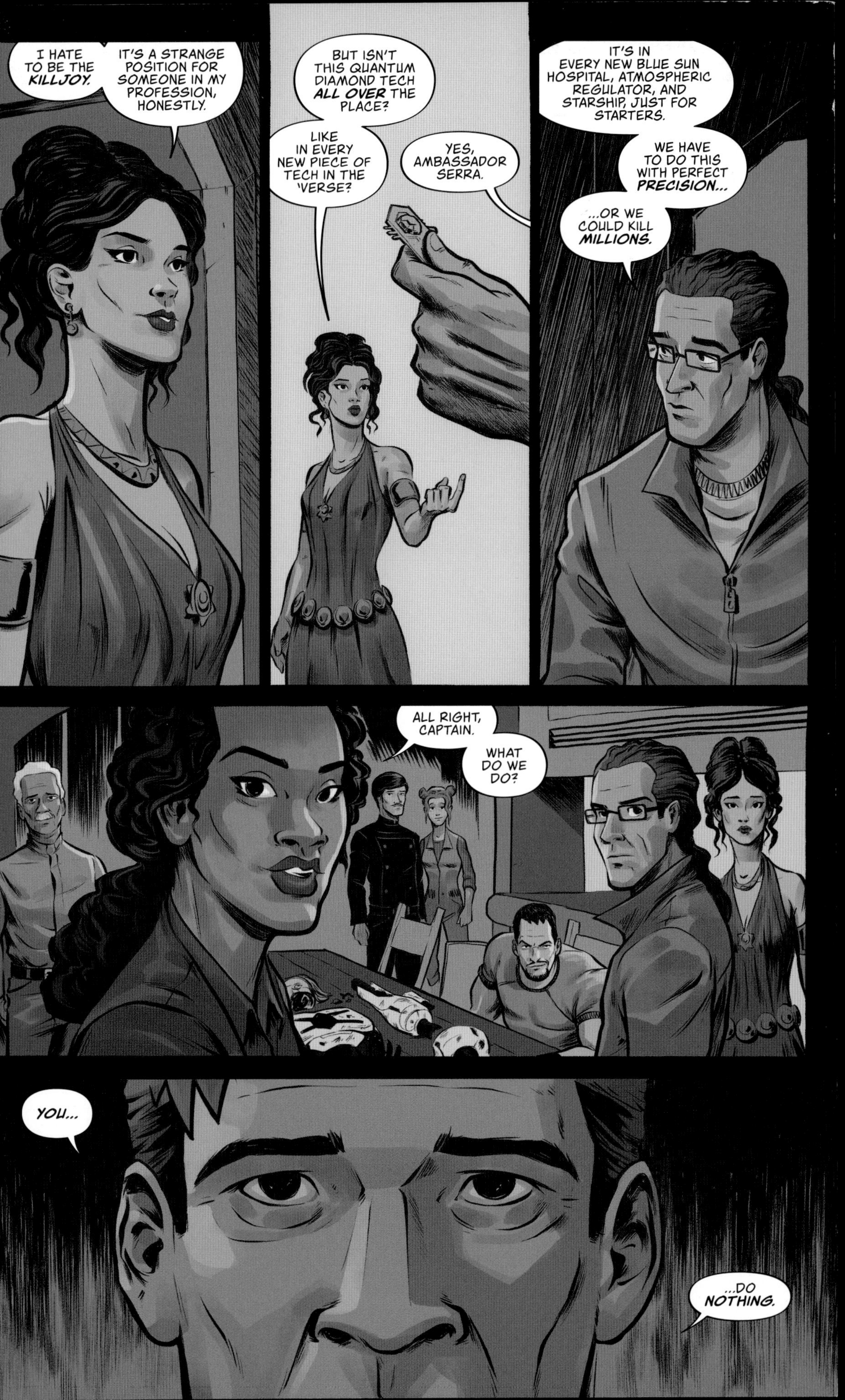
I HATE TO BE THE KILLJOY.
IT'S A STRANGE POSITION FOR SOMEONE IN MY PROFESSION, HONESTLY.
BUT ISN'T THIS QUANTUM DIAMOND TECH ALL OVER THE PLACE?
LIKE IN EVERY NEW PIECE OF TECH IN THE 'VERSE?
YES, AMBASSADOR SERRA.
IT'S IN EVERY NEW BLUE SUN HOSPITAL, ATMOSPHERIC REGULATOR, AND STARSHIP, JUST FOR STARTERS.
WE HAVE TO DO THIS WITH PERFECT PRECISION...
...OR WE COULD KILL MILLIONS.
ALL RIGHT, CAPTAIN.
WHAT DO WE DO?
YOU...
...DO NOTHING.

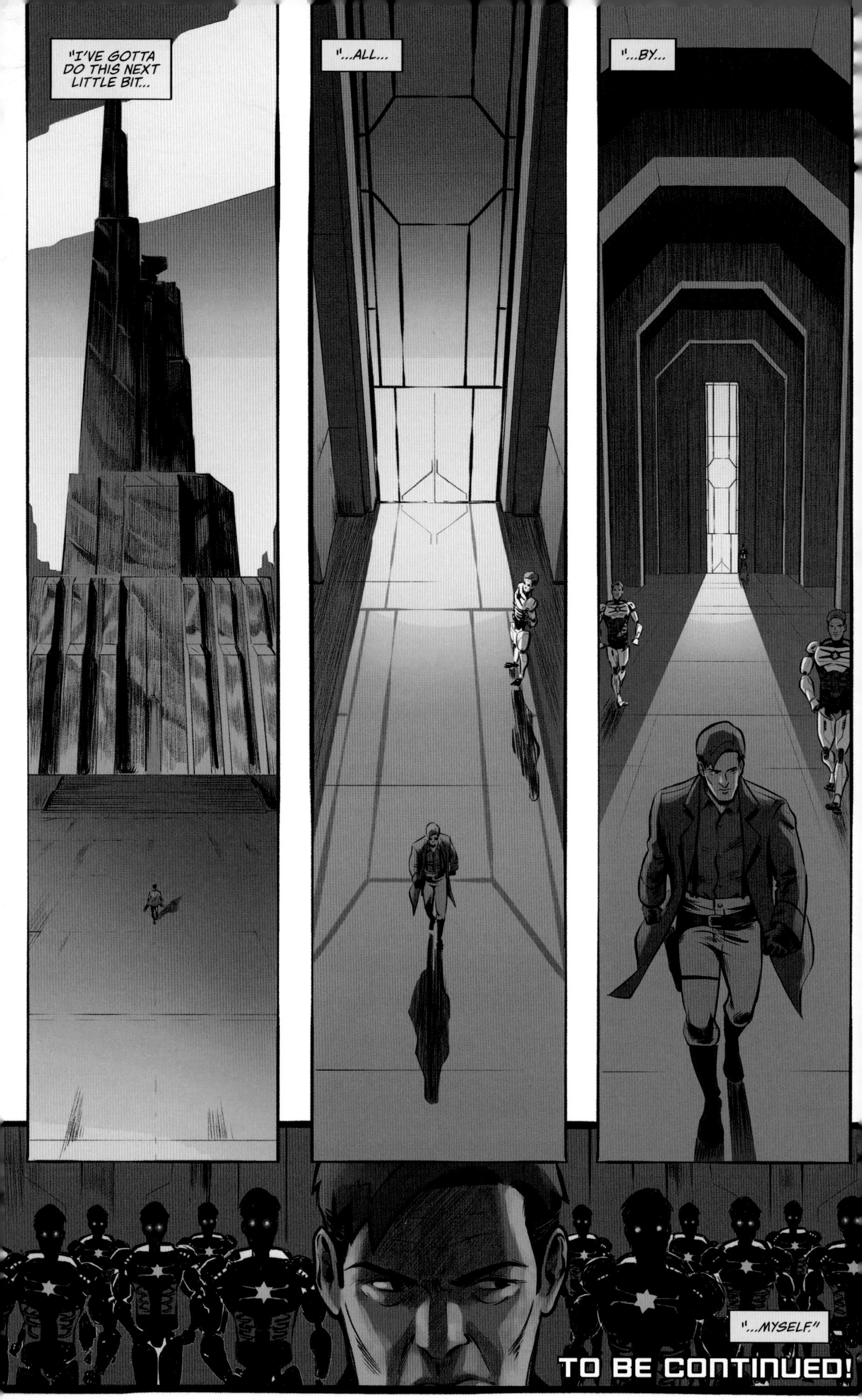
"I'VE GOTTA DO THIS NEXT LITTLE BIT...
"...ALL...
"...BY...
"...MYSELF."
TO BE CONTINUED!

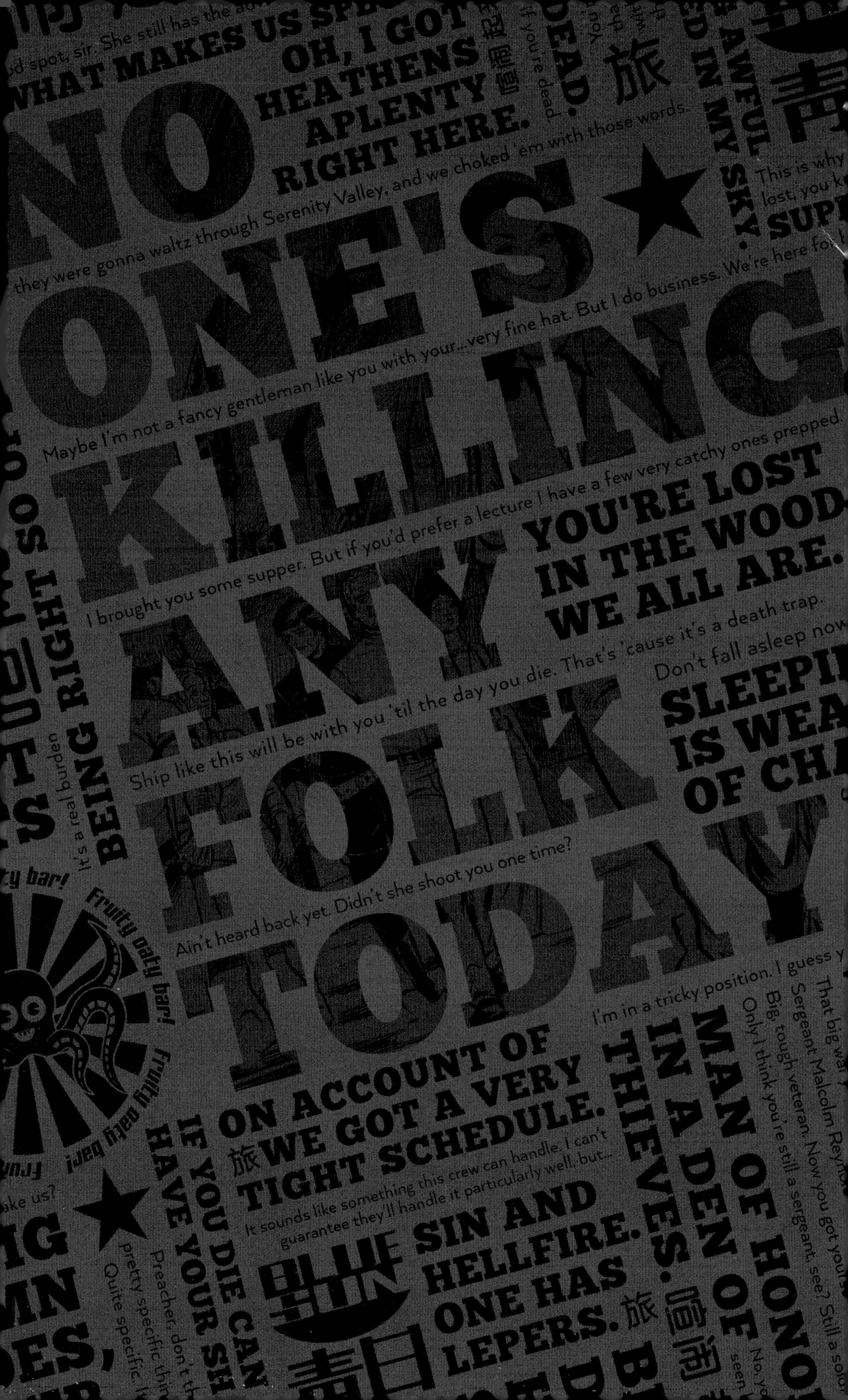

WHAT MAKES US SP
OH, I GOT HEATHENS APLENTY RIGHT HERE.
If you're dead
DEAD.
旅
AWFUL
ED IN MY SKY.
NO ONE'S ★ KILLING ANY FOLK TODAY
they were gonna waltz through Serenity Valley, and we choked 'em with those words.
This is why
lost, you k
SUP
Maybe I'm not a fancy gentleman like you with your...very fine hat. But I do business. We're here fo
I brought you some supper. But if you'd prefer a lecture I have a few very catchy ones prepped.
YOU'RE LOST IN THE WOOD WE ALL ARE.
Ship like this will be with you 'til the day you die. That's 'cause it's a death trap.
Don't fall asleep now
SLEEPI IS WEA OF CHA
BEING RIGHT
It's a real burden
Ain't heard back yet. Didn't she shoot you one time?
Fruity oaty bar!
I'm in a tricky position. I guess y
That big war
Sergeant Malcolm Reyno
Big, tough veteran. Now you got yours
Only I think you're still a sergeant, see? Still a sold
MAN OF HONO
IN A DEN OF
THIEVES.
ON ACCOUNT OF WE GOT A VERY TIGHT SCHEDULE.
It sounds like something this crew can handle. I can't guarantee they'll handle it particularly well, but...
IF YOU DIE CAN
HAVE YOUR SH
SIN AND HELLFIRE. ONE HAS LEPERS.
BLUE SUN
Preacher, don't th
pretty specific
Quite specific thi

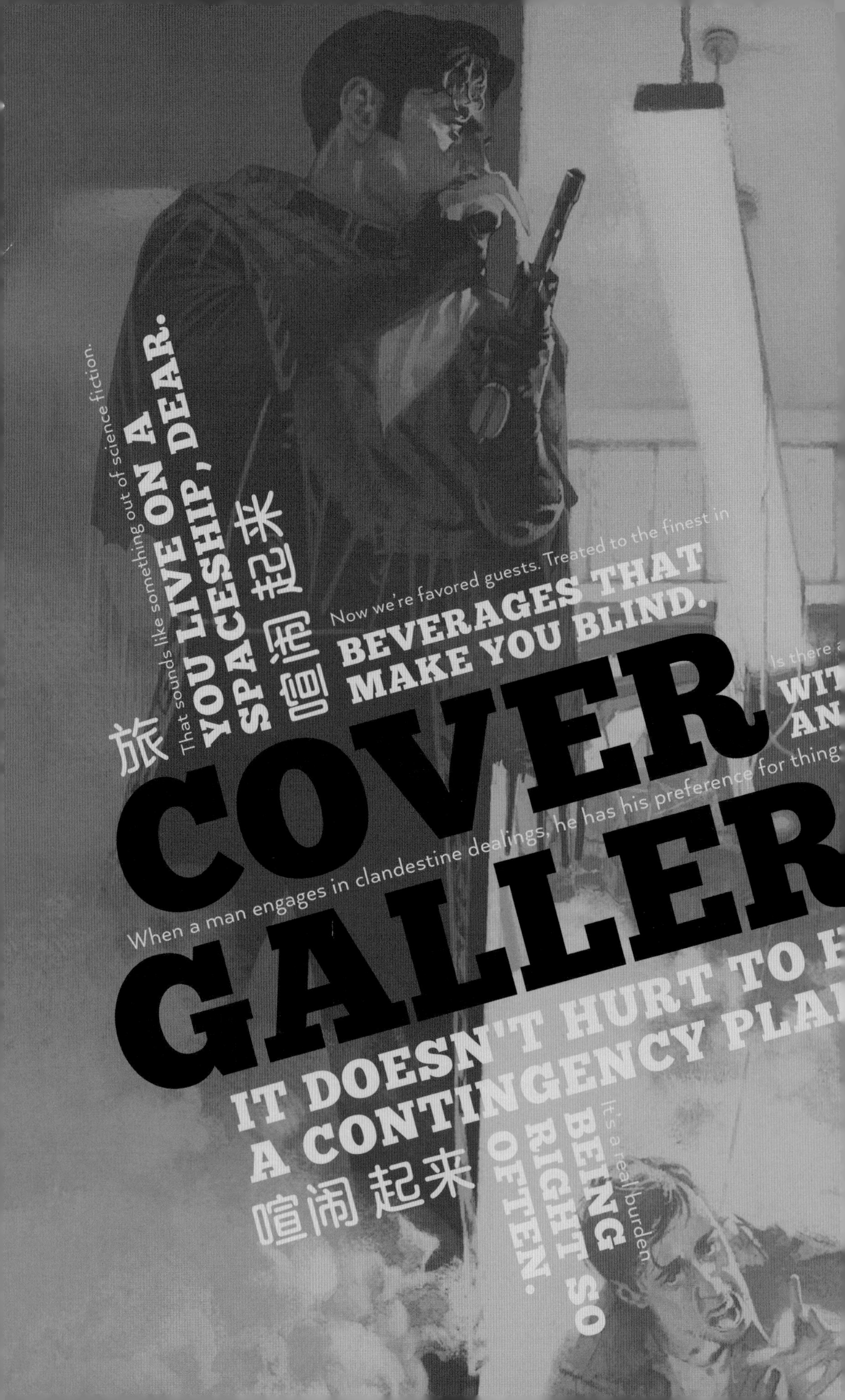

旅
That sounds like something out of science fiction.
YOU LIVE ON A SPACESHIP, DEAR.
喧闹 起来
Now we're favored guests. Treated to the finest in
BEVERAGES THAT MAKE YOU BLIND.
Is there a
WIT
AN
COVER
GALLER
When a man engages in clandestine dealings, he has his preference for thing
IT DOESN'T HURT TO H
A CONTINGENCY PLA
喧闹 起来
It's a real burden
BEING RIGHT SO OFTEN.

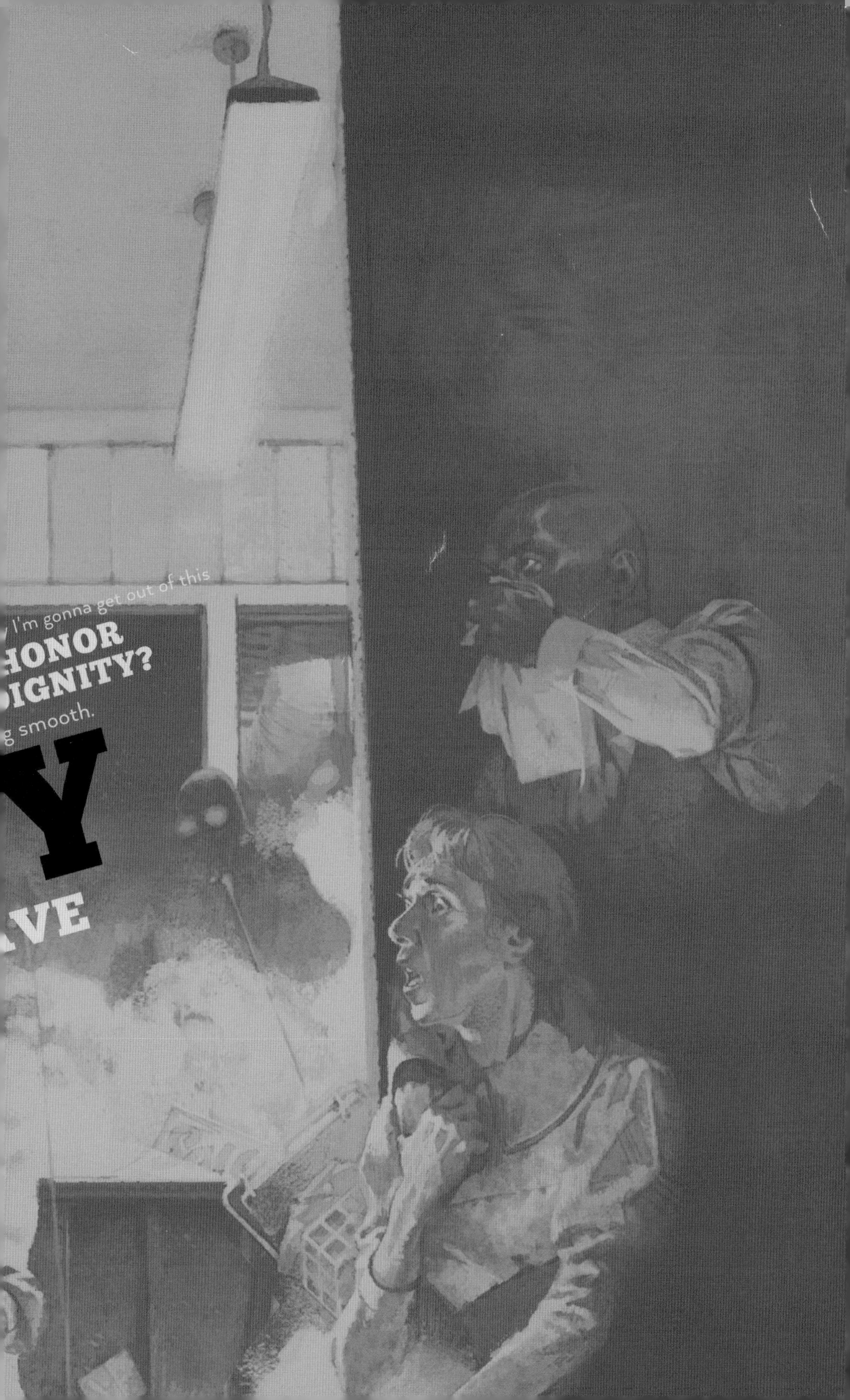

I'm gonna get out of this
HONOR
IGNITY?
g smooth.
Y
VE

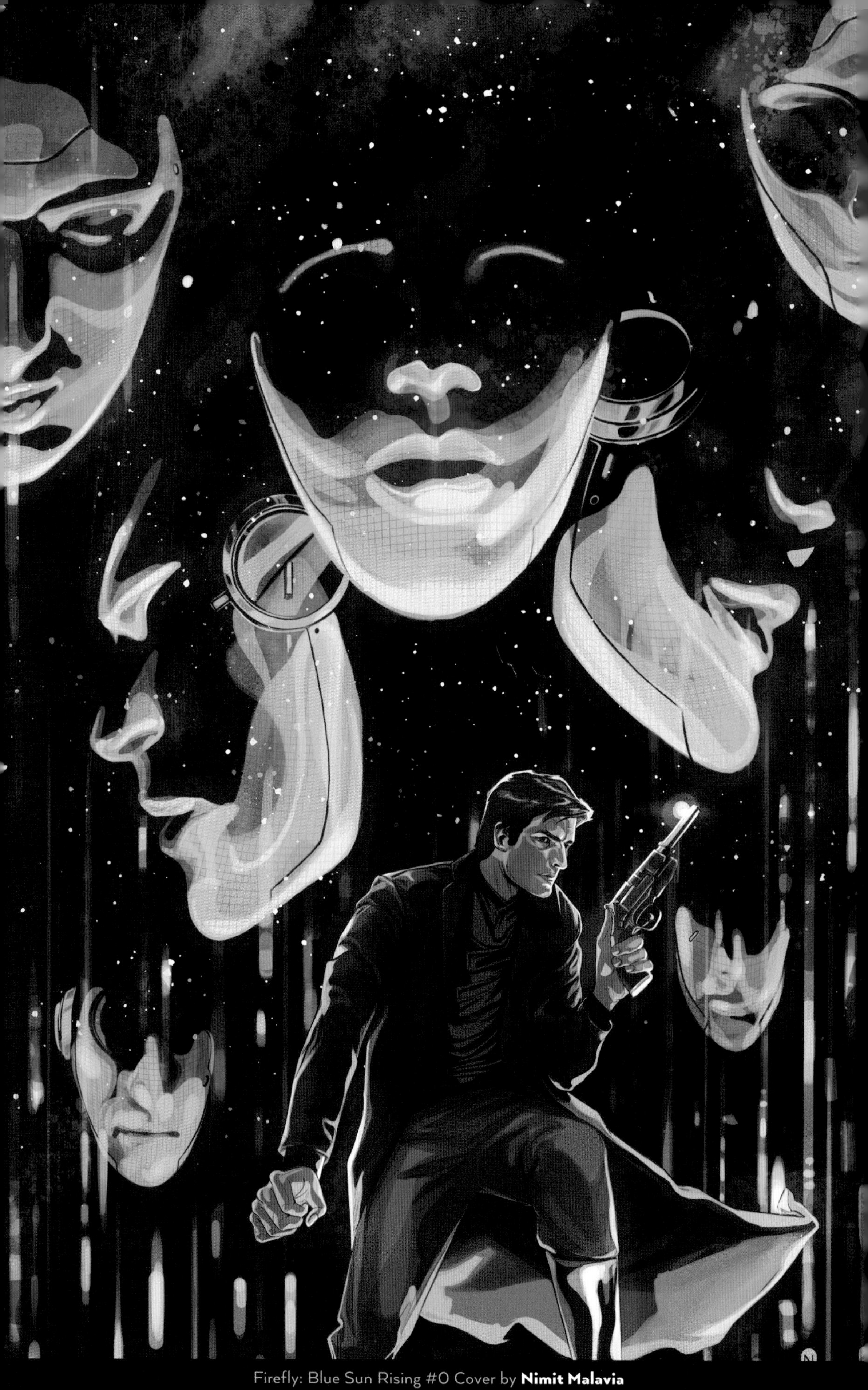

Firefly: Blue Sun Rising #0 Cover by **Nimit Malavia**

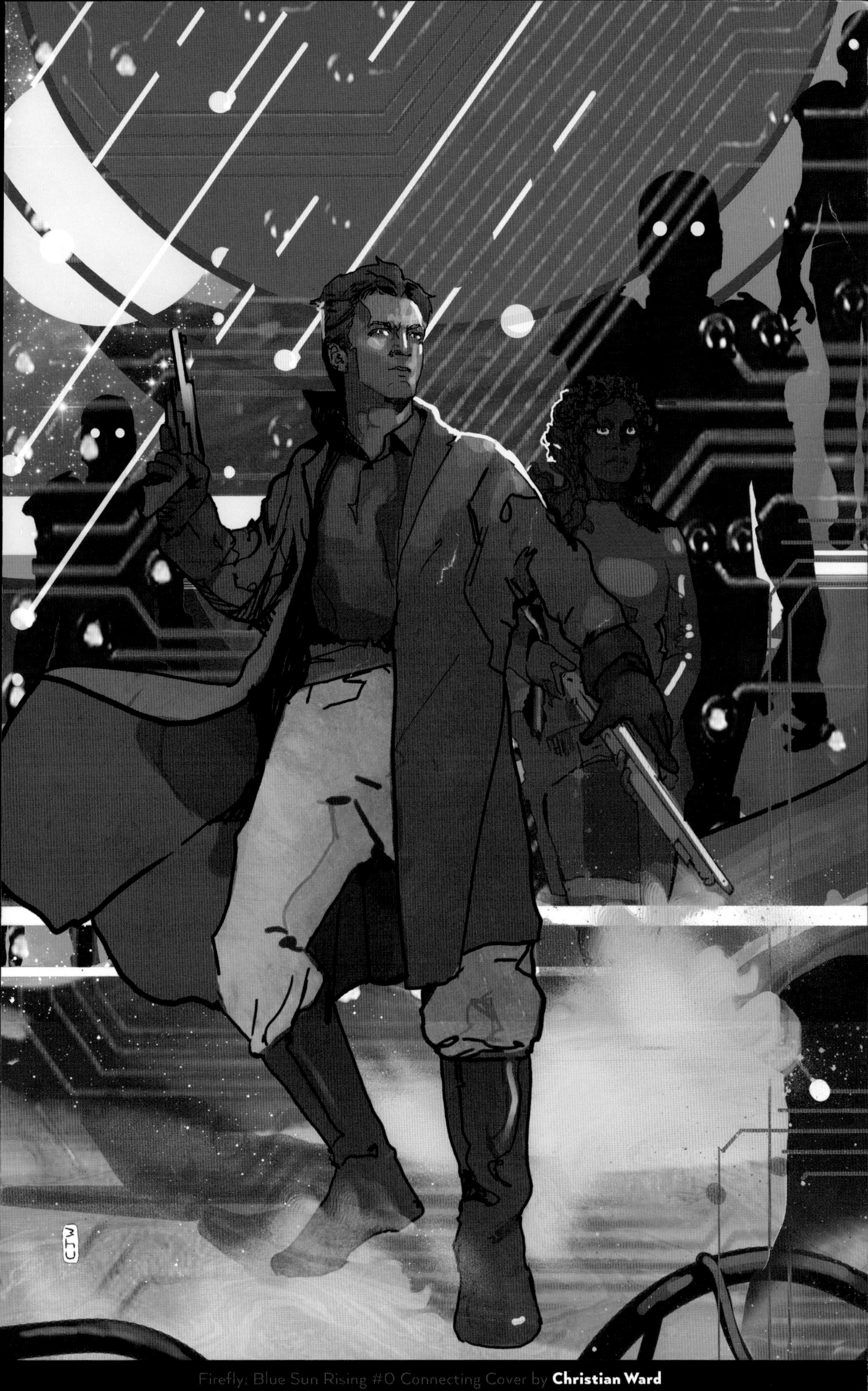

Firefly: Blue Sun Rising #0 Connecting Cover by **Christian Ward**

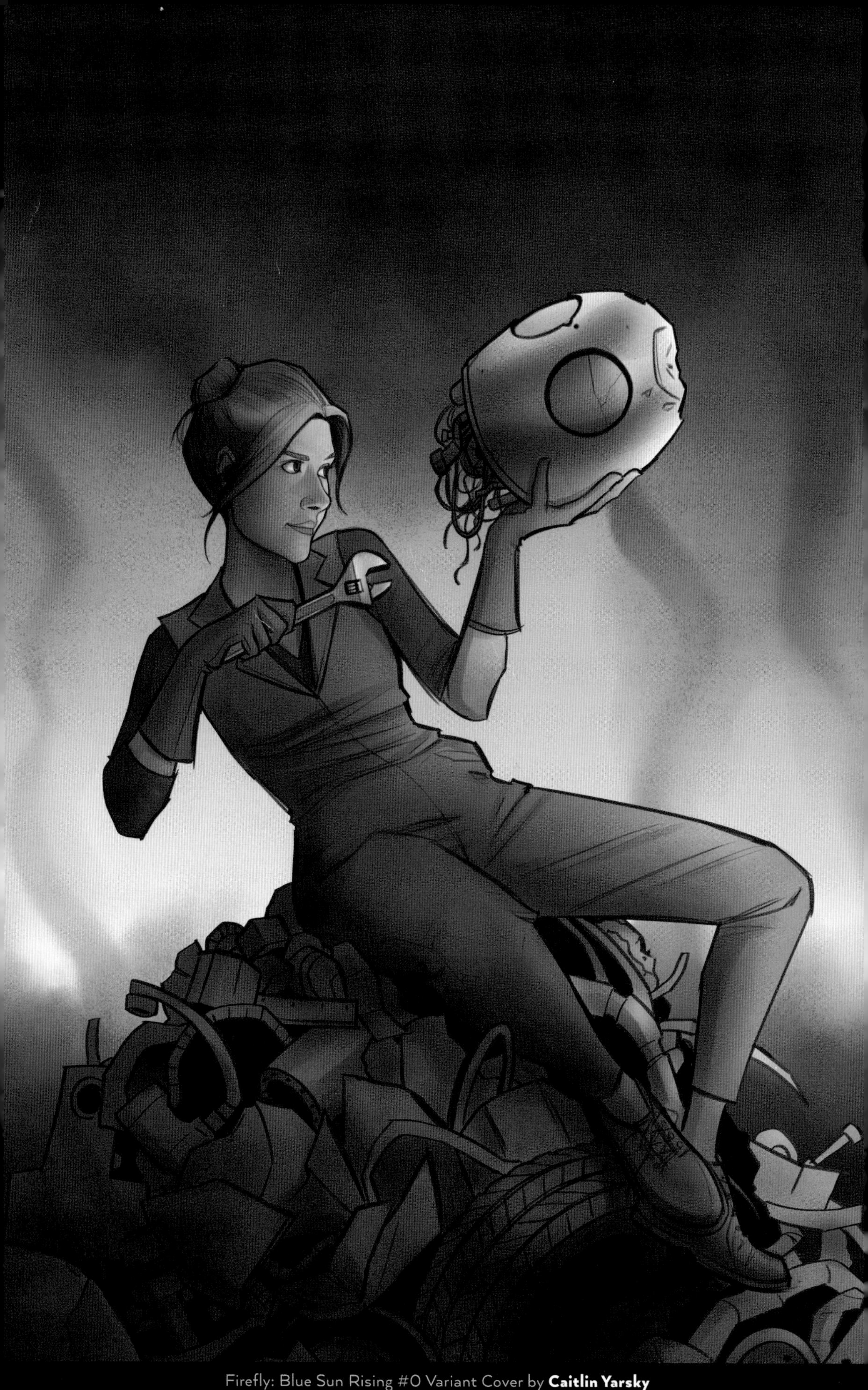

Firefly: Blue Sun Rising #0 Variant Cover by **Caitlin Yarsky**

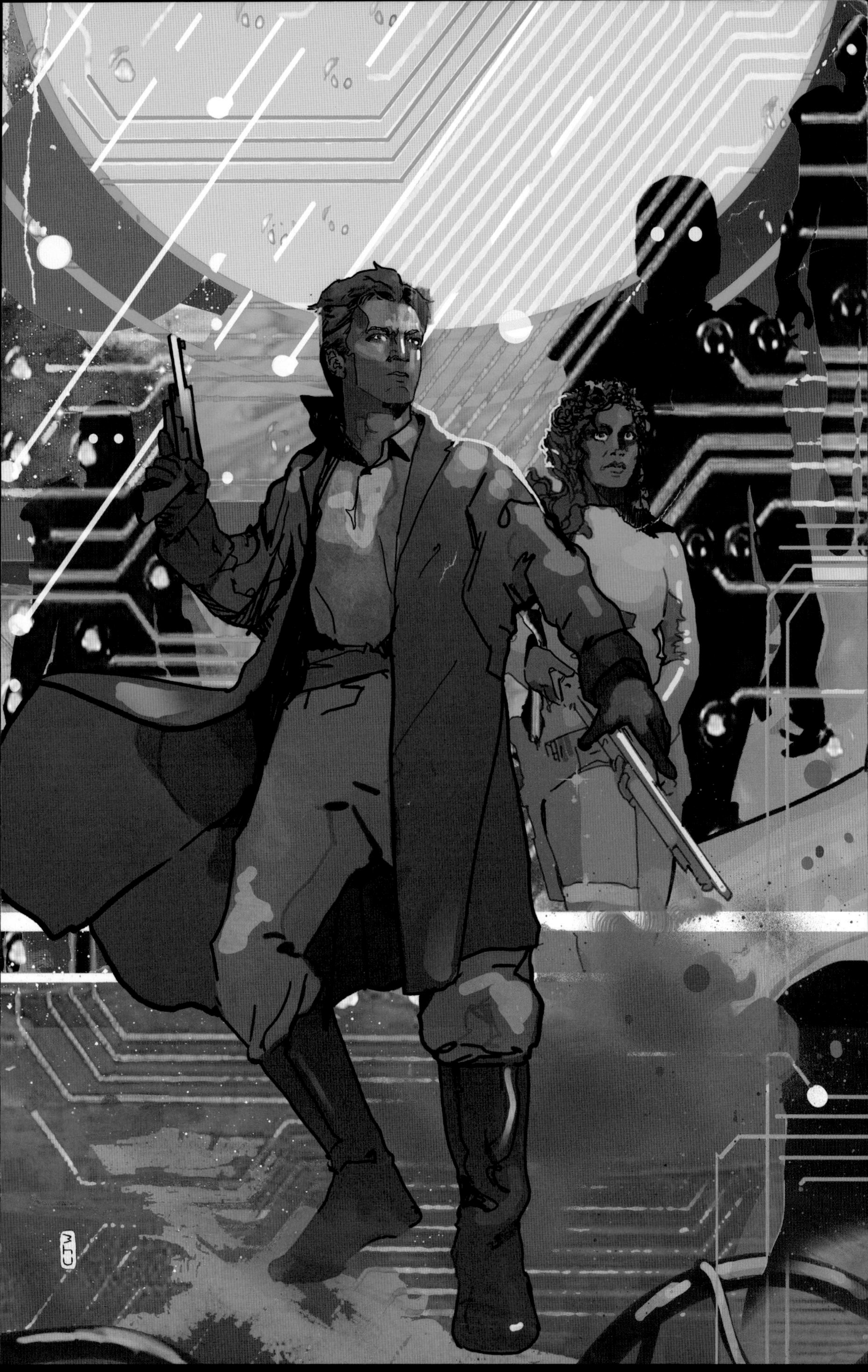

Firefly: Blue Sun Rising #0 Connecting Color Variant Cover by **Christian Ward**

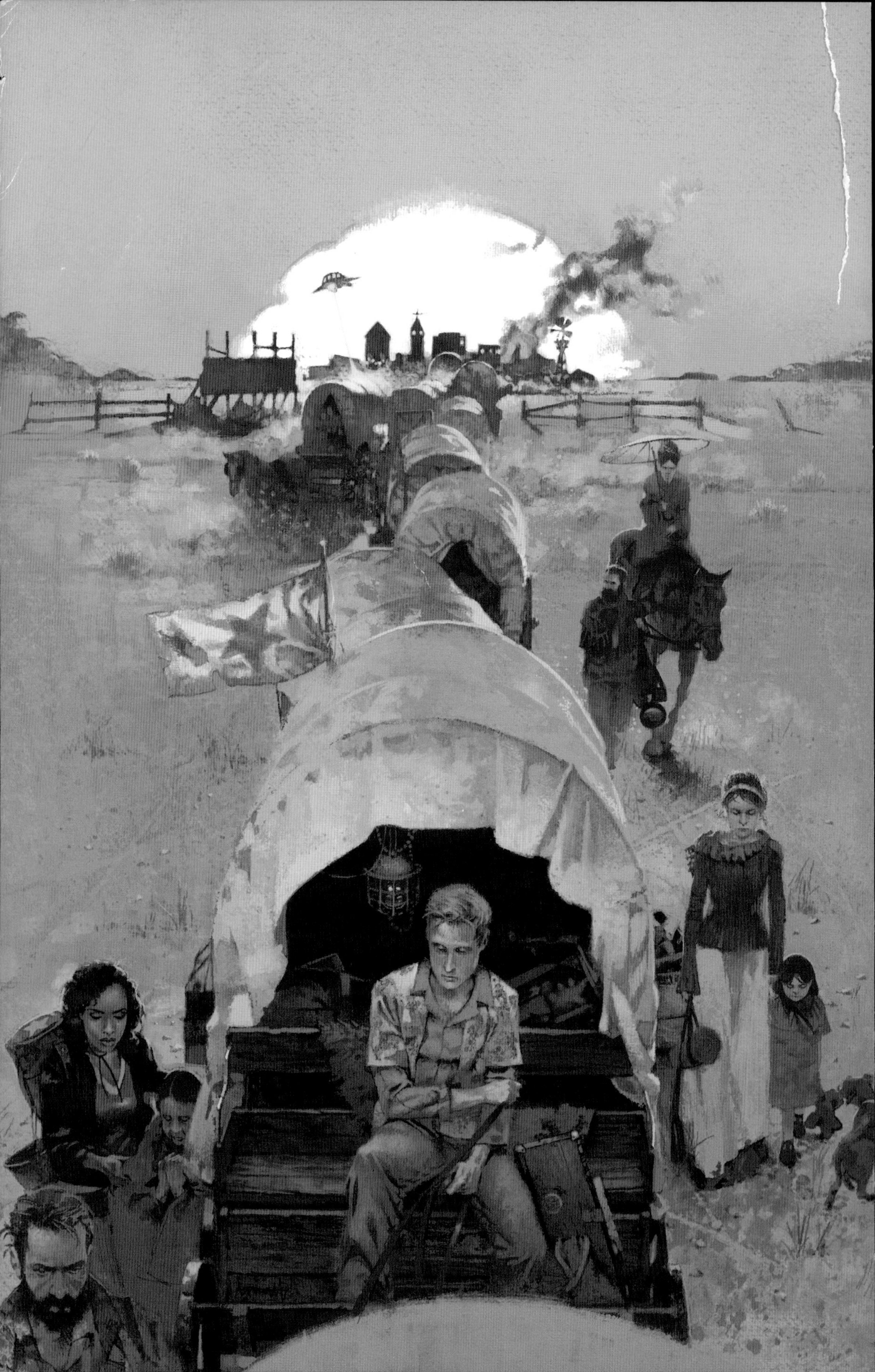

Firefly #21 Cover by **Marc Aspinall**

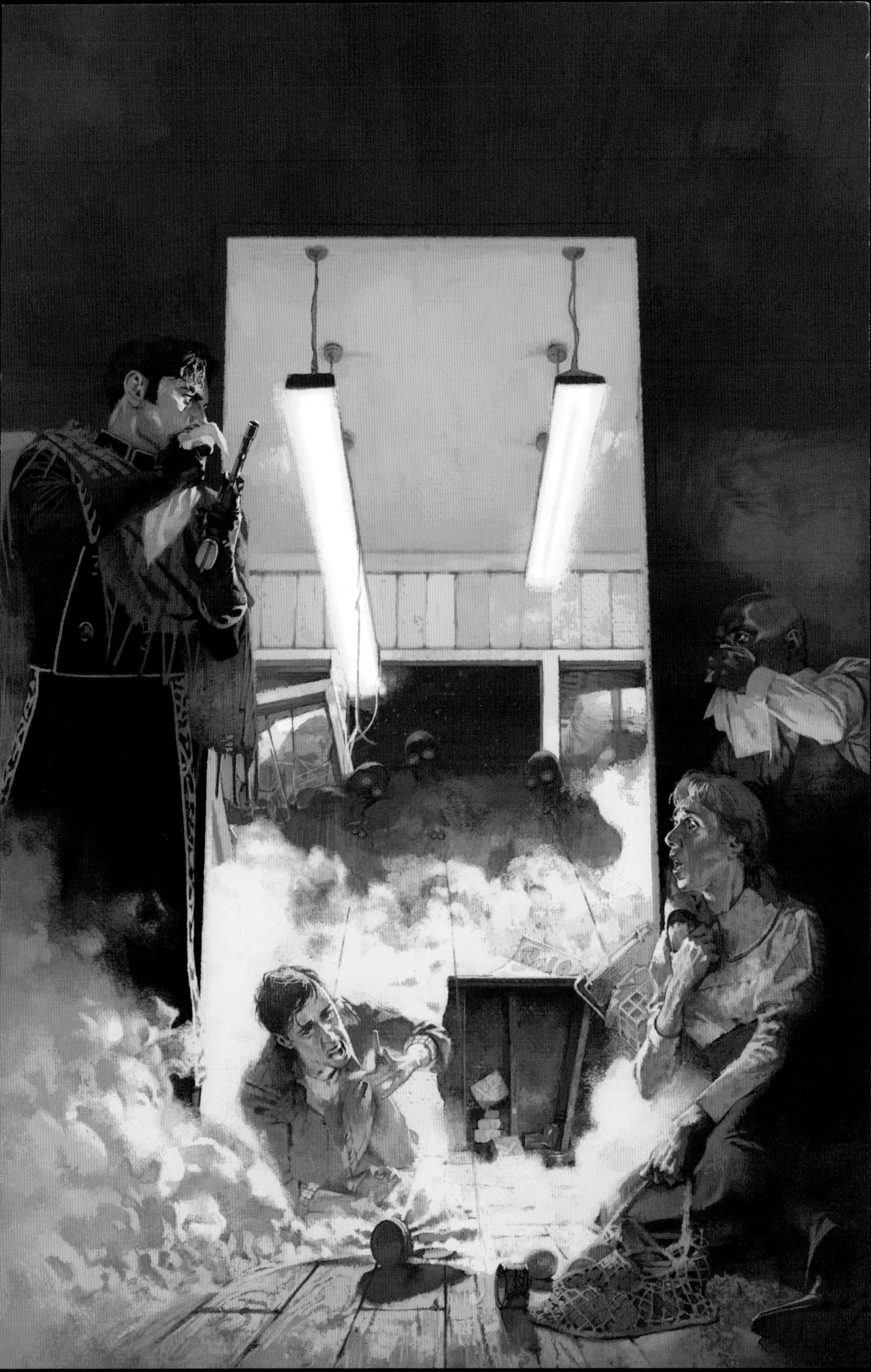

Firefly #22 Cover by **Marc Aspinall**

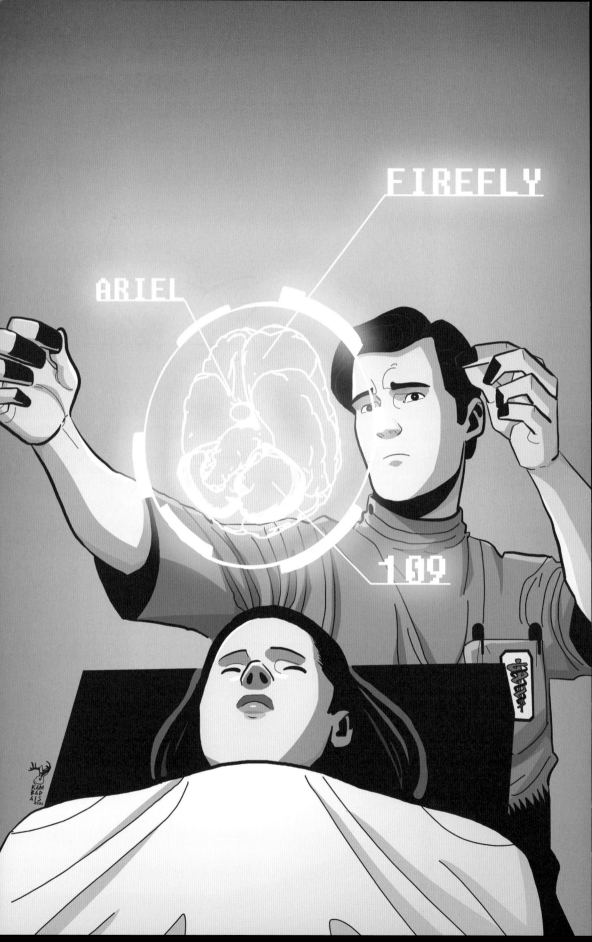

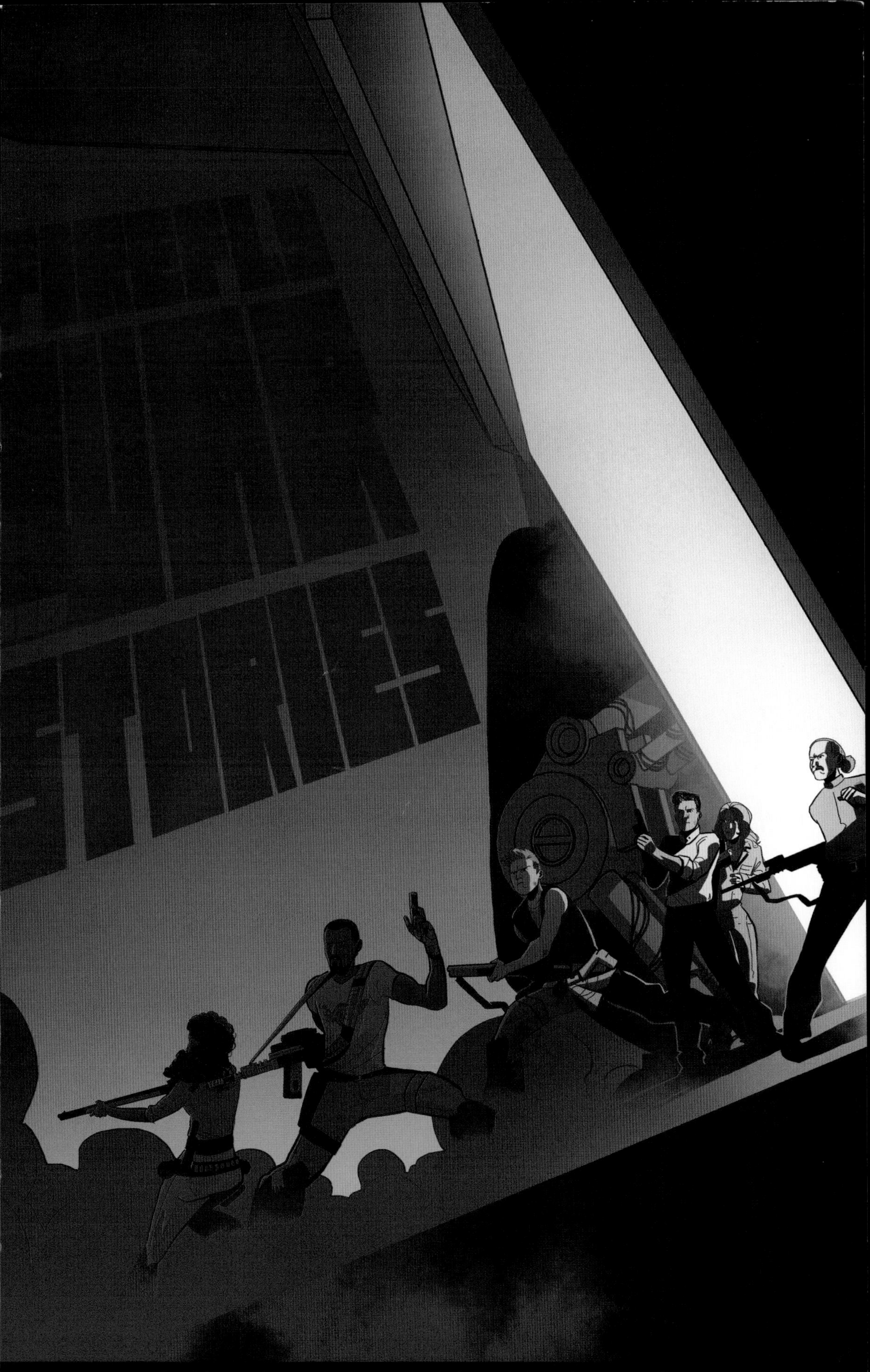

Firefly #22 Episode Cover by **George Kambadais** with Colors by **Joana Lafuente**

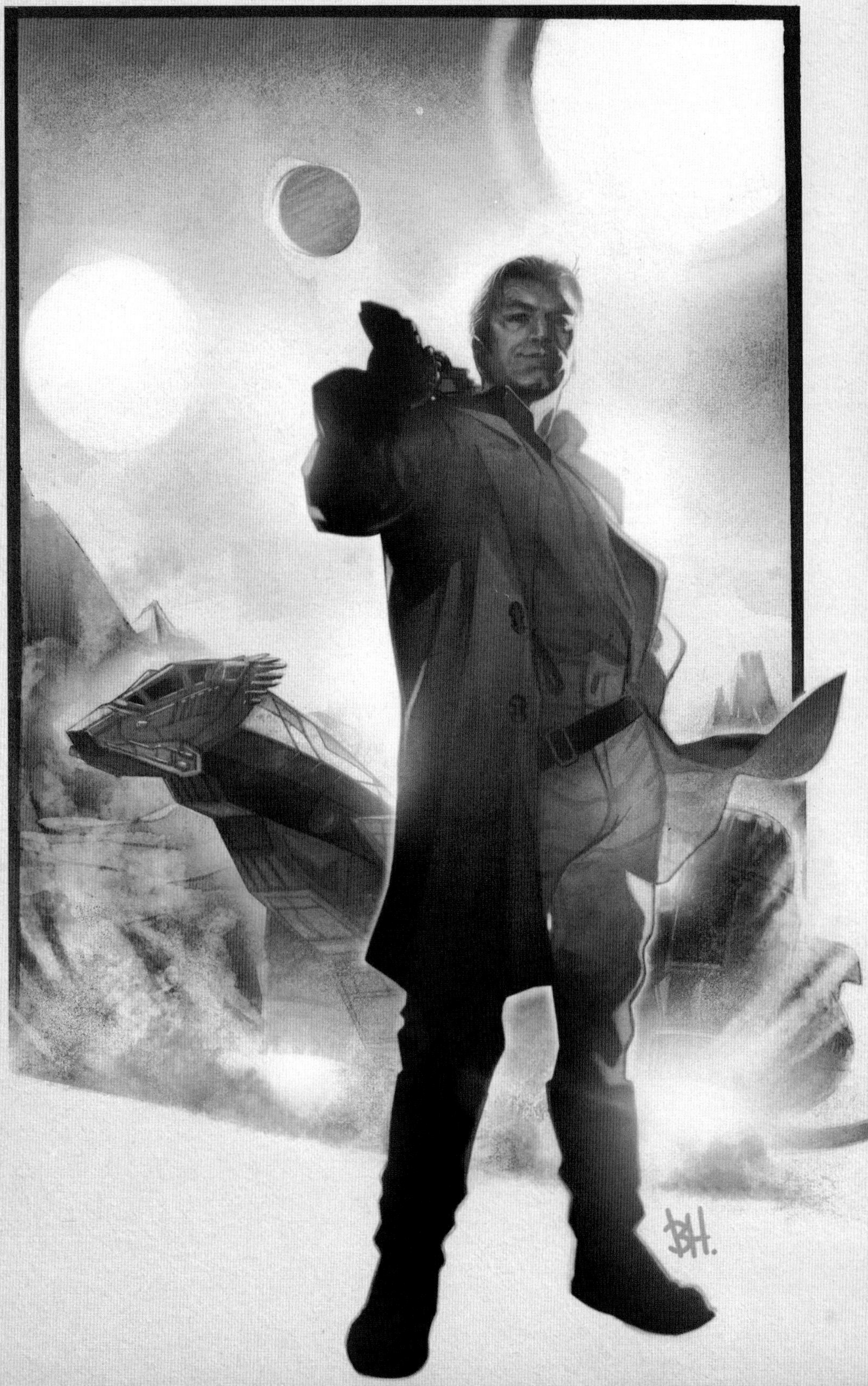

Firefly #21 Variant Cover by **Ben Harvey**

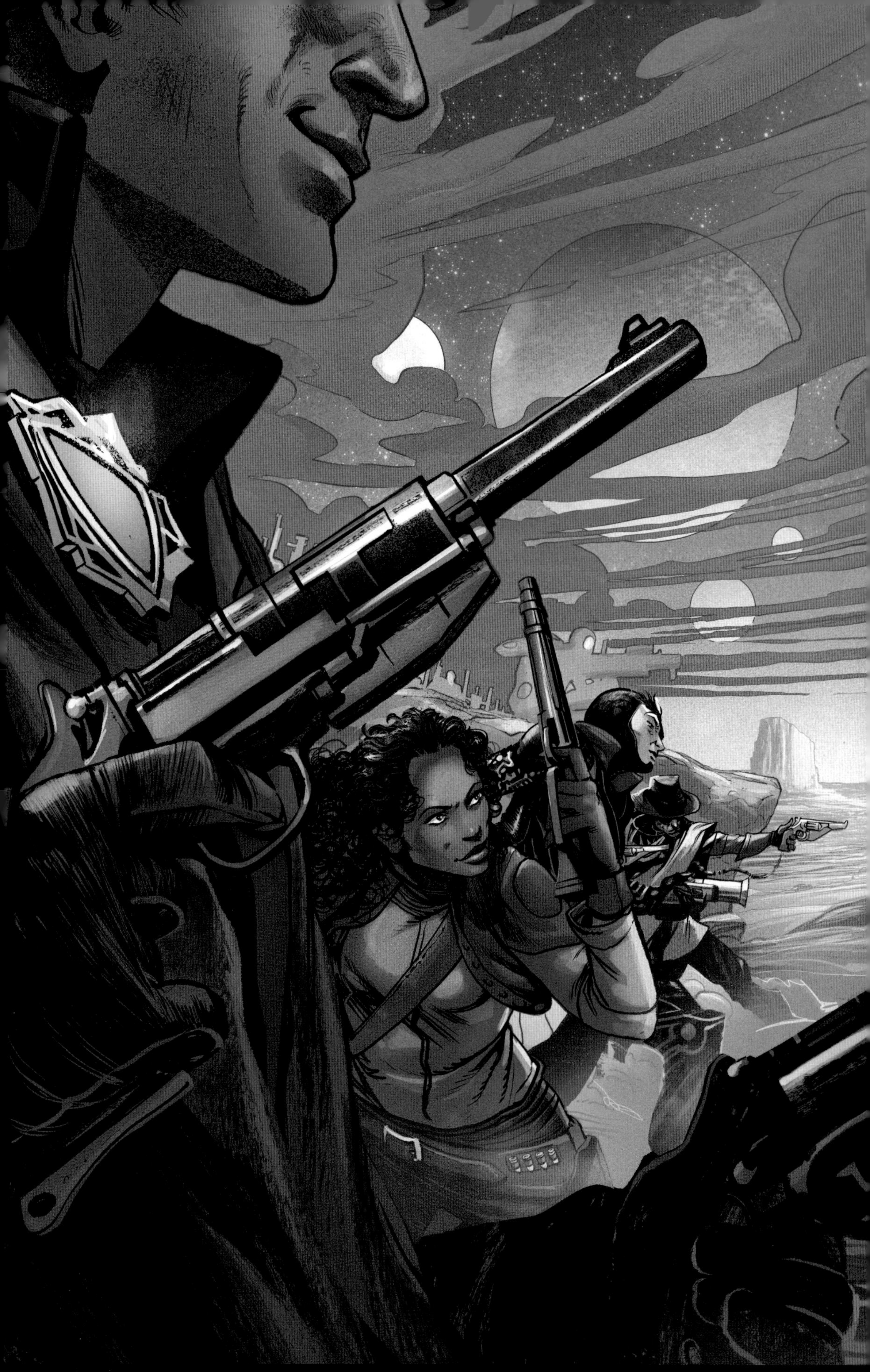

Firefly #22 Variant Cover by **Dex Pramanik** with Colors by **Alex Guimarães**

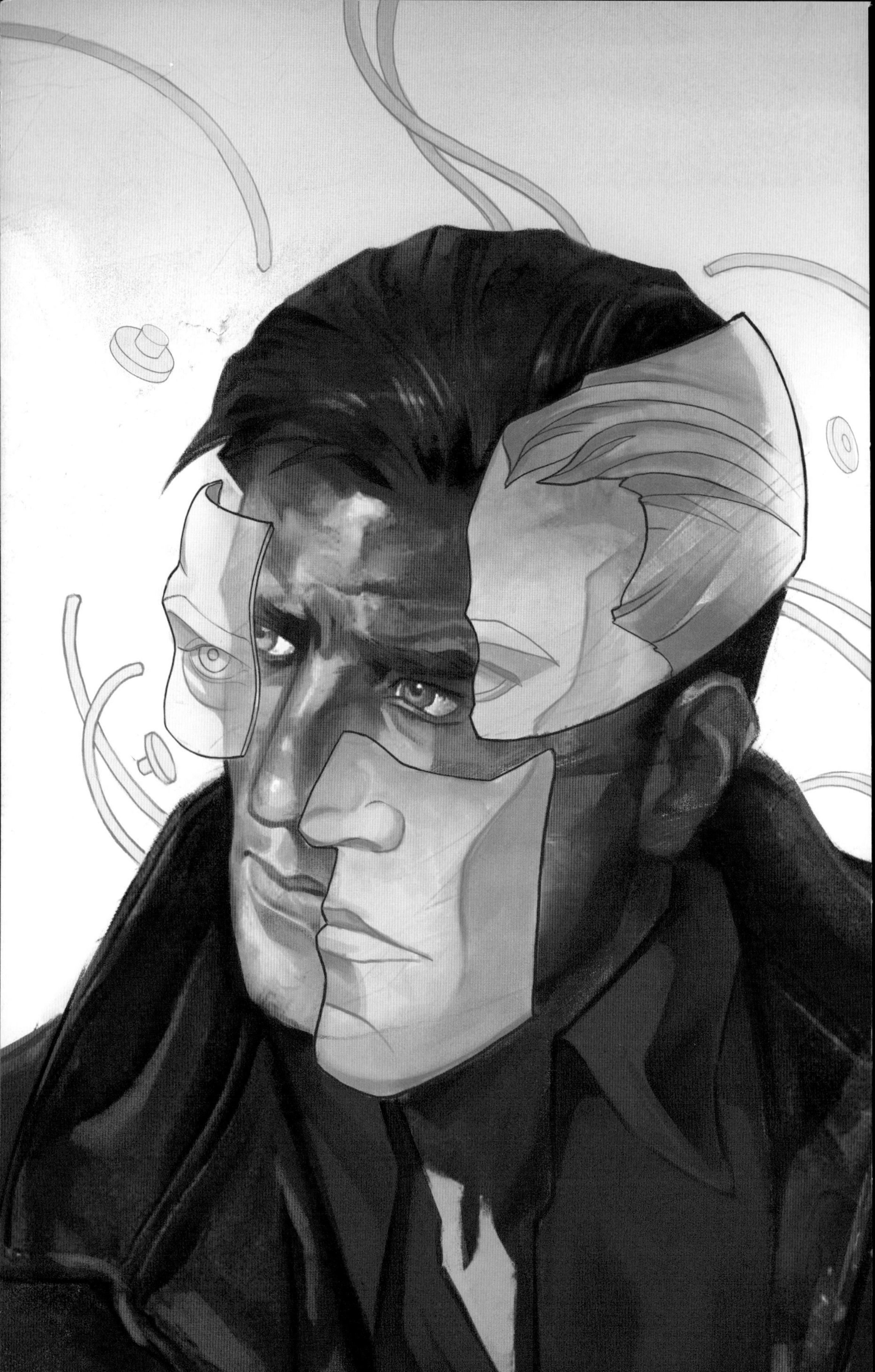

Firefly #21 Variant Cover by **Qistina Khalidah**

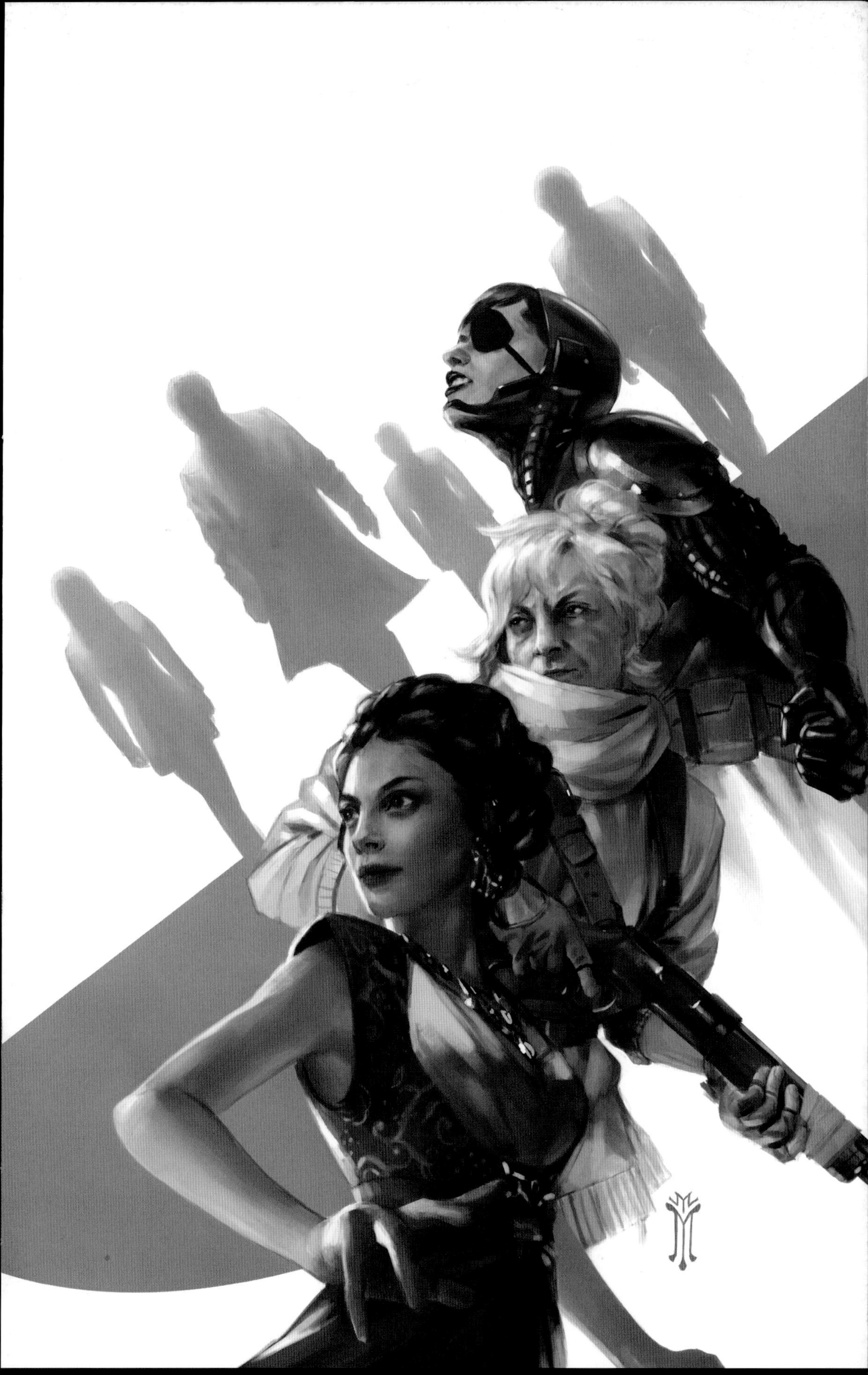

Firefly #22 Variant Cover by **Miguel Mercado**

SNEAK PREVIEW

firefly

WATCH HOW I SOAR

THE LAND

Written and Illustrated by
Ethan Young

Lettered by
Fábio Amelia

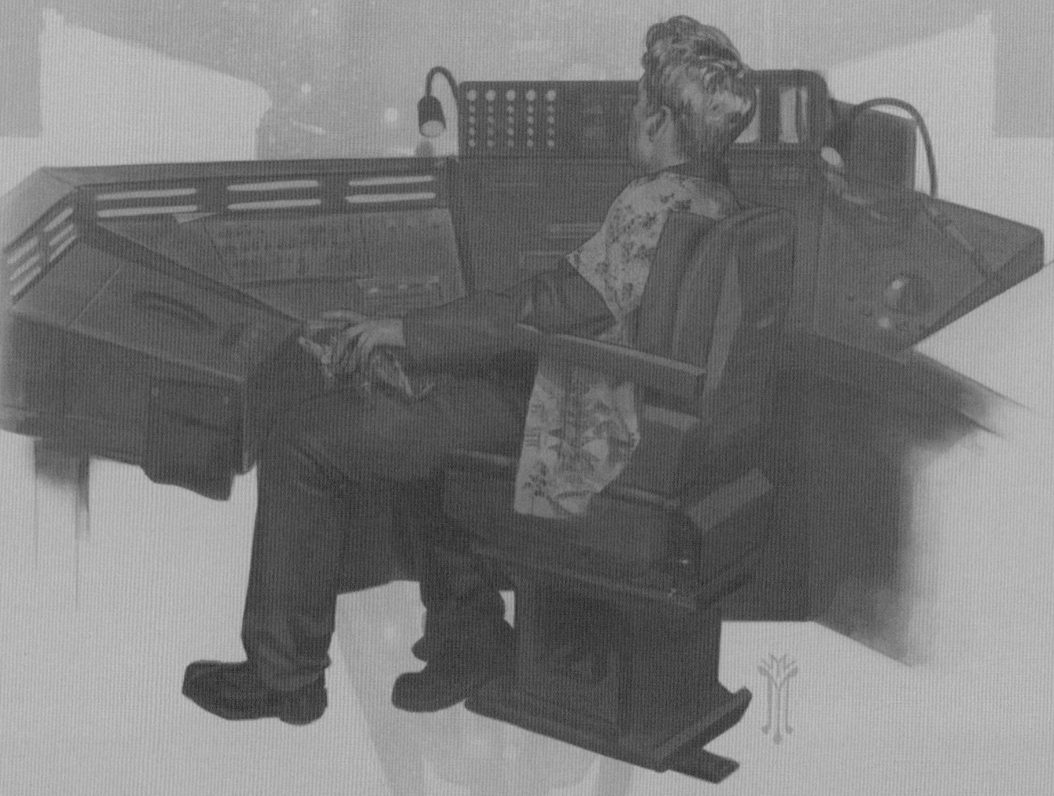

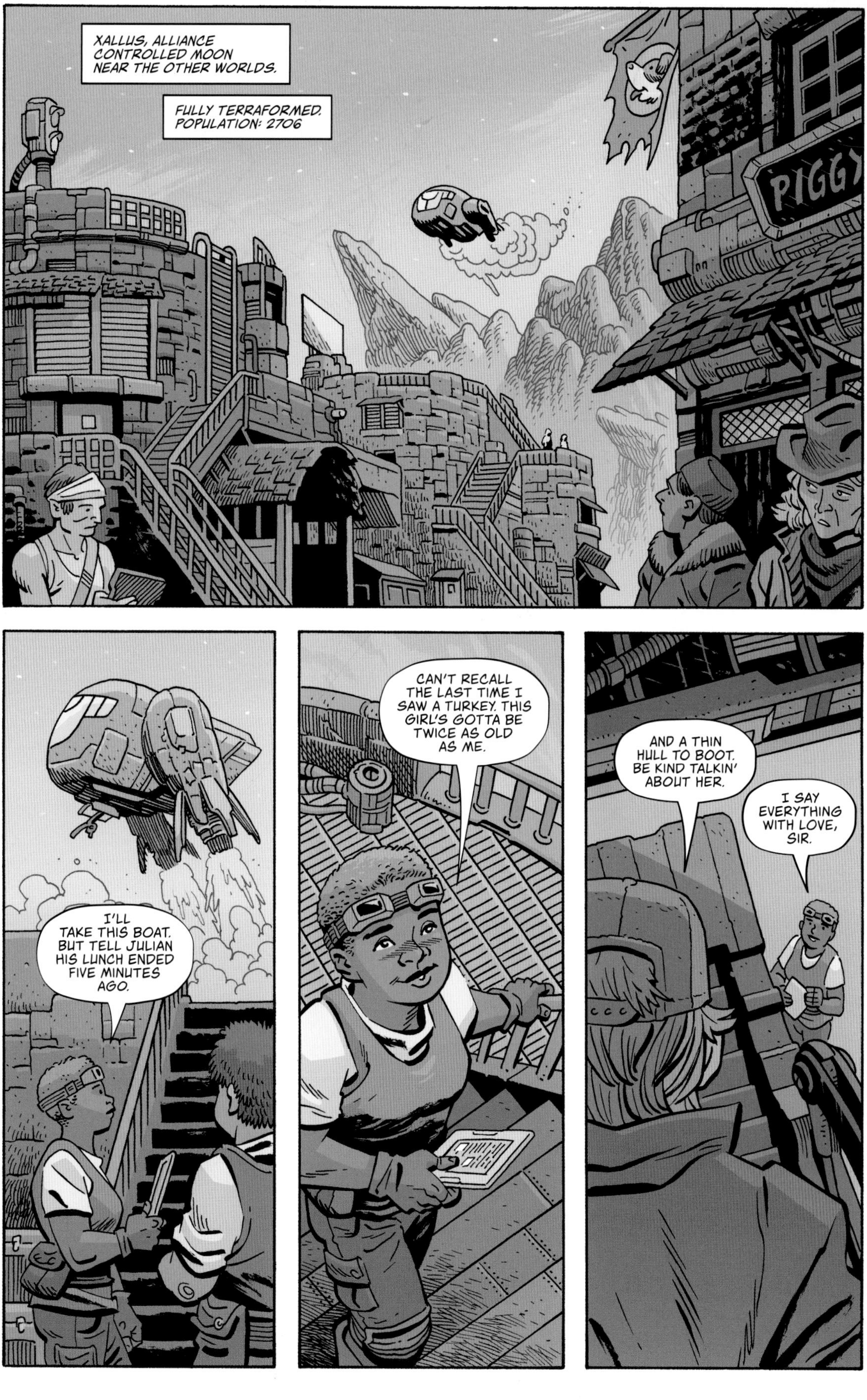
XALLUS, ALLIANCE CONTROLLED MOON NEAR THE OTHER WORLDS.
FULLY TERRAFORMED. POPULATION: 2706
PIGGY
I'LL TAKE THIS BOAT. BUT TELL JULIAN HIS LUNCH ENDED FIVE MINUTES AGO.
CAN'T RECALL THE LAST TIME I SAW A TURKEY. THIS GIRL'S GOTTA BE TWICE AS OLD AS ME.
AND A THIN HULL TO BOOT. BE KIND TALKIN' ABOUT HER.
I SAY EVERYTHING WITH LOVE, SIR.

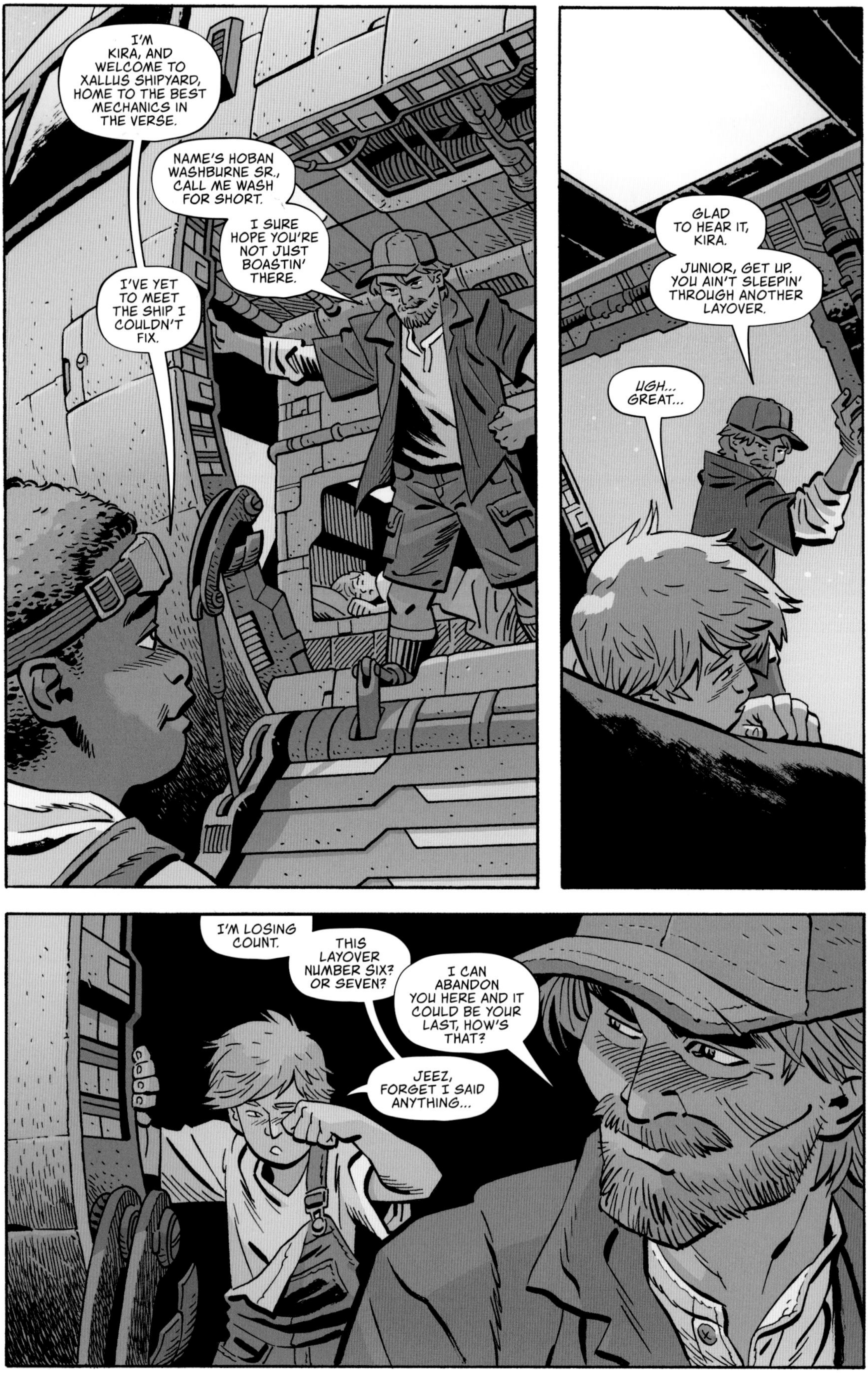
I'M KIRA, AND WELCOME TO XALLUS SHIPYARD, HOME TO THE BEST MECHANICS IN THE VERSE.
NAME'S HOBAN WASHBURNE SR., CALL ME WASH FOR SHORT.
I SURE HOPE YOU'RE NOT JUST BOASTIN' THERE.
I'VE YET TO MEET THE SHIP I COULDN'T FIX.
GLAD TO HEAR IT, KIRA.
JUNIOR, GET UP. YOU AIN'T SLEEPIN' THROUGH ANOTHER LAYOVER.
UGH... GREAT...
I'M LOSING COUNT.
THIS LAYOVER NUMBER SIX? OR SEVEN?
I CAN ABANDON YOU HERE AND IT COULD BE YOUR LAST, HOW'S THAT?
JEEZ, FORGET I SAID ANYTHING...

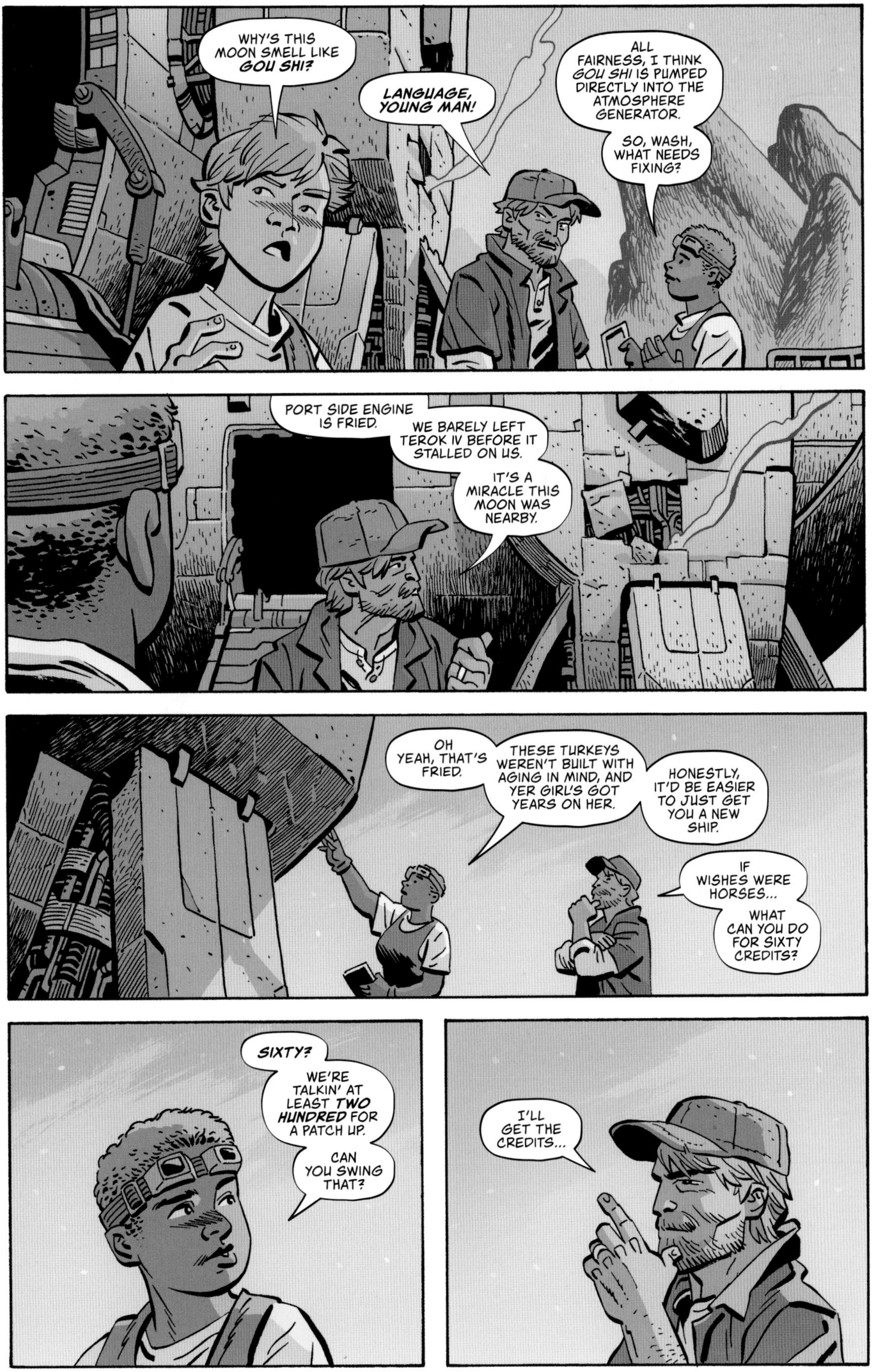
WHY'S THIS MOON SMELL LIKE GOU SHI?
LANGUAGE, YOUNG MAN!
ALL FAIRNESS, I THINK GOU SHI IS PUMPED DIRECTLY INTO THE ATMOSPHERE GENERATOR.
SO, WASH, WHAT NEEDS FIXING?
PORT SIDE ENGINE IS FRIED.
WE BARELY LEFT TEROK IV BEFORE IT STALLED ON US.
IT'S A MIRACLE THIS MOON WAS NEARBY.
OH YEAH, THAT'S FRIED.
THESE TURKEYS WEREN'T BUILT WITH AGING IN MIND, AND YER GIRL'S GOT YEARS ON HER.
HONESTLY, IT'D BE EASIER TO JUST GET YOU A NEW SHIP.
IF WISHES WERE HORSES...
WHAT CAN YOU DO FOR SIXTY CREDITS?
SIXTY?
WE'RE TALKIN' AT LEAST TWO HUNDRED FOR A PATCH UP.
CAN YOU SWING THAT?
I'LL GET THE CREDITS...

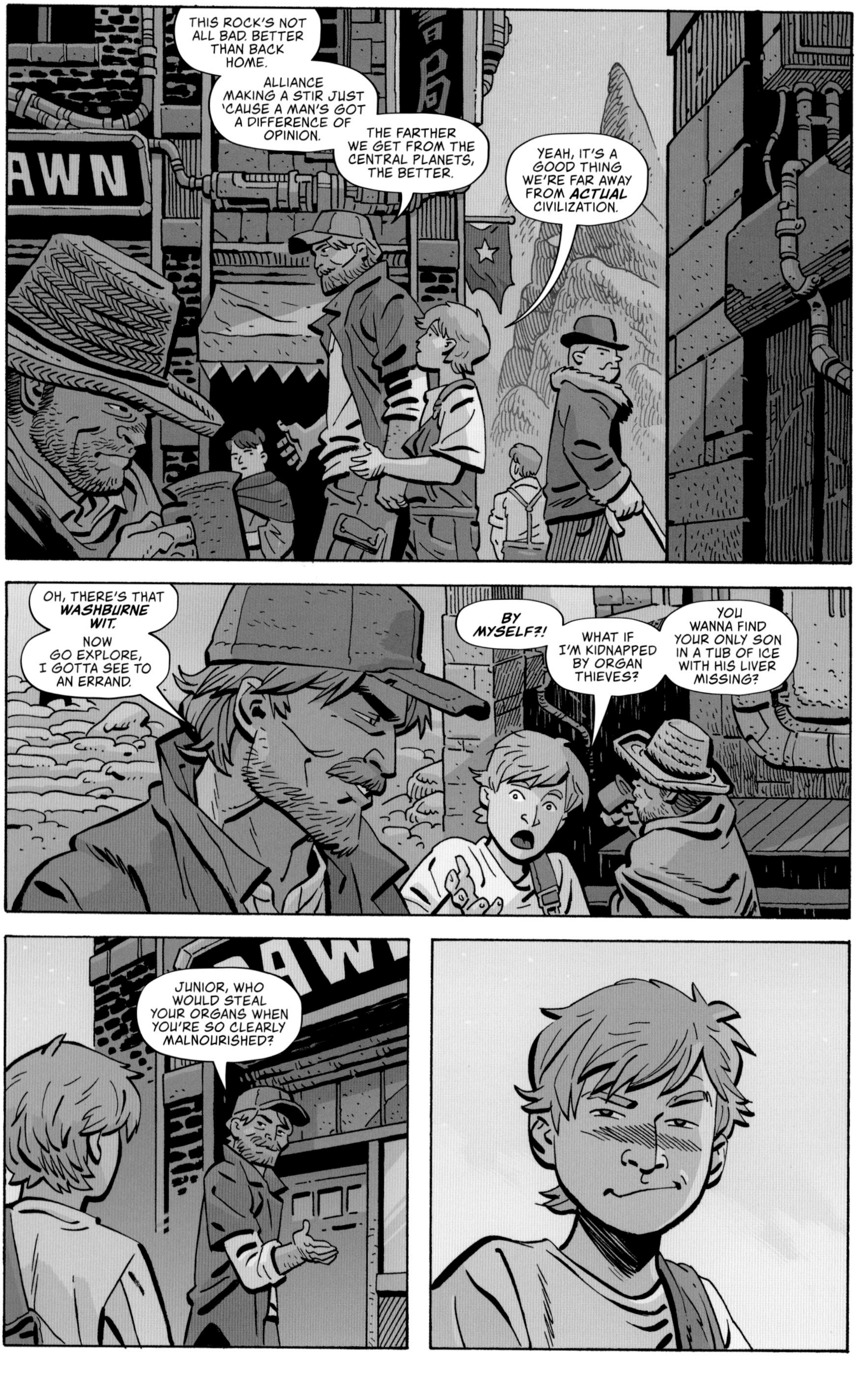
THIS ROCK'S NOT ALL BAD. BETTER THAN BACK HOME.
ALLIANCE MAKING A STIR JUST 'CAUSE A MAN'S GOT A DIFFERENCE OF OPINION.
THE FARTHER WE GET FROM THE CENTRAL PLANETS, THE BETTER.
YEAH, IT'S A GOOD THING WE'RE FAR AWAY FROM **ACTUAL** CIVILIZATION.
OH, THERE'S THAT **WASHBURNE WIT.**
NOW GO EXPLORE, I GOTTA SEE TO AN ERRAND.
BY MYSELF?!
WHAT IF I'M KIDNAPPED BY ORGAN THIEVES?
YOU WANNA FIND YOUR ONLY SON IN A TUB OF ICE WITH HIS LIVER MISSING?
JUNIOR, WHO WOULD STEAL YOUR ORGANS WHEN YOU'RE SO CLEARLY MALNOURISHED?

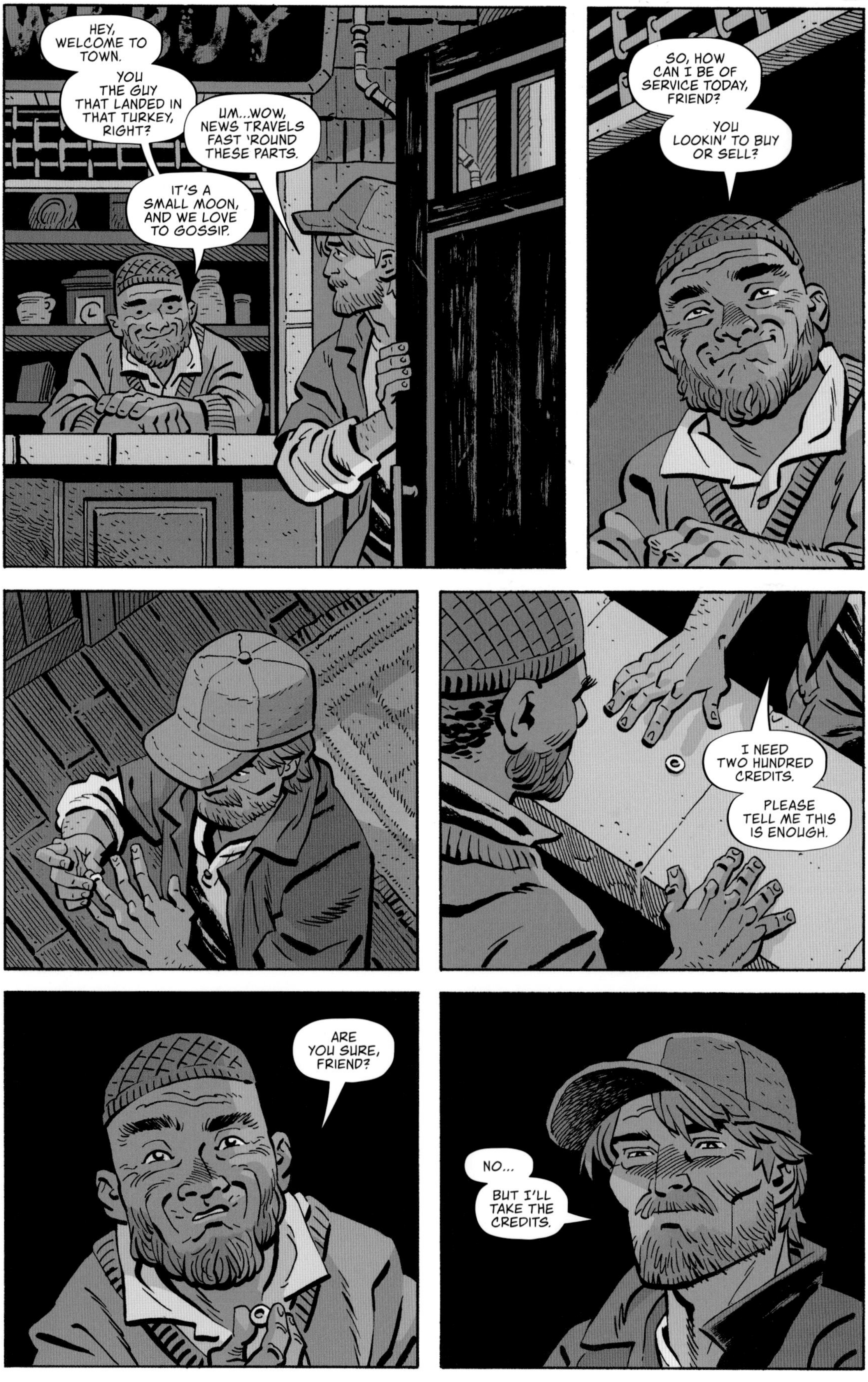
WE BUY
HEY, WELCOME TO TOWN.
YOU THE GUY THAT LANDED IN THAT TURKEY, RIGHT?
UM...WOW, NEWS TRAVELS FAST 'ROUND THESE PARTS.
IT'S A SMALL MOON, AND WE LOVE TO GOSSIP.
SO, HOW CAN I BE OF SERVICE TODAY, FRIEND?
YOU LOOKIN' TO BUY OR SELL?
I NEED TWO HUNDRED CREDITS.
PLEASE TELL ME THIS IS ENOUGH.
ARE YOU SURE, FRIEND?
NO...
BUT I'LL TAKE THE CREDITS.

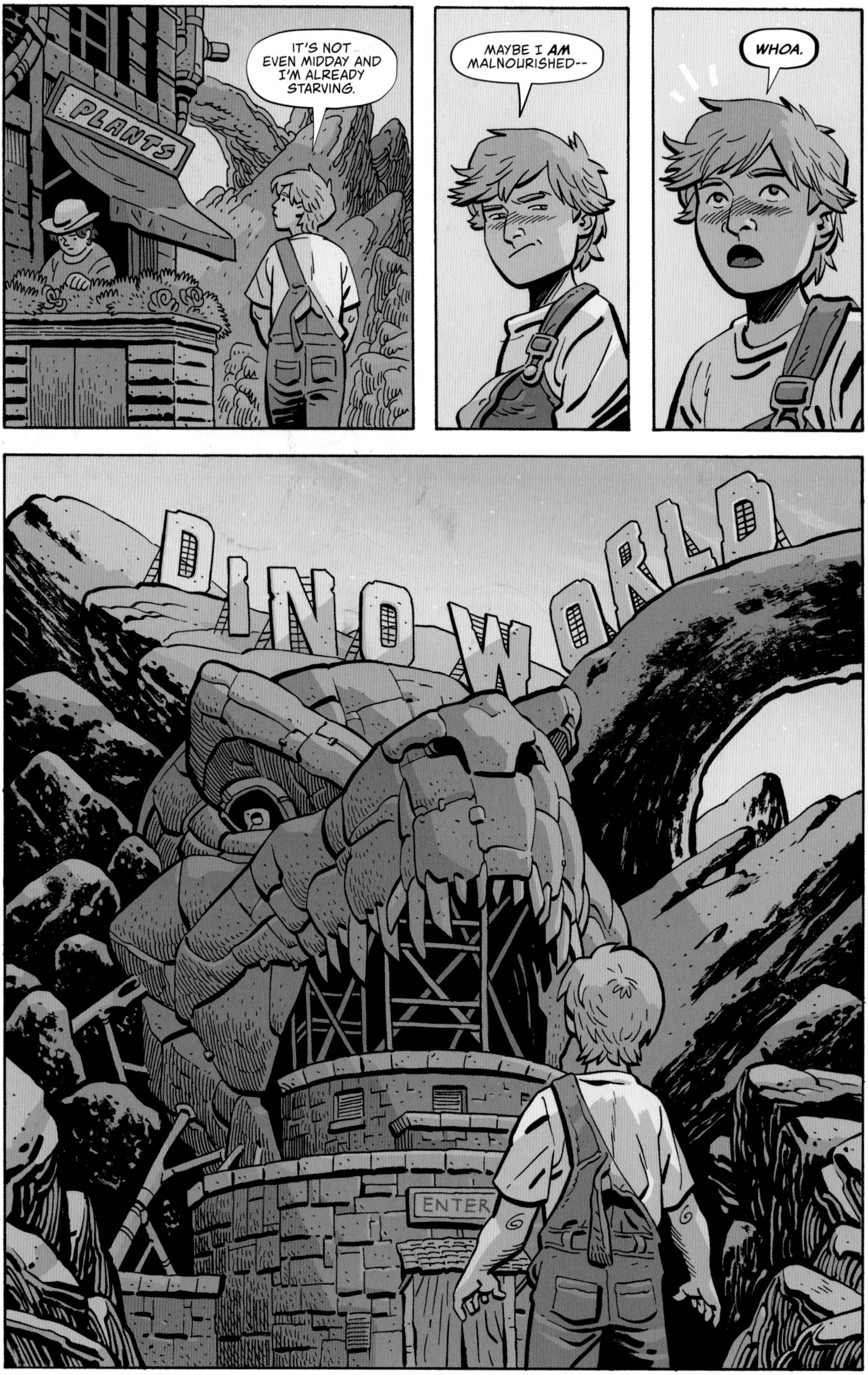

IT'S NOT EVEN MIDDAY AND I'M ALREADY STARVING.
PLANTS
MAYBE I AM MALNOURISHED--
WHOA.
DINO WORLD
ENTER

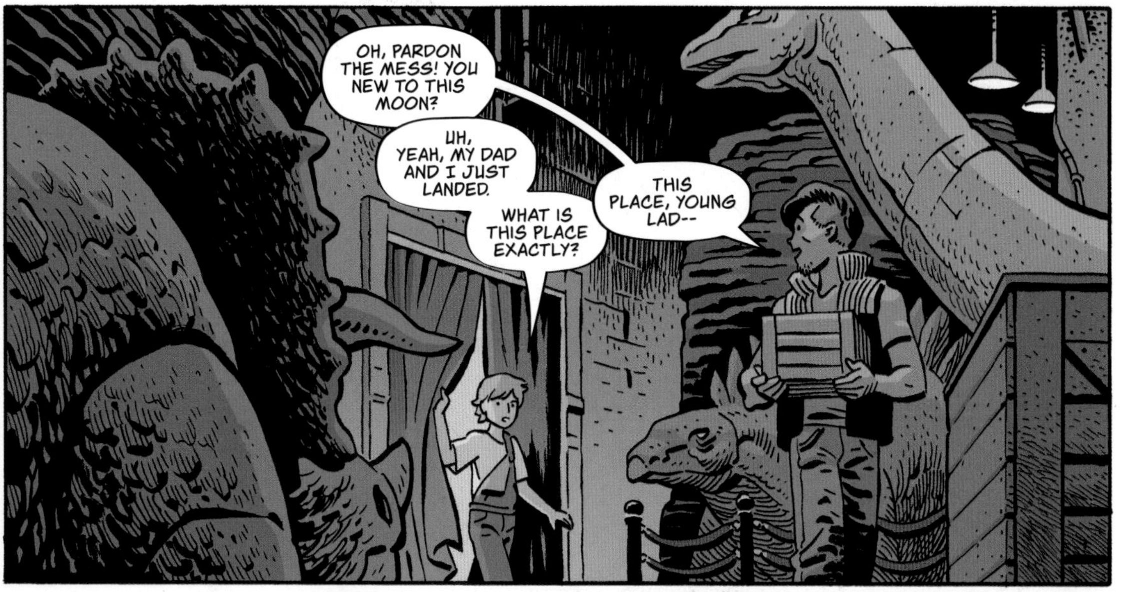
OH, PARDON THE MESS! YOU NEW TO THIS MOON?
UH, YEAH, MY DAD AND I JUST LANDED.
WHAT IS THIS PLACE EXACTLY?
THIS PLACE, YOUNG LAD--

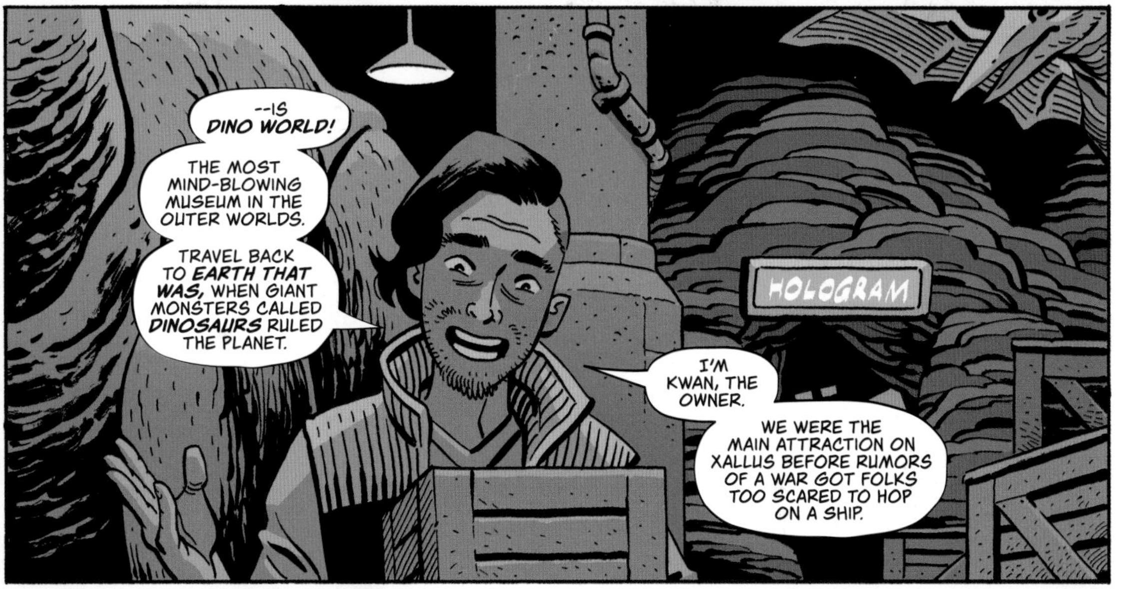
--IS DINO WORLD!
THE MOST MIND-BLOWING MUSEUM IN THE OUTER WORLDS.
TRAVEL BACK TO EARTH THAT WAS, WHEN GIANT MONSTERS CALLED DINOSAURS RULED THE PLANET.
HOLOGRAM
I'M KWAN, THE OWNER.
WE WERE THE MAIN ATTRACTION ON XALLUS BEFORE RUMORS OF A WAR GOT FOLKS TOO SCARED TO HOP ON A SHIP.

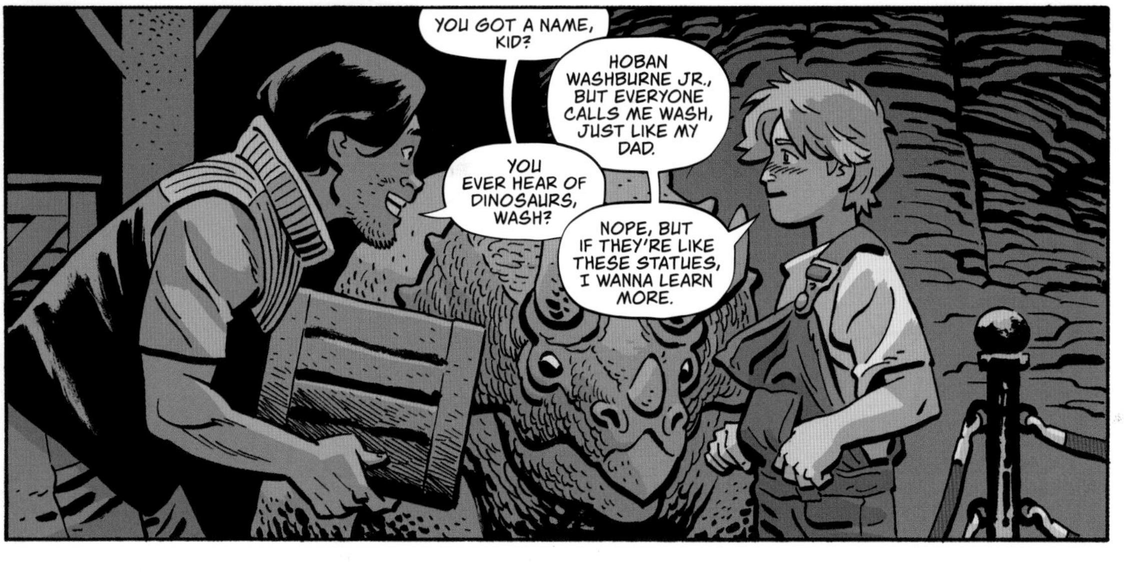
YOU GOT A NAME, KID?
HOBAN WASHBURNE JR., BUT EVERYONE CALLS ME WASH, JUST LIKE MY DAD.
YOU EVER HEAR OF DINOSAURS, WASH?
NOPE, BUT IF THEY'RE LIKE THESE STATUES, I WANNA LEARN MORE.

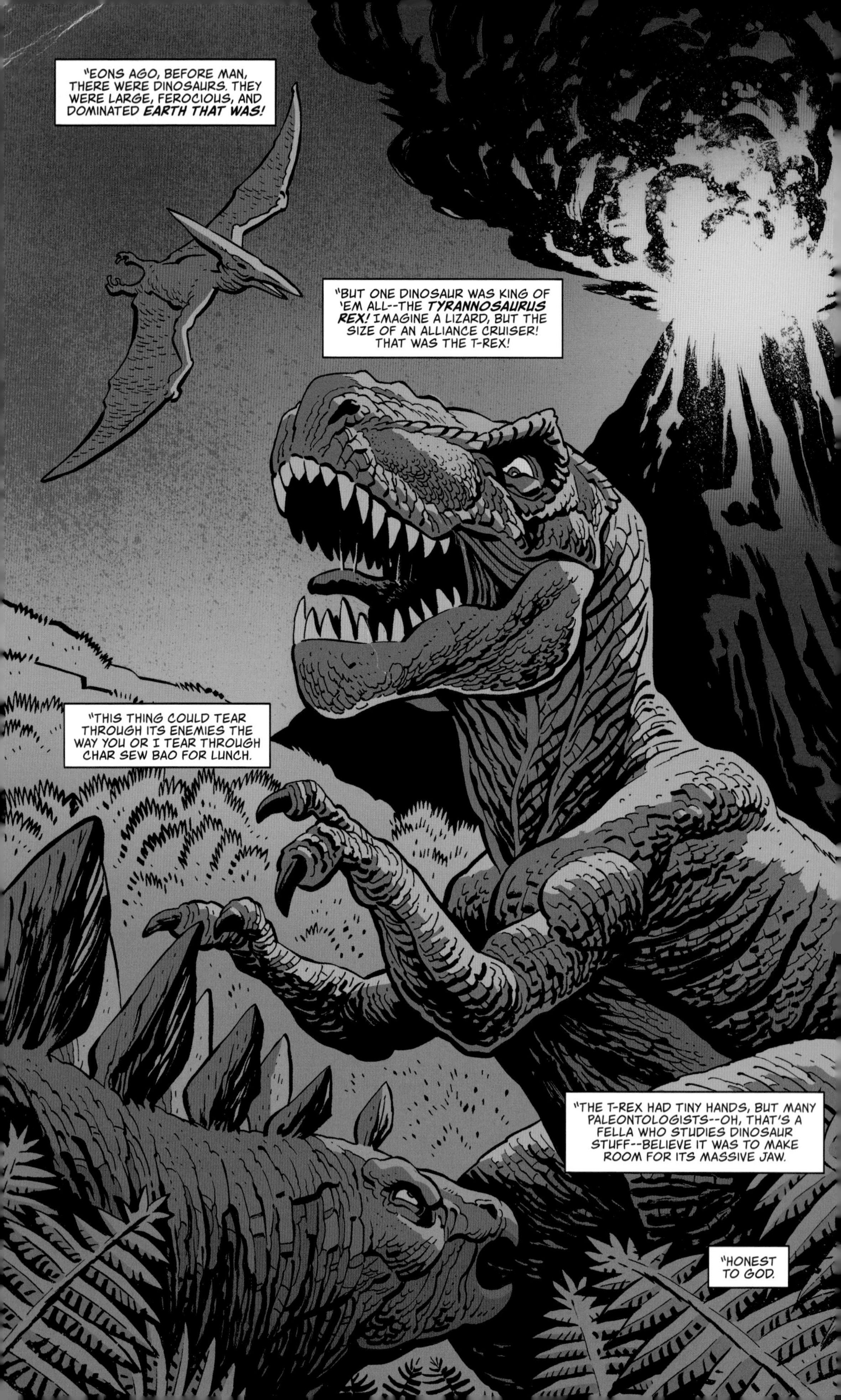
"EONS AGO, BEFORE MAN, THERE WERE DINOSAURS. THEY WERE LARGE, FEROCIOUS, AND DOMINATED EARTH THAT WAS!
"BUT ONE DINOSAUR WAS KING OF 'EM ALL--THE TYRANNOSAURUS REX! IMAGINE A LIZARD, BUT THE SIZE OF AN ALLIANCE CRUISER! THAT WAS THE T-REX!
"THIS THING COULD TEAR THROUGH ITS ENEMIES THE WAY YOU OR I TEAR THROUGH CHAR SEW BAO FOR LUNCH.
"THE T-REX HAD TINY HANDS, BUT MANY PALEONTOLOGISTS--OH, THAT'S A FELLA WHO STUDIES DINOSAUR STUFF--BELIEVE IT WAS TO MAKE ROOM FOR ITS MASSIVE JAW.
"HONEST TO GOD.

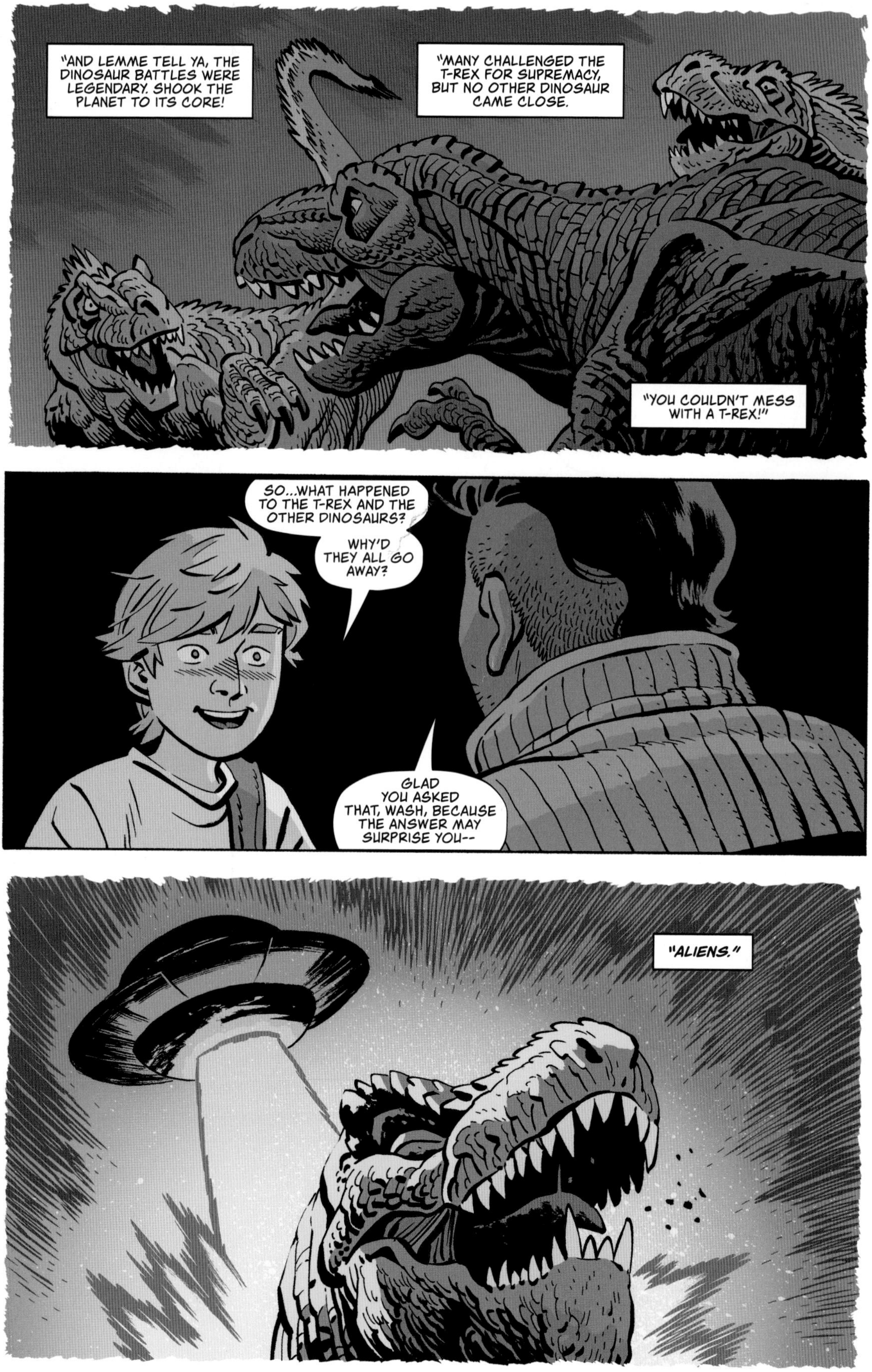
"AND LEMME TELL YA, THE DINOSAUR BATTLES WERE LEGENDARY. SHOOK THE PLANET TO ITS CORE!
"MANY CHALLENGED THE T-REX FOR SUPREMACY, BUT NO OTHER DINOSAUR CAME CLOSE.
"YOU COULDN'T MESS WITH A T-REX!"
SO...WHAT HAPPENED TO THE T-REX AND THE OTHER DINOSAURS?
WHY'D THEY ALL GO AWAY?
GLAD YOU ASKED THAT, WASH, BECAUSE THE ANSWER MAY SURPRISE YOU--
"ALIENS."

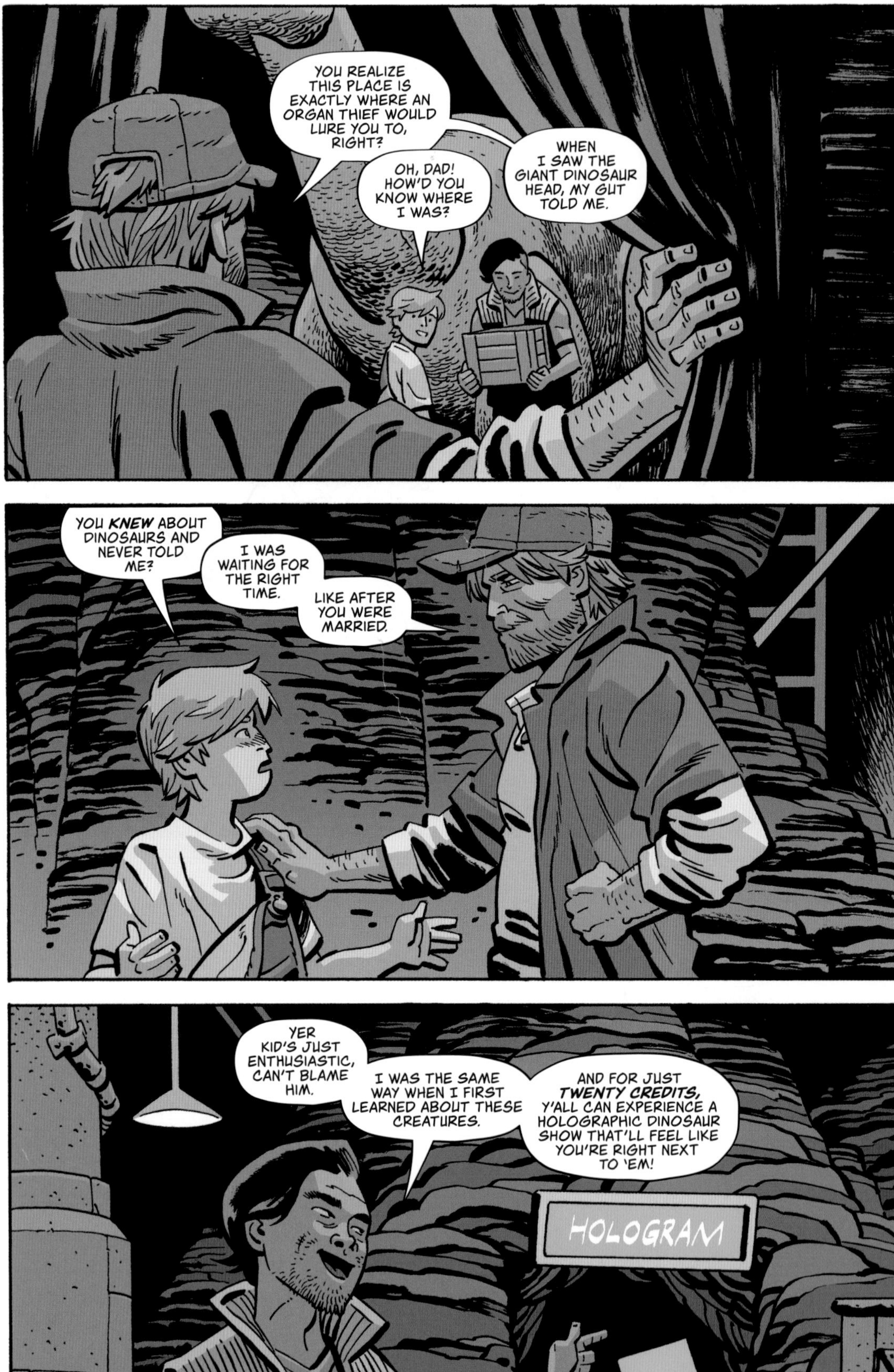
YOU REALIZE THIS PLACE IS EXACTLY WHERE AN ORGAN THIEF WOULD LURE YOU TO, RIGHT?
OH, DAD! HOW'D YOU KNOW WHERE I WAS?
WHEN I SAW THE GIANT DINOSAUR HEAD, MY GUT TOLD ME.
YOU **KNEW** ABOUT DINOSAURS AND NEVER TOLD ME?
I WAS WAITING FOR THE RIGHT TIME.
LIKE AFTER YOU WERE MARRIED.
YER KID'S JUST ENTHUSIASTIC, CAN'T BLAME HIM.
I WAS THE SAME WAY WHEN I FIRST LEARNED ABOUT THESE CREATURES.
AND FOR JUST ***TWENTY CREDITS,*** Y'ALL CAN EXPERIENCE A HOLOGRAPHIC DINOSAUR SHOW THAT'LL FEEL LIKE YOU'RE RIGHT NEXT TO 'EM!
HOLOGRAM

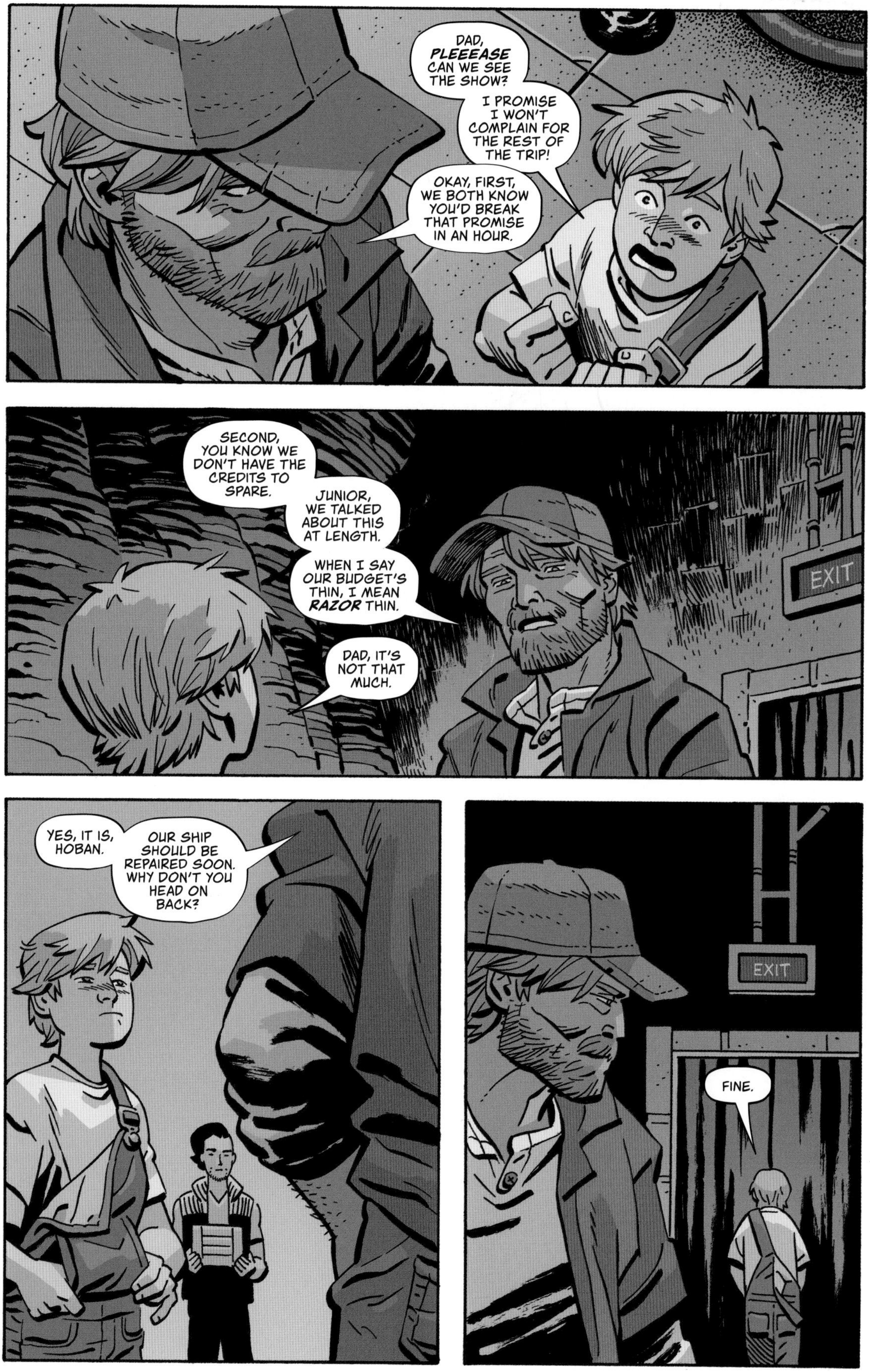
DAD, *PLEEEASE* CAN WE SEE THE SHOW?
I PROMISE I WON'T COMPLAIN FOR THE REST OF THE TRIP!
OKAY, FIRST, WE BOTH KNOW YOU'D BREAK THAT PROMISE IN AN HOUR.
SECOND, YOU KNOW WE DON'T HAVE THE CREDITS TO SPARE.
JUNIOR, WE TALKED ABOUT THIS AT LENGTH.
WHEN I SAY OUR BUDGET'S THIN, I MEAN *RAZOR* THIN.
DAD, IT'S NOT THAT MUCH.
EXIT
YES, IT IS, HOBAN.
OUR SHIP SHOULD BE REPAIRED SOON. WHY DON'T YOU HEAD ON BACK?
EXIT
FINE.

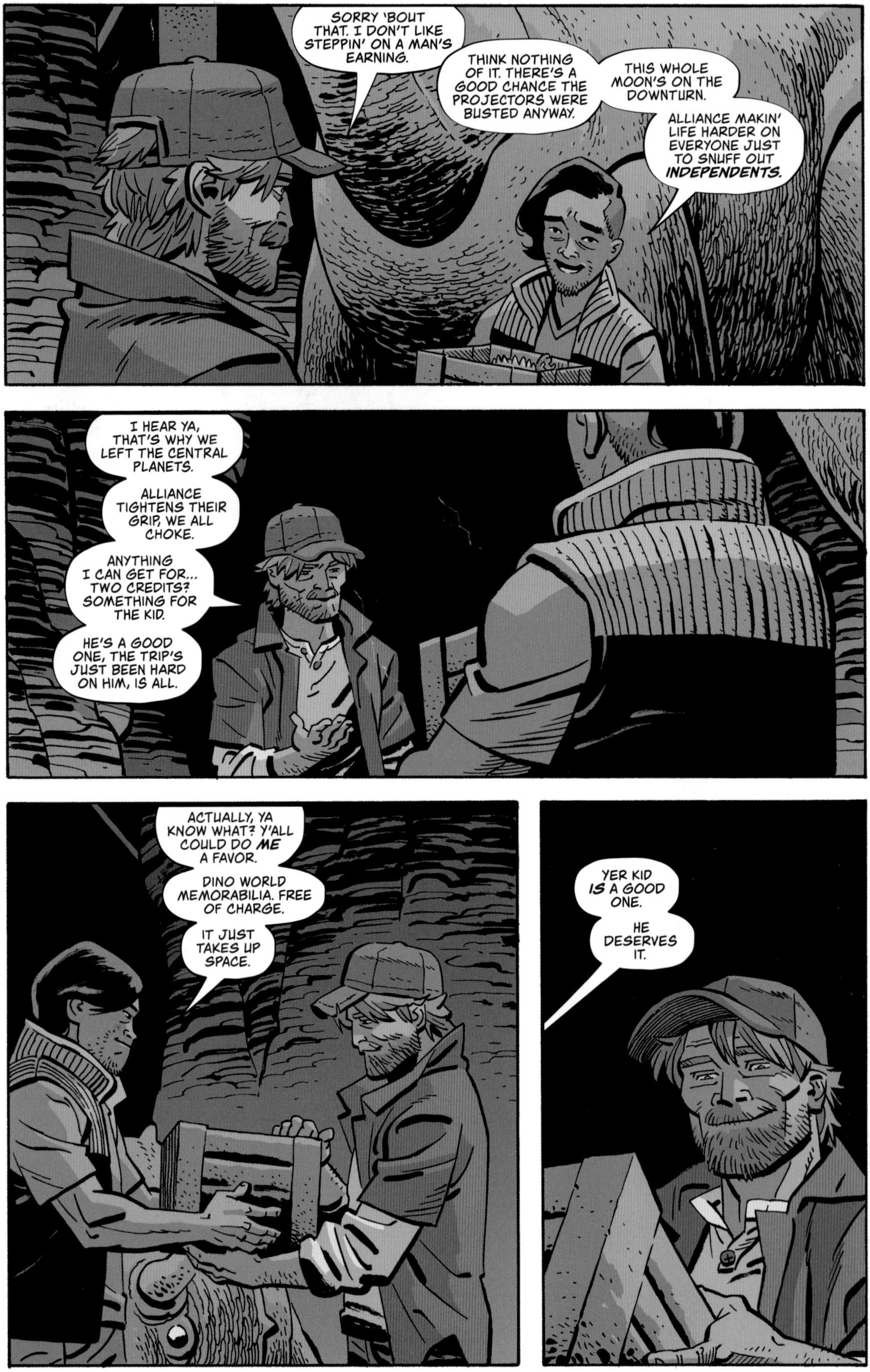
SORRY 'BOUT THAT. I DON'T LIKE STEPPIN' ON A MAN'S EARNING.
THINK NOTHING OF IT. THERE'S A GOOD CHANCE THE PROJECTORS WERE BUSTED ANYWAY.
THIS WHOLE MOON'S ON THE DOWNTURN.
ALLIANCE MAKIN' LIFE HARDER ON EVERYONE JUST TO SNUFF OUT ***INDEPENDENTS.***
I HEAR YA, THAT'S WHY WE LEFT THE CENTRAL PLANETS.
ALLIANCE TIGHTENS THEIR GRIP, WE ALL CHOKE.
ANYTHING I CAN GET FOR... TWO CREDITS? SOMETHING FOR THE KID.
HE'S A GOOD ONE, THE TRIP'S JUST BEEN HARD ON HIM, IS ALL.
ACTUALLY, YA KNOW WHAT? Y'ALL COULD DO ***ME*** A FAVOR.
DINO WORLD MEMORABILIA. FREE OF CHARGE.
IT JUST TAKES UP SPACE.
YER KID ***IS*** A GOOD ONE.
HE DESERVES IT.

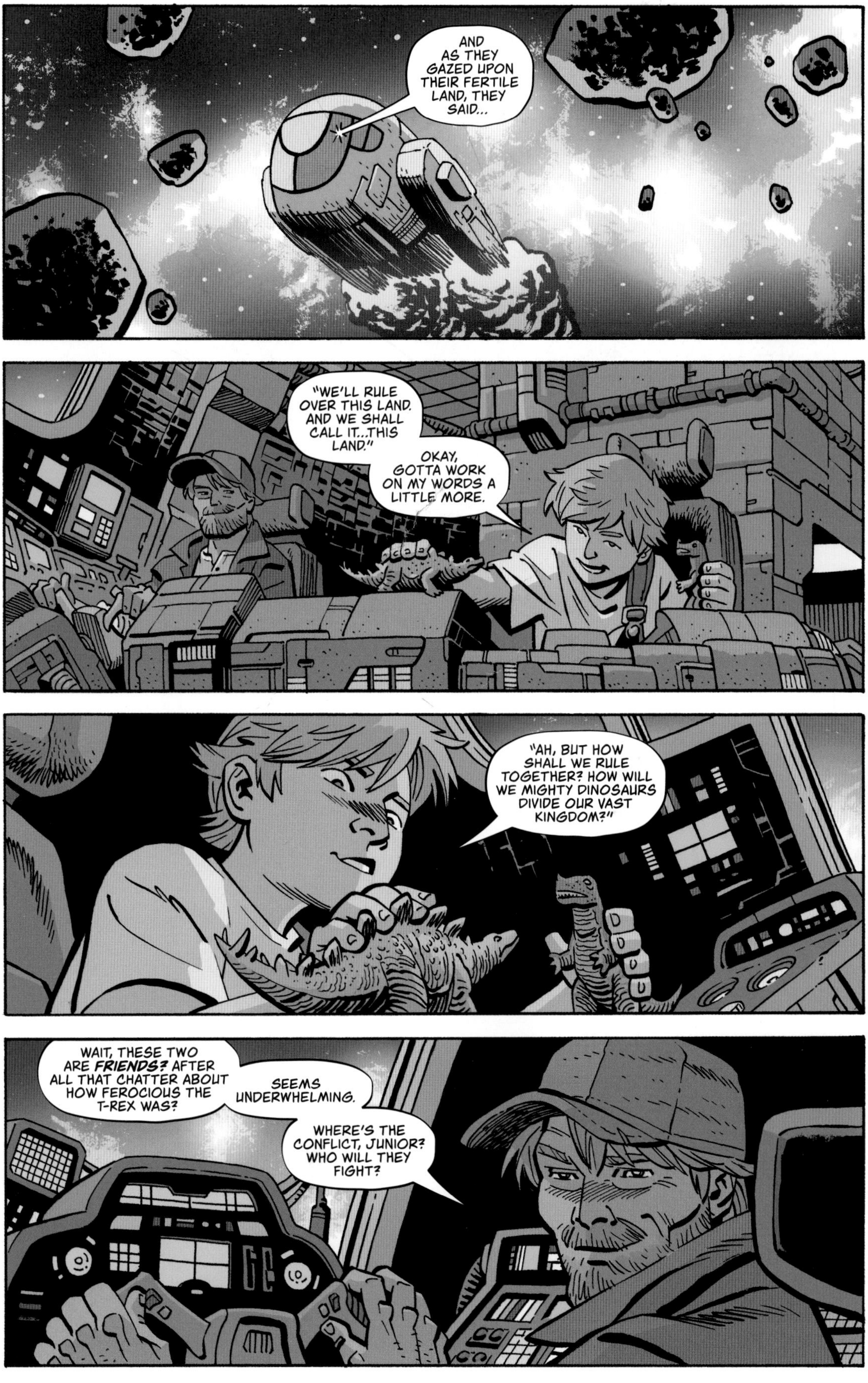

AND AS THEY GAZED UPON THEIR FERTILE LAND, THEY SAID...
"WE'LL RULE OVER THIS LAND. AND WE SHALL CALL IT...THIS LAND."
OKAY, GOTTA WORK ON MY WORDS A LITTLE MORE.
"AH, BUT HOW SHALL WE RULE TOGETHER? HOW WILL WE MIGHTY DINOSAURS DIVIDE OUR VAST KINGDOM?"
WAIT, THESE TWO ARE ***FRIENDS?*** AFTER ALL THAT CHATTER ABOUT HOW FEROCIOUS THE T-REX WAS?
SEEMS UNDERWHELMING.
WHERE'S THE CONFLICT, JUNIOR? WHO WILL THEY FIGHT?

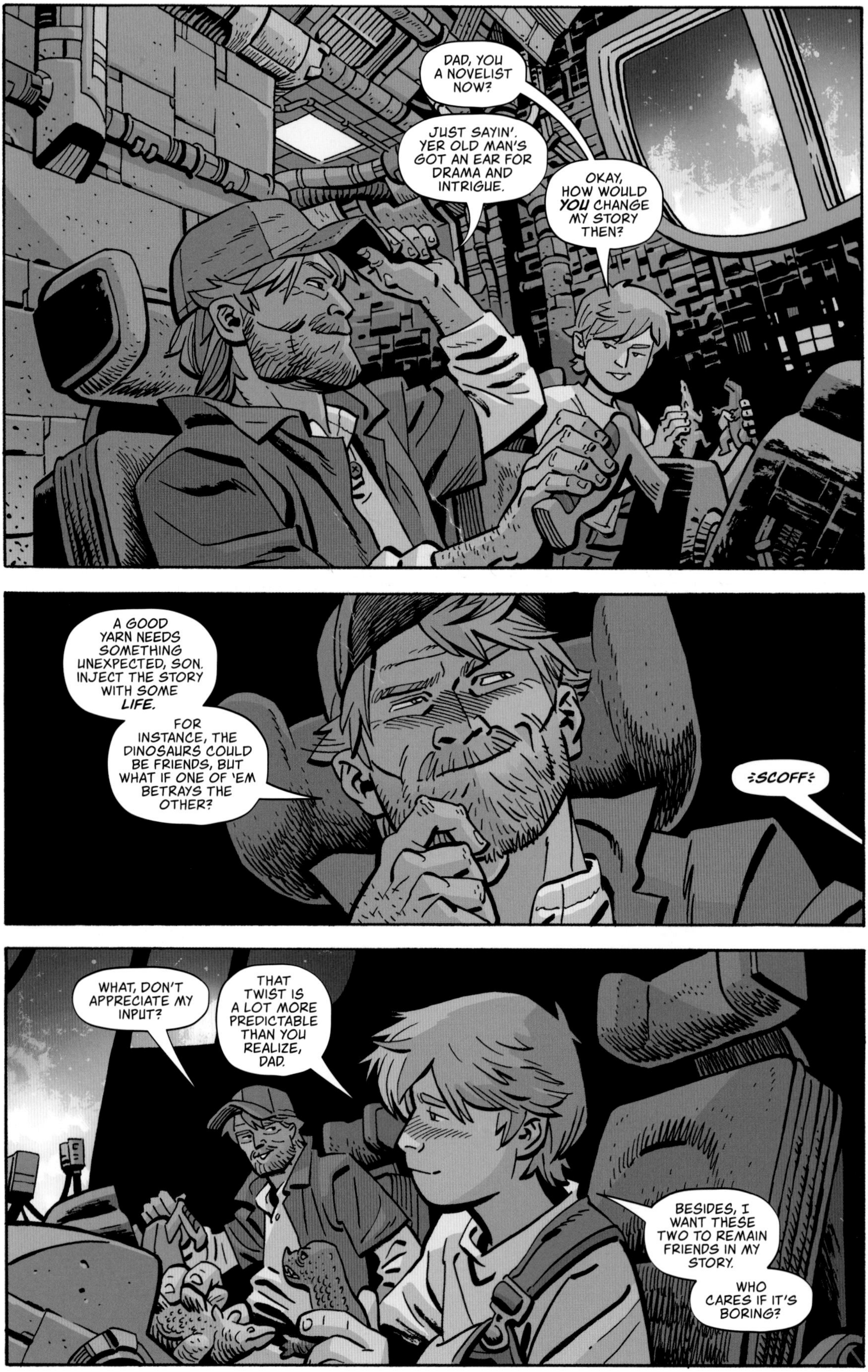
DAD, YOU A NOVELIST NOW?
JUST SAYIN'. YER OLD MAN'S GOT AN EAR FOR DRAMA AND INTRIGUE.
OKAY, HOW WOULD YOU CHANGE MY STORY THEN?
A GOOD YARN NEEDS SOMETHING UNEXPECTED, SON. INJECT THE STORY WITH SOME LIFE.
FOR INSTANCE, THE DINOSAURS COULD BE FRIENDS, BUT WHAT IF ONE OF 'EM BETRAYS THE OTHER?
SCOFF
WHAT, DON'T APPRECIATE MY INPUT?
THAT TWIST IS A LOT MORE PREDICTABLE THAN YOU REALIZE, DAD.
BESIDES, I WANT THESE TWO TO REMAIN FRIENDS IN MY STORY.
WHO CARES IF IT'S BORING?

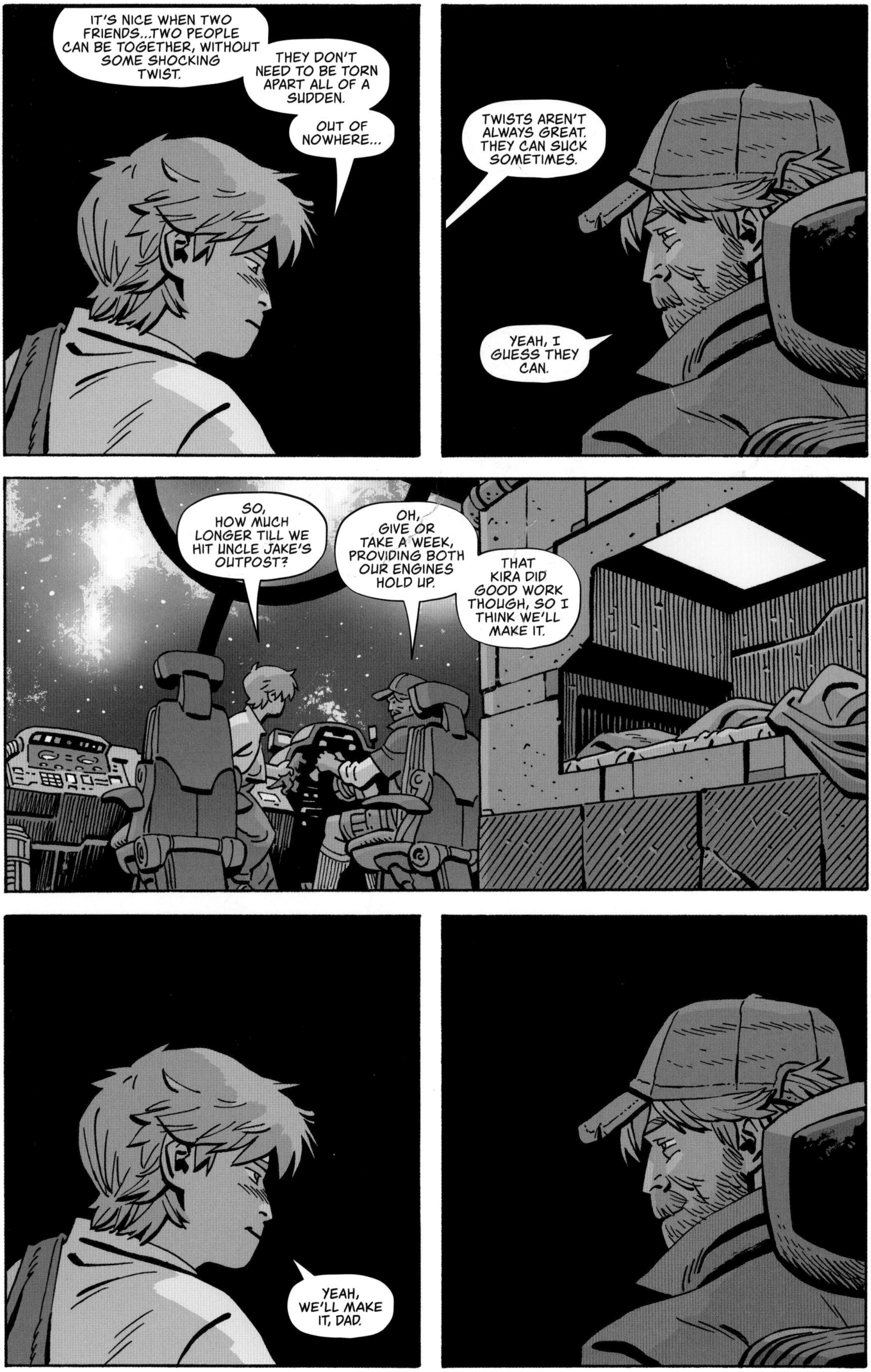
IT'S NICE WHEN TWO FRIENDS...TWO PEOPLE CAN BE TOGETHER, WITHOUT SOME SHOCKING TWIST.
THEY DON'T NEED TO BE TORN APART ALL OF A SUDDEN.
OUT OF NOWHERE...
TWISTS AREN'T ALWAYS GREAT. THEY CAN SUCK SOMETIMES.
YEAH, I GUESS THEY CAN.
SO, HOW MUCH LONGER TILL WE HIT UNCLE JAKE'S OUTPOST?
OH, GIVE OR TAKE A WEEK, PROVIDING BOTH OUR ENGINES HOLD UP.
THAT KIRA DID GOOD WORK THOUGH, SO I THINK WE'LL MAKE IT.
YEAH, WE'LL MAKE IT, DAD.

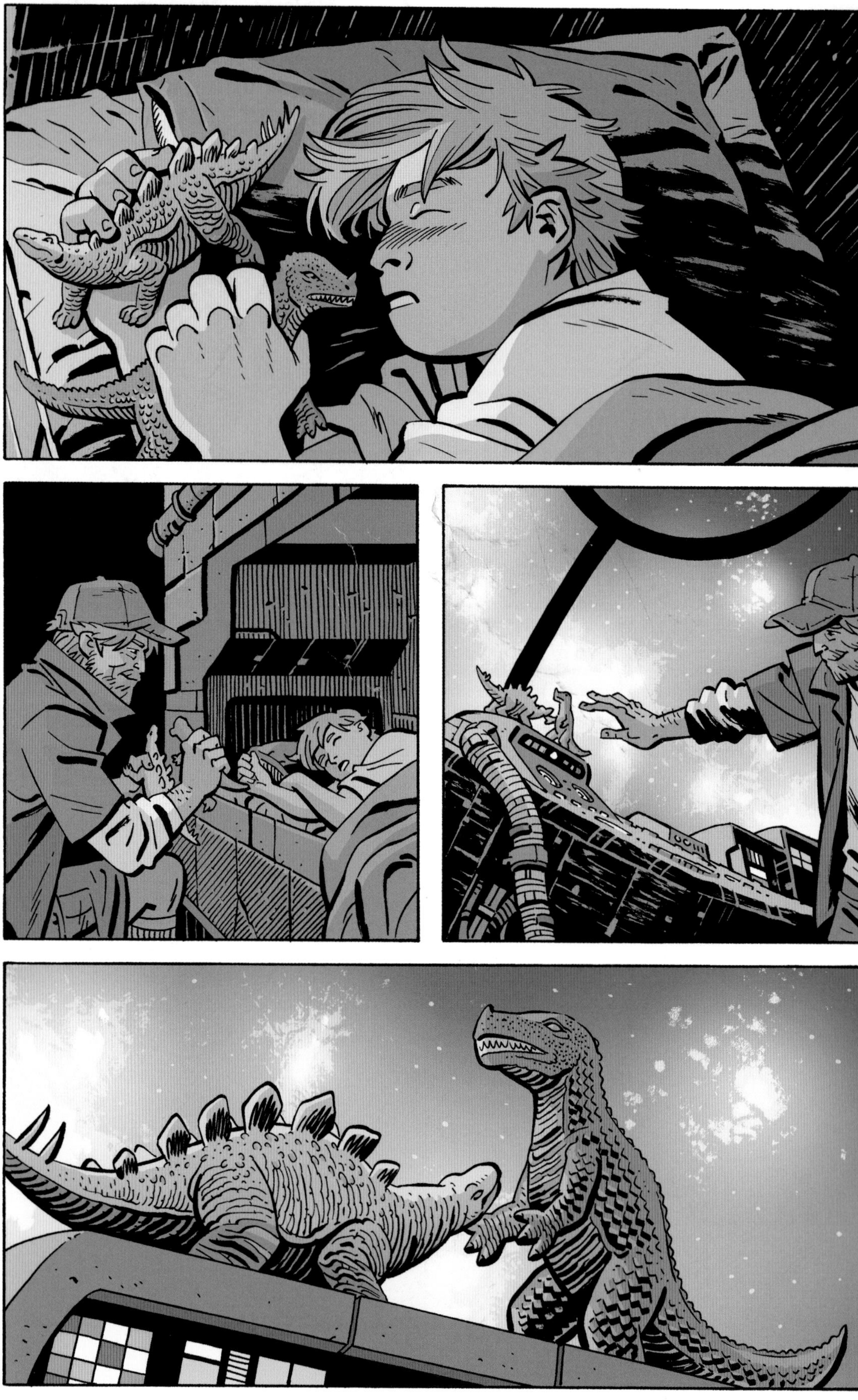

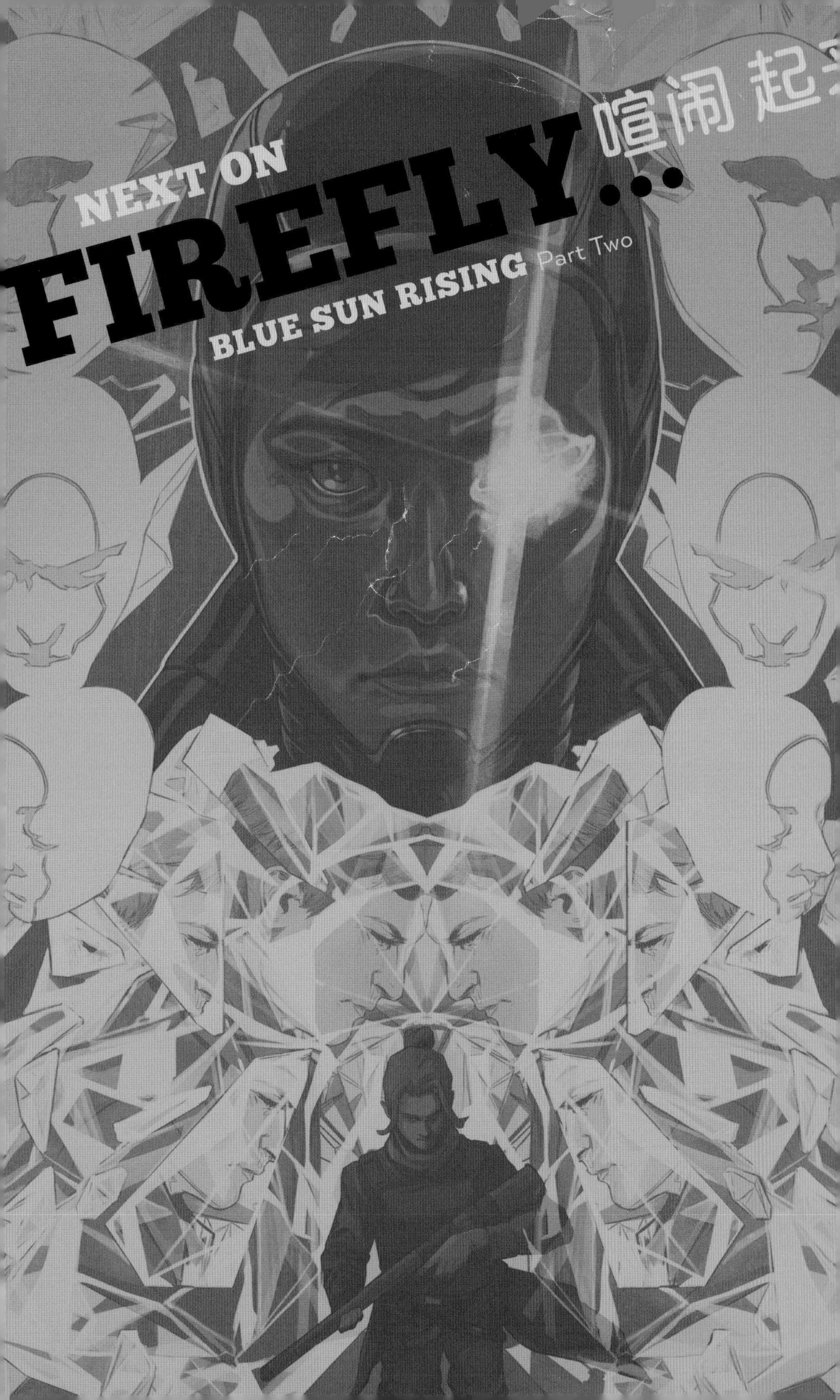
NEXT ON
FIREFLY...
喧闹起
BLUE SUN RISING Part Two

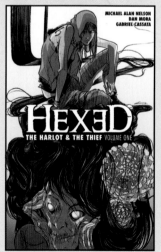